Ageing, Dementia and Time in Film

For my Ah Ma

Ageing, Dementia and Time in Film

Temporal Performances

MaoHui Deng

EDINBURGH
University Press

Edinburgh University Press is one of the leading university presses in the UK. We publish academic books and journals in our selected subject areas across the humanities and social sciences, combining cutting-edge scholarship with high editorial and production values to produce academic works of lasting importance. For more information visit our website: edinburghuniversitypress.com

© MaoHui Deng, 2023, 2024

Edinburgh University Press Ltd
13 Infirmary Street
Edinburgh EH1 1LT

First published in hardback by Edinburgh University Press 2023

Typeset in 12 on 14pt Arno Pro and Myriad Pro by
Cheshire Typesetting Ltd, Cuddington, Cheshire

A CIP record for this book is available from the British Library

ISBN 978 1 4744 8697 2 (hardback)
ISBN 978 1 4744 8698 9 (paperback)
ISBN 978 1 4744 8699 6 (webready PDF)
ISBN 978 1 4744 8700 9 (epub)

The right of MaoHui Deng to be identified as author of this work has been asserted in accordance with the Copyright, Designs and Patents Act 1988 and the Copyright and Related Rights Regulations 2003 (SI No. 2498).

Contents

List of Figures	vi
Acknowledgements	viii
Introduction: A Temporally Relational Worldview	1
1. Performing Time/Performed by Time	18
2. The Shape of Dementia Narratives and Deleuze's Third Synthesis of Time	42
3. A Kind of Radical Empathy	65
4. Ecologies of Temporal Performances	85
5. Reading the Digital Index in a Hesitant Way	105
6. The Trope of Wandering and the Temporalities of a Nation	128
Coda: My Grandparents	145
Bibliography	152
Filmography	169
Index	172

Figures

1.1 Su-jin lost in a sea of working people in *A Moment to Remember* — 30
1.2 Piya repeatedly refreshed by the rain and the wiper in *U Me Aur Hum* — 33
1.3 Ajay repeatedly refreshed by the rain and the wiper in *U Me Aur Hum* — 37
1.4 Cheol-su and the man at the beginning of *A Moment to Remember* — 38
1.5 Cheol-su and the man towards the end of *A Moment to Remember* — 40
2.1 A different kind of textured surface in *Memories of Tomorrow* — 46
2.2 Maria crying silently in *Memoir of a Murderer* — 49
2.3 Eun-hee's view in *Memoir of a Murderer* — 55
2.4 The mirror from Eun-hee's point of view in *Memoir of a Murderer* — 57
3.1 Not necessarily a point-of-view shot in *The Mourning Forest* — 70
3.2 Aunty Fanny's environment as out of focus in *Happiness* — 75
4.1 A landscape that is sonically buzzing with vitality in *Pandora's Box* — 90
4.2 Georges, Eve and the fleeting presence of the album in *Happy End* — 97
4.3 Ecologies of temporal performances in the final moments of *Happy End* — 101
4.4 The ambiguous final shot of *Pandora's Box* — 102
4.5 The enchanting landscape in *Pandora's Box* — 103
5.1 The grandmother in her armchair at the far end of the room in *The Visit* — 108
5.2 The visual irruption of a man in *The Taking of Deborah Logan* — 110
5.3 Subtitling Deborah's prosopopoeia in *The Taking of Deborah Logan* — 111

5.4 The grandmother by the oven in *The Visit* 116
5.5 Material degradation in *The Taking of Deborah Logan* 125
6.1 Ismail engulfed by the architecture of Chung Cheng High in *Parting* 134
6.2 Temporal collision between the past and the present in *Parting* 142

Acknowledgements

This book started its life as a doctoral project at the University of Manchester. The project was funded by the University's President's Doctoral Scholarship and was supervised and advised by David Butler, Felicia Chan and Jackie Stacey. It was examined by Vicky Lowe and Sue Harris. I am grateful for their wonderful advice, for their endless capacity to believe in my ability to complete the thesis, and for their support as I turned the thesis into a monograph. I am also thankful for my colleagues at Manchester who have been nothing but supportive. Special thanks go to both Maggie Gale and Jenny Hughes, who sacrificed so much of their time to sharpen the many drafts that I sent their way.

Rajinder Dudrah, who has been nothing but an excellent human being, introduced me to the wonderful world of the British Association of Film, Television and Screen Studies. The people at BAFTSS have also been excellent mentors and providers of opportunities. Likewise, I have been fortunate enough to have met so many scholars working in cultural gerontology through the Dementia and Cultural Narrative Network. These include Sarah Falcus, Katsura Sako, Sue Vice, Janet Gibson and Raquel Medina, who have been great sources of inspiration.

I am very thankful for having the opportunity to work with the excellent editors at Edinburgh University Press. Gillian Leslie's advice on how to reshape the thesis into a monograph did indeed work wonders! I would also like to thank the feedback of the anonymous reviewer for their very helpful and constructive feedback.

Lastly, I am grateful to my friends and family in both the UK and Singapore, who supported me through the whole journey. Special thanks go to Jacqueline and Anthony, who not only found it bearable to live with me for so many years but were also constant sources of creative energy that pushed me through. I played quite a bit of dodgeball with the Manchester Bees Dodgeball Club as I wrote this book. I am not very good at it – and indeed have been sent to the A&E once because I was hit in the head a few too many times – but the sport offered me time away from the book and to return to it in a more refreshed and energised manner. Thank you, too, to Sonny, who is always a great source of comfort.

Introduction
A Temporally Relational Worldview

This book makes the argument that films about dementia encourage a temporally relational worldview. To make this claim, this introduction begins with the Clock Drawing Test (CDT), which is one of the most common tests administered to people suspected to be living with dementia. The CDT requires the individual to draw a clock, fill in the numbers and, after which, set the clock to a specified time (usually at ten past eleven). The test is deceptively simple but actually examines multiple cognitive functions that highlight the neurodegeneration experienced by people living with dementia: it requires the person to have adequate auditory language skills in order to comprehend the verbal instructions; to retrieve and reconstruct the visual representation of the clock in their visual memory; to coordinate their visuospatial system with their graphomotor skills in order to translate their visual image into drawing; to possess a certain level of numerical knowledge so as to label the hours on the clock face accurately; to be able to think abstractly so that ten past eleven can be understood temporally; to be able to resist and suppress the perceptual pull towards the number ten on the clock face so that the hour hand can be positioned correctly; and, finally, to be able to concentrate.[1]

A clock drawn by someone without dementia will largely be able to accurately lay out the numbers in an ascending order on the clock face and identify the correct prescribed time (though the length of the hour and minute hand might not necessarily be adequately distinguished). A clock drawn by the person living with dementia, on the other hand, might include extra numbers, have the hours laid out in an incorrect order, and not tell the correct time at all. Furthermore, as Morris Freedman et al. observe, 'patients with more severe dementia show more deficits on clock drawings as compared to those with mild impairment' (Freedman et al. 1994: 63). Put differently, the chances of an individual being diagnosed with dementia become more certain when they are unable to tell the time on the clock, a device that conditions and locks us into thinking about time linearly and homogeneously.

Clocks, according to Kevin K. Birth, are cognitive artefacts that demonstrate 'the potential of constraining thought through the mediation between thought and what is thought about' but, in addition, 'also hide the ways in which thought is directed and constrained' (Birth 2012: 20). Expanding on this argument, Birth posits that the design of the clock 'subordinated the determination of moments and timings to the measure of duration', which in turn heightened the dominance of linear, homogeneous time to 'the modern construction of knowledge' (Birth 2012: 40–1). In addition to this, the simplicity of the clock's design gave people an easy and quick way to tell time, which meant that the skills to calculate time through considering different temporalities quickly atrophied after the popularisation of clocks. Lastly, Birth also observes that although the clock gives off the impression that it is designed to measure the earth's rotation, clock time has actually been set to the atomic cycle of caesium atoms since 1967 as the earth's rotation was simply too irregular for time-keeping; in other words, this understanding of homogeneous, linear time as 'natural' is actually a highly calculated and regulated consideration of time.

With the clock being a pervasively strong symbol of linear, homogeneous time, the CDT, designed to measure a wide variety of cognitive functions in a person suspected to be living with dementia, becomes an example to highlight the ways in which the person living with dementia is subjected to the disciplines of linear, homogeneous time and, in failing to conform to this chronological understanding of time, the person living with dementia is put under the watchful medical gaze. In addition to this, much scientific research has not only demonstrated that people living with dementia display a loss of temporal perception early on in the diagnosis, where 'the temporal relationships and coherence of past, present and future were often unclear and vague', but also suggested multiple techniques in which carers and people living with dementia can adopt to keep to linear, homogeneous time (Nygård and Johansson 2000: 89).[2] In other words, as 'time past, present and future blur together like watercolours washed in the rain', the person living with dementia gets increasingly out of sync of modern society's understanding of time that progresses in a chronological manner, and is in turn feared and stigmatised (Hayes 2011: 47). Clocks for the person living with dementia and their carers, then, become 'another reminder of a shattered world' as the tension/negotiation between linear time and non-linear time is exacerbated (Orona 1990: 1254).

Clock time, as we understand it today, where a day is divided into twenty-four hours and an hour into sixty minutes, gained traction with the rise of the mechanical clock in Europe. Throughout the fourteenth century, church and public clocks were erected in cities and towns throughout Europe, and they measured the passing of time visually and aurally, regulating the movements in these places with 'militant imperiousness' (Schafer 1994: 56). Gradually, clocks were introduced to the workplace during the Industrial Revolution, in part, as E.P. Thompson argues, due to the demands of the changing technology that necessitated a highly regulated understanding of time and in part 'as a means of labour exploitation' (Thompson 1967: 80). Concurrently, as trains and electricity became more commonplace in the nineteenth and early twentieth centuries, time began to be standardised across the world: for example, almost all English railway stations agreed to follow Greenwich Mean Time (GMT) in 1848 so that people across England could have a standardised schedule to follow in order to catch their trains; the International Meridian Conference was held in 1884 and GMT was adopted as the prime meridian (France only adopted GMT in 1911 due to political differences with Britain) so as to facilitate global trades and communication. The Eiffel Tower transmitted the first time signal to the whole world in 1913, which allowed the global synchronisation of time to happen.[3] The late nineteenth and early twentieth centuries, therefore, saw an accelerated and dramatic change in the reconsideration of time in relation to space. As Stephen Kern writes, the 'independence of local times began to collapse once the framework of a global electronic network was established' (Kern 2003: 14). In turn, the Western world encountered a modernity characterised by the 'empty, homogeneous time' of the clock, where every single minute, hour and day is the same, and where time is experienced linearly predominantly in the service of capitalism (Benjamin 1992: 244–55).

In the same period, cinema, as a brand new form of art/technology, began participating in 'modernity's reconceptualization of time and its representability' (Doane 2002: 4). For Tom Gunning, early Western cinema – the cinema of attractions – had 'one basic temporality, that of the alternation of presence/absence which is embodied in the act of display' (Gunning 1993: 6). According to Gunning, unlike films from the classical paradigm where narrative is dominant, the desire to display in the cinema of attractions meant that early cinema 'is limited to the pure present tense of its appearance' (Gunning 1993: 7). However, faced with the enormous growth of nickelodeon exhibition spaces and an economic reorganisation to regulate the film industry (the founding of the Motion Picture Patents Company) from around 1908 onwards, Gunning argues, cinema began to focus more on its capabilities to tell narratives. Consequently, the temporality of cinema moved from that of irruption to that of linear development (Gunning 1993: 7).

This process of empty, homogeneous time creeping into, and becoming dominant over, the temporality of cinema is furthered with the introduction of synchronised sound technology. Prior to synchronised sound, non-synchronised sound films were projected at different frame rates, ranging from 16 to 24 frames per second (fps). However, synchronised sound technology, with the introduction of the narrow strip of soundtrack running down the side of the celluloid film stock, 'demanded an absolutely consistent projection speed of 24fps', which meant that any non-synchronised sound films had to be sped up in order to be screened by the new projection technology (Napper 2017: 5–6). The strict adherence to a highly regulated frame rate, for Bliss Cua Lim, meant that cinema can be thought of as 'a kind of clockwork mechanism' that reduces time to the homogeneity of measurable space' (Lim 2009: 11). Yet, beyond the linearity of the cinematic apparatus, as Mary Ann Doane observes, there are also the temporality of the diegesis, wherein 'time is represented by the image, the varying invocations of present, past, future, historicity', and the temporality of the reception, which 'encourages the spectator to honor the relentless temporality of the apparatus' (Doane 2002: 30). That is to say, in cinema, there too is a constant negotiation between clock and non-clock time.

In this book, these messy temporal negotiations as evinced by cinema and the experiences of dementia that fleet, constantly and consistently, between linearity and non-linearity, past and present, absence and presence, and there and here are filtered through the prism of performance. Performance, as defined by Richard Schechner, is 'twice-behaved behaviour' (Schechner 1985: 36). For Schechner, performance is 'living behaviour treated as a film director treats a strip of film' (Schechner 1985: 35). These strips of behaviour, or strips of film in the case of the metaphor employed by Schechner, 'can be rearranged or reconstructed', like the ways in which each frame can be moved around within the reel to create, at each edit, a different film, as time is cut out of joint and re-joined again (Schechner 1985: 35). In other words, as Elin Diamond puts it, performances are 'always a doing and a thing done' (Diamond 1996: 1). They are cultural processes that 'conservatively reinscribe or passionately reinvent the ideas, symbols, and gestures that shape social life' – performances are, in a sense, intricate 'negotiations with regimes of power' (Diamond 1996: 2).[4]

Understood as performances in the widest sense possible, both the cultural processes and understandings of cinema and the experiences of dementia can be comprehended through the framework of temporal negotiation, where times are done onto *and* times are being done. Each interaction, as performance, Peggy Phelan writes, 'in a strict ontological sense is nonreproductive': each event is different, and each negotiation is ever changing, in a constant state of becoming (Phelan 2003: 148). In cinema, film (itself a complex negotiation between the clock-like linearity of the mechanical apparatus and the multifarious temporal explorations of the film's formal properties and narratives) enact a certain kind of temporality onto the audience; likewise, audiences and their individual spectatorships bring to the mix different times, proliferating the ways a film might be varyingly watched. Similarly, the person living with dementia experiences and lives their sense of non-linear temporalities while individuals of the wider society variously prescribe different intensities of linear clock time on to the person living with dementia. Consequently, films about dementia, in part concerned about cinema and in part concerned about dementia, surface the complex push and pull between multiple entangled times and temporalities, and highlight the ways in which the person living with dementia might be performing time and is performed by time.

In arguing that films about dementia encourage a temporally relational worldview, this book suggests that people living with dementia experience time differently. In order to make this proposition in a way that does not Other, this book carefully develops and elaborates a theoretical framework of change and ephemerality which maintains that *everyone* experiences time differently as multiple categories of temporalities come together to structure/affect/implicate an individual subject's identification, where identification, following Jackie Stacey, is understood as a constant process of negotiation between the self and the other that take place within the psychic imagination and at the level of cultural activity (Stacey 1994: 306–7). At the heart of my discussion of films about dementia, then, is an examination of the ways in which everyone and everything, enmeshed in extended ecologies, is engaged in different performances of time, as they each negotiate with different temporalities in relation to their surrounding world.

Films about dementia in the new millennium

Dementia, as commonly understood, is an umbrella term that points to a wide range of neurodegenerative diseases that are variously characterised by degrees of memory loss, problems with communication and meaning and mood changes. Predominantly affecting people in later life, dementia refers to a wide range of diseases that include Alzheimer's disease, frontotemporal dementia, dementia with Lewy bodies, vascular dementia, mixed dementia, Creutzfeld-Jakob disease and Huntington's disease, to name just a few. In this book, I consider narrative films that explicitly identify characters living with dementia, such as *Iris* (Richard Eyre, 2001, UK/USA), *Thanmathra* (Blessy, 2005, India), *The Savages* (Tamara Jenkins, 2007, USA), *Pandora's Box* (Yeşim Ustaoğlu, 2008, Turkey), *Poetry* (Lee Chang-dong, 2010, South Korea), *A Separation* (Asghar Farhadi, 2011, Iran/France), *Amour* (Michael Haneke, 2012, Austria/France/Germany), *Robot and Frank* (Jake Schreier, 2012, USA), *Still Mine* (Michael McGowan, 2012, Canada), *Pecoross' Mother and Her Days* (Azuma Morisaki, 2013, Japan), *Passage of Life* (Diego Corsini, 2015, Argentina/Spain), *The Olive Tree* (Icíar Bollaín, 2016, Spain/Germany) and *Shed Skin Papa* (Roy Szeto, 2016, Hong Kong). I also examine narrative films that have characters who display traits of dementia but are never explicitly identified as living with dementia, such as *Nebraska* (Alexander Payne, 2013, USA), *Magallanes* (Salvador del Solar, 2015, Peru/Argentina/Spain), *The Mimic* (Huh Jung, 2017, South Korea), *Marjorie Prime* (Michael Almereyda, 2017, USA) and *Happy End* (Michael Haneke, 2017, France/Austria/Germany).

Throughout I predominantly refer to films made from 2000 onwards, though there are, of course, films about dementia made pre-2000, such as *On Golden Pond* (Mark Rydell, 1981, UK/USA), *Gray Sunset* (Shunya Itô, 1985, Japan), *Summer Snow* (Ann Hui, 1995, Hong Kong), *Travelling Companion* (Peter Del Monte, 1996, Italy) and *After Life* (Hirokazu Koreeda, 1998, Japan). My focus on films released in the new millennium is down to a few reasons. In part, this is due to a heightened awareness in the ageing population across almost every advanced industrialised country in the world as the Baby Boomer generation began to enter their sixties in the 2000s, prompting the United Nations to describe the ageing population as 'one of the most significant social transformations of the twenty-first century' (United Nations 2015: 1).[5] In turn, with the world's population getting greyer in the new millennium, and with the ageing of stars and celebrities, there is a significant increase in films about ageing in later life. Cinema, traditionally associated with the 'younger' age group, started to tell stories about the older population. Genre films such as *The Expendables* franchise (2010–), the *Red* series (2010–), *Twilight Gangsters* (Kang Hyo-jin, 2010, South Korea), *Star Wars: Episode VII – The Force Awakens* (J. J. Abrams, 2015, USA) and *Blade Runner 2049* (Denis Villeneuve, 2017, USA/UK/Hungary/Canada/Spain) put old age at the front of the narrative whereas *The Alzheimer Case* (Erik Van Looy, 2003, Belgium), *The Bodyguard* (Sammo Hung, 2010, Hong Kong/China), *Ashes* (Mat Whitecross, 2012, UK) and *Logan* (James Mangold, 2017, USA) go one step further and feature characters who live with dementia at the core of these geri-action films.[6] Likewise, geri-animations such as *Millennium Actress* (Satoshi Kon, 2001, Japan), *The Triplets of Belleville* (Sylvain Chomet, 2003, France/Belgium/Canada/UK/Latvia/USA), *Howl's Moving Castle* (Hayao Miyazaki, 2004, Japan), *Up* (Pete Docter, 2009, USA), *My Dog Tulip* (Paul Fierlinger, 2009, USA) and *The Illusionist* (Sylvain Chomet, 2010, France/UK) have also started telling stories about older characters, whilst *Wrinkles* (Ignacio Ferreras, 2011, Spain), *Ethel and Ernest* (Roger Mainwood, 2016, UK) and *Coco* (Lee Unkrich, 2017, USA) specifically focus on the experiences of dementia.

Concomitantly, cinemas across the world have also discovered the purchasing power of the 'grey pound'.[7] In the UK alone, for instance, films about older people primarily aimed at older people such as *The King's Speech* (Tom Hooper, 2010, UK/USA/Australia), *The Best Exotic Marigold Hotel* (John Madden, 2011, UK/USA/UAE), *Quartet* (Dustin Hoffman, 2012, UK), *Philomena* (Stephen Frears, 2013, UK/USA/France) and *The Lady in the Van* (Nicholas Hytner, 2015, UK) have proven financially lucrative and successful with the 55-plus audience group. Significantly, 45 per cent of the audiences for *The King's Speech* in the year of its UK release were above the age of fifty-five and heralded a substantial upwards trend in film viewership for the 55-plus audience demographics in the UK, going from 8.3 per cent of the cinema admissions in 2011 to 11.5 per cent in 2014 (BFI 2015: 4). Likewise, *The Best Exotic Marigold Hotel* made £20.4 million in the year it was released in the UK and 53 per cent of the audiences were made up of people aged above fifty-five (BFI 2013: 169) whereas *Quartet* made £8.6 million in the year of its UK release and the 55-plus audience group made up 87 per cent of its audience demographics (BFI 2014: 162).[8]

Put differently then, following the scholarship of gerontologists Christopher Gilleard and Paul Higgs, as the Baby Boomer generation is confronted with older age and as the world becomes more conscious of the benefits and/or disadvantages of the ageing population,

> ageing has come to occupy such a central position within postmodern culture because there is more 'age' about than ever before, more varied resources to shape its experience, more commonalities across the whole of adulthood established by post-war consumer culture and more sources of 'conflict' around the social regulation and expression of ageing. (Gilleard and Higgs 2000: 9)[9]

Although, in drawing from Gilleard and Higgs, films about ageing in later life made post-2000 do feature a wide array of themes and narratives, Sally Chivers observes that a substantial portion of these films – which she describes as the 'silvering screen' – regularly encourage audience members to 'negotiate the cultural panic of the silver tsunami, personal fear at the prospect of ageing, and social guilt about their own care choices in relation to older characters' (Chivers 2011: 76). Further to the articulation of these anxieties about older age, Chivers notes that these films also demonstrate a 'heightened awareness of time passing' (Chivers 2011: xvi). For Chivers, these films 'value and evaluate the present primarily in relation to a distant past' and, additionally, 'illuminate time' by 'continually featuring clocks, visually noting seasons, including birthdays in the plot' (Chivers 2011: xvi).

Here, I focus on the silvering screen's obsession with time – with clocks, with calendrical seasons, with birthdays – vis-à-vis ageing so as to make a point about films about dementia and their relationship with clock time. In his research into ageing and time, Jan Baars notes that although people are continuously aged by chronological time in culture, 'aging is poorly indicated by higher chronological ages' (Baars 2009: 88). As an alternative to chronological time, Baars proposes to think about older age in terms of the biological clock, which has its 'own rhythm of living and aging' (Baars 1997: 289). Baars concedes that although the biological clock is not a specific 'clock' to begin with because different people show signs of wearing and tearing at different stages of their lives, the metaphor of the clock used in gerontology is still unfortunate as it hints at a chronometric outlook towards ageing. This constant deployment of the clock as metaphor for ageing, Baars argues, can lead to the aim of transforming the human body into 'a perfect clock' that would 'tick on forever without any functional "aging"', in turn leading to 'a neglect of finite life' (Baars 2017: 288). Similarly, Naomi Woodspring, in exploring the Baby Boomer generation's relationship with time and ageing, notes that 'there was an evident tension between the chronological and cultural narratives of old age and the lived experiences of participants' (Woodspring 2016: 170). On the one hand, the Baby Boomers acknowledge that, in following the modern, homogeneous understanding of time, they are now considered 'old'; on the other hand, the Baby Boomers *do not feel* 'old'. What both Baars and Woodspring highlight is the aged body's constant negotiation between the body and the multiple forms of temporal experiences.

Expounding on this notion, Amelia DeFalco, in adopting a psychoanalytic approach towards old age, proposes that the process of ageing is achieved through 'confrontations with temporality' (DeFalco 2010: 7).[10] According to DeFalco, the process of ageing in later life creates a split in the subject as tensions between the body and the self become increasingly evident, resulting in 'a new or intensified awareness of the differences between the past and present selves' (DeFalco 2010: 7). In turn, this split causes the ageing body to experience the profound sense of the uncanny as the subject adapts themselves to older age. Arguing along similar lines, Lynne Segal suggests that, in addition to the uncanny, 'the timelessness of the unconsciousness, the persistence of the psychic past within the present', accordingly ensures 'that there will always be some sense of temporal vertigo within our experiences of ageing' (Segal 2014: 183). For Segal, then, to really acknowledge older age is to recognise that there is more past than future, to be out of time, and to accept 'that we are unlikely to remain the autonomous, independent and future-oriented individuals most of us once liked to imagine that we were' (Segal 2014: 184). Going even further, E. Ann Kaplan takes this argument towards ageing and time to the extreme and proposes to think of the ageing process as a form of trauma. She writes: 'The trauma of aging consists in being *in time* and unable to get out of it' (Kaplan 1999: 173; emphasis in original).

Whilst I would not go as far as Kaplan to compare ageing to trauma, I do want to highlight the common thread that is emerging from the discussions of the process of growing older in later life. For DeFalco, Segal and Kaplan, as the subject ages, and as the tension between the body and time increases, the chasm between the past and the present becomes bigger while the prospect of a future diminishes; yet, despite recognising the failure of a linear understanding of time, where the present is preceded by the past and followed by the future, the subject is largely locked into this comprehension of linearity and is unable to get out of it. Put differently, to age is to get increasingly out of sync with (clock) time, and to age is to continuously engage in a particular performance of time, where the linear time done unto the subject is put in negotiation with the non-adherence to chronological linearity that the subject is doing. Where the silvering screen is concerned, then, with their general gloominess about older age and the abundant presence of clock and calendrical time, films about older age can therefore be seen as articulating the fear of losing control over time and losing control to time.

Seen in this light, films about dementia made from the year 2000 onwards, as a subset of the silvering screen, come to occupy a very interesting relationship with time and temporality. On one layer, following DeFalco, dementia can be seen as 'a grotesque exaggeration of what human temporality, our condition as aging subjects, enacts', as people living with dementia's experiences of time increasingly pull away from the understanding of modern, homogeneous time (DeFalco 2010: 56). On another layer, it is important to note that dementia – more specifically, early onset dementia – does affect people who are in their thirties or forties; in fact, early onset dementia makes a regular appearance in dementia cinema through films such as *Beautiful Memories* (Zabou Breitman, 2001, France), *A Moment to Remember* (John H. Lee, 2004, South Korea), *Memories of Tomorrow* (Yukihiko Tsutsumi, 2006, Japan), *U Me Aur Hum* (Ajay Devgan, 2008, India), *Evim Sensin* (Özcan Deniz, 2012, Turkey) and *Still Alice* (Richard Glatzer and Wash Westmoreland, 2014, USA/UK/France). Yet, as Patricia Mc Parland, Fiona Kelly and Anthea Innes suggest, although dementia does affect 'younger' people, the diagnosis of early onset dementia 'has the potential to conceptually catapult the younger person into the terrain or imagery associated with the most vulnerable old' (Mc Parland et al. 2017: 260). In other words, *all* dementia is synonymised with older age. Consequently, films about dementia heighten the fear of losing authority over/to time for dementia is suggested as something that can happen to anyone at any time in their life (despite significantly fewer cases of early onset dementia in comparison to, say, Alzheimer's disease, which is a form of predominantly late onset dementia that affect people from age sixty-five and onwards). As such, films about dementia in the new millennium can be understood as being doubly apprehensive with being out of time, in turn indexing and highlighting the temporal negotiations at work.

Experiencing time differently

In thinking about films about dementia in relation to the wider experiences and structures of time, this book builds on the burgeoning research about ageing, dementia and cinema by scholars such as Chivers (2011), Timothy Shary and Nancy McVittie (2016) and Raquel Medina (2018).[11] Chivers's monograph *The Silvering Screen*, for example, traces 'the cultural imagination as captured in filmic representations of older age in order to think about what such films can spark in the imaginations of audiences' (Chivers 2011: xxii). In a similar vein, Shary and McVittie's *Fade to Gray* (2016) explores the changing representations of old age throughout the history of Hollywood cinema, surfacing the socio-political factors in America that engender the largely negative portrayals of older people. More directly, perhaps, is Medina's *Cinematic Representations of Alzheimer's Disease* (2018), which looks at the ways in which the disease is represented on screen or used as a cultural metaphor to discuss certain societal issues.

These studies of cinematic representations of dementia have provided much foundation for the field, and have opened up many avenues for further investigation. Where my book differs from the previous research is my outlook towards cinema. The above scholarship, coming from a representational angle, often understands the subject matter as mediated and constructed by the film's form. According to Richard Rushton, these representational approaches understand cinematic images as 'culturally constructed in the same way that language are' (Rushton 2011: 131). In turn, Rushton argues, cinema is seen as secondary to real life, where films 'in themselves have no reality but can only refer to or reflect the realities of life that exist outside, beyond, or behind them', and thus there is always a tendency to insist that all films are grounded in their respective socio-political contexts (Rushton 2011: 8).

By contrast, I draw from Gilles Deleuze's philosophy of time and characterisation of cinema. For Deleuze, cinema is made up of what he terms 'signaletic material' that 'includes all kinds of modulation features, sensory (visual and sound), kinetic, intensive, affective, rhythmic, tonal, and even verbal (oral and written)' (Deleuze 2013b: 29). When language gets hold of the signaletic material, Deleuze writes:

> it gives rise to utterances which come to dominate or even replace the images and signs, and which refer in turn to pertinent features of the language system, syntagms and paradigms, completely different from those we started with. (Deleuze 2013b: 29)

Simply put, cinema is not separate from the material world as a second order of representation. Rather, cinematic audio-visual images are no different from the world beyond the frame – the temporalities embedded in cinema are also the temporalities of the surrounding material world, and vice versa.[12] In this sense, borrowing from Maud Ceuterick, 'cinema acts as "a way of thinking" towards the world' and reveals 'a world in constant transformation' (Ceuterick 2020: 12). In turn, cinema becomes similarly and equally entangled in multiple viewpoints. As such, throughout the book, discourses on cinema, dementia and cultural narratives about dementia are treated in the same way as I draw from various disciplines and fleet from one to another, putting them in dialogue.[13]

In examining the ways in which the filmic treatment of people living with dementia can be understood as what Janet Gibson describes as 'creative adaptations rather than just as deficit exemplars of insidious diseases', the book holds the concept of relationality at its core (Gibson 2020: 256). A relational approach, in dementia studies and in cultural gerontology, constitutes a development from Tom Kitwood's influential work on person-centred care that seeks to reaffirm the personhood of the person living with dementia (Kitwood 1997). Since Kitwood, there has been a gradual move towards also considering 'the interdependencies and reciprocities that underpin caring relationships' (Nolan et al. 2002: 203). For instance, Kate White, drawing from social psychology, advocates for a relationship centred framework that offers the person living with dementia – whom she describes as 'being disoriented-in-time' (White 2018: 23) – and their carer 'an opportunity as a couple to renew, recover and revitalise their attachment relationship' (White 2018: 15). In another example, dementia studies scholars John David Keady et al. attempt to understand the ways the person living with dementia might be 'in the moment', where to be in a moment is to encounter a 'relational, embodied and multi-sensory experience' (Keady et al. 2022: 687). For Keady et al. such a moment can be conceptualised as part of a 'continuum of moments with transitional, temporal and, potentially, cyclical properties' (Keady et al. 2022: 687). Altogether, in the relational turn, there is a concerted effort to reaffirm the social citizenship and agency of people living with dementia (Kontos et al. 2017).[14]

Whilst this book finds affinity with many of the ideas from the above-mentioned scholarship, I make my argument by specifically suggesting that the person living with dementia, like the person not living with dementia and other (non-)living phenomena, is experiencing time *differently*. This attitude towards difference draws inspiration from Deleuze's call to think of difference from that of negation to that of affirmation. He writes:

> difference is affirmation. This proposition, however, means many things: that difference is an object of affirmation; that affirmation itself is multiple; that it is creation but also that it must be created, as affirming difference, as being difference in itself. It is not the negative which is the motor. Rather, there are positive differential elements which determines the genesis of both the affirmation and the difference affirmed. (Deleuze 1994: 55)

This is to say, difference is not 'not like this thing' but, rather, is almost the same but not quite. Seen from this point of view, difference as affirmation works to recognise the elements that are common between multiple animate and non-animate things, and the ways in which these mutual components might manifest in multiple actual forms due to different performances. Consequently, difference, celebrated, becomes a route to acknowledging a shared world despite the multiple variations of the actual forms that inhabit the world – in recognising the heterogeneous commonalities through a Deleuzian philosophy of difference, Othering becomes harder.

To think deeply with and through cinema, this book consciously places the analysis of the filmic form at the foreground of research into films about dementia. This is because, in aligning with Lee Carruthers (2016) and Matilda Mroz (2012), close textual analysis of films is a way to allow the durations and rhythms of cinema to surface.[15] I elaborate on this framework of temporal performances by zooming into the details of the case study films to tease out the ways in which these minutiae might provoke and evoke a way of thinking about time that does not completely reject linearity nor non-linearity. As I approach the films about dementia through close textual analysis, exploring the significance of each audio-visual detail, I pause and hesitate, thinking about all the possible nuances and the wider temporal implications that might be attached to each detail. As I hesitate, I pause, and carefully tease out the multifaceted performances of time imbricated in the films about dementia, thinking through the networks of power and relations of cultural processes that are embedded in these temporal negotiations. Put differently, as Alia Al-Saji would argue, hesitation becomes a means 'to feel one's way tentatively and receptively', and to unfurl time (Al-Saji 2014: 143).

Beyond a methodological approach to read films, hesitation offers the potential for a deeply ethical stance to actualise. According to Al-Saji, hesitation interrupts 'habitual action', as one's automated habits are brought to a temporary standstill (Al-Saji 2014: 143). In an encounter with my grandmother, for instance, I might expect her to behave in ways that I have come to habitually presume of her. However, if, in that moment, my grandmother does not acknowledge me as her grandson but as someone else, a sense of hesitation will be induced in me, as I tentatively feel for a solution and to try and make sense of the unexpected behaviour. For Al-Saji, after that momentary pause, I could choose to respond in two ways. Firstly, I can insist on 'maintaining the normative organization of the field' and insist that I am her grandson (Al-Saji 2014: 155). Conversely, I can react 'by receptively allowing an event to insinuate itself into our vision as the dimension according to which the visual field is restructured' (Al-Saji 2014: 155). In the latter, Al-Saji argues, hesitation offers an opportunity to expand my critical-ethical vision by allowing my 'perceptual field' to be 'reoriented by others' (Al-Saji 2014: 161). Put differently, through hesitation, and through allowing myself to be performed by my grandmother, I am putting both my worldview and my grandmother's new worldview into a relational conversation so as to engender a 'reconfiguration of the network of attachments' (Al-Saji 2014: 159). As I will insist throughout the book, I advocate for such an ethical and relational encounter with people living with dementia so as to not Other.

In doing so, *Ageing, Dementia and Time in Film* takes up Linn J. Sandberg and Barbara L. Marshall's challenge to actively imagine 'radically different aging futures that might accommodate difference' (Sandberg and Marshall

2017: 8). To think about the person living with dementia as experiencing time differently is to work through the ways in which everyone and everything is embedded in multiple temporal performances. To work through the different layers of this proposal, the monograph is structured like that of a scaffold, where the arguments put forward in Chapter Two are built on the arguments in Chapter One, and so on and so forth. Therefore, I recommend approaching the book in a chronological order so as to allow the complexities of the proposed ideas to slowly gain its nuances over the course of reading (though, of course, each chapter can be read as stand-alone chapters with a tightly focused research question).

In Chapter One I look at *U Me Aur Hum* (Ajay Devgn, 2008, India) and *A Moment to Remember* (John H. Lee, 2004, South Korea), two films that depict early onset Alzheimer's disease, so as to examine the issue of agency in relation to the person living with dementia. I propose to think of the agency of the person living with dementia through the concept of change and becoming, and I link this discussion to Henri Bergson's notion of pure duration, consequently articulating these concerns with agency and identification through the concept of time as performance. Ultimately, I lay the foundation for the rest of the book by putting forward the notion of temporal identification and argue that a subject is always performing time and performed by time.

I expand on this notion of temporal performance alongside questions of narratives about dementia in Chapter Two. The chapter explores the narrative structures of both *Memories of Tomorrow* (Yukihiko Tsutsumi, 2006, Japan) and *Memoir of a Murderer* (Won Shin-yeon, 2017, South Korea), two films that largely attempt to narrativise the experiences of dementia from the subjective viewpoint of the person living with dementia, alongside Deleuze's three syntheses of time. I suggest that the narratives of these two films about dementia can be understood as that of the virtual past (a pure past that is shared and experienced by all the actual entities in the world) returning differently, opening up the narratives of dementia to future invention and change.

The arguments put forward in the first two chapters are then tied together in Chapter Three through an analysis of *Happiness* (Andy Lo, 2016, Hong Kong) and *The Mourning Forest* (Naomi Kawase, 2007, Japan), two films about a stranger caring for, and becoming family with, a person living with dementia. The chapter suggests that films about dementia, in highlighting the multiple temporal performances on and off screen, aestheticise what Matthew Ratcliffe describes as 'radical empathy', which 'involves engaging with someone else's experiences, rather than one's own, while at the same time suspending the usual assumption that both parties share the same space of possibilities' (Ratcliffe 2015: 242). In turn, I argue, films about dementia draw our attention to how we can empathetically relate to our shared world differently.

In Chapter Four I significantly expand the parameters of the framework of temporal performances from that of human relationality to that of the more-than-human, and I do this through an examination of *Pandora's Box* (Yeşim Ustaoğlu, 2008, Turkey/France/Germany/Belgium) and *Happy End* (Michael Haneke, 2017, France/Austria/Germany). In both films, the narrative arc of the person living with dementia is not just performed by the people around them but is also significantly performed by their material surround, and vice versa. Consequently, the chapter argues that a subject's temporal identification is situated in wider ecologies of temporal performances. In turn, borrowing from Jacques Rancière (2004), films about dementia encourage a creative engagement with the heterogeneous temporalities embedded in them so as to make sensible new ways of imagining the lives of dementia.

Seen from this perspective, Chapter Four opens the possibility of enabling a rhizomatic worldview that eschews hierarchies, where anywhere can be centre and anywhere can be periphery. This is the focus of Chapter Five, which looks at the experiences of dementia through the lens of generic horror, exploring two found footage horror films – *The Taking of Deborah Logan* (Adam Robitel, 2014, USA) and *The Visit* (M. Night Shyamalan, 2015, USA) – and the ways in which the experiences of dementia threaten to explode the seeming separation between the past and the present. I propose that the temporalities indexed by the person living with dementia and the person not living with dementia, where the past co-exists alongside the present, are predominantly evinced and surfaced through a mode of hesitant encounter. Consequently, I suggest that to think about time through the prism of performance is to de-centre a Western-centric worldview and to allow for a rhizomatic understanding of a world where anywhere can be centre and anywhere can be periphery. In turn, through thinking about the performance of time, the buried/neglected pasts across the world are surfaced.

In exploring the ways in which the person living with dementia experiences time differently through Chapters One to Five, the book gradually puts forward a methodological approach that hesitantly explores, where hesitation, according to Al-Saji, is 'not only an interruption of the present but also a *critical reconfiguration of the past*' (Al-Saji 2018: 338; emphasis in original). To hesitate is to think through the entangled temporalities of the world, where everyone and everything is performed and performed by various intersections of time, and to hesitate is to open up new lines of temporal performances. In Chapter Six, I weave all these threads together with an in-depth case study of Singapore and Singapore cinema vis-à-vis *Parting* (Boo Junfeng, 2015, Singapore). In particular, I focus on the trope of the person living with dementia wandering, which is a regular feature in various films about dementia and in the wider cultural imaginary, and argue that the trope enacts a particular performance of time in relation to the film's contextual surround so as to enter and traverse the nation's discursive sphere of history and historiography. Ultimately, then, the concept of time as performance not only becomes a way to think of the world through a philosophy of difference but is also a category of analysis that offers the potential for hidden and forgotten pasts to be surfaced and remembered again, differently.

One final note: as is evident, although most of the films seem to fall within the umbrella of 'Asian cinema', the films analysed in the individual chapters are grouped by their thematic concerns. This predominant focus on cinemas across Asia is largely due to the presence of existing research done on films about dementia across Europe, North America and South America, but it is also down to the intersections of my research interests and subjectivity as a postcolonial subject who grew up in Singapore and is now living in the UK. Here, in the analyses of all these films, I make no claims about anything that can be universally applied to all discourses about dementia for, as has been much discussed, the concept of universality is a notion that privileges imperialist and Western-centric worldviews.[16] Rather, the performances of time that I explore in the case study films are all heterogeneously connected, each but a performance (or many singular performances) of time, variously different and variously related – it is in this spirit that I have subtitled the book *Temporal Performances*.

Notes

1 See Freedman et al. 1994, Shulman 2000 and Kim and Chey 2010 on the Clock Drawing Test.
2 See also Levy and Dreier 1997, Nygård and Borell 1998, Topo et al. 2007, Iwamoto and Hoshiyama 2012 and Bohn et al. 2016.
3 The history and cultures of clock time have been widely written about. See also Le Goff 1980, Landes 2000, Bartky 2000, Kern 2003, Hassan 2003, Hassan and Ronald 2007, Glennie and Thrift 2009, Nanni 2012, Sharma 2014 and Ogle 2015.
4 Richard Schechner takes a broad spectrum approach towards the theory of performance: 'Theater is only one node on a continuum that reaches from the ritualizations of animals (including humans) through performances in everyday life – greetings, displays of emotion, family scenes, professional roles, and so on – through

to play, sports, theater, dance, ceremonies, rites, and performances of great magnitude' (Schechner 2003: xvii). For a more comprehensive overview of the concept of performance and the debates within the field of performance studies, see also Goffman 1990, Read 1993, Carlson 2003, Striff 2003, Harding and Rosenthal 2011, Schneider 2011 and Schechner 2015.

5   The Baby Boomer generation typically refers to people who were born from the mid-1940s to the mid-1960s, where the end of the Second World War saw a spike in birth rates occurring across the world.

6   See Crossley and Fisher 2021 and Dudrah 2021 on geri-action cinema.

7   Maktoba Omar, Nathalia C. Tjandra and John Ensor observe that the disposable income of consumers over fifty has increased 25 per cent in 2012 since the 2008 economic recession as compared to the meagre 2 per cent increment for those under fifty (Omar et al. 2014: 754). Separately, the notion of films targeted at the 'grey pound' started to gain traction in British newspapers in the early noughties (see Cox 2012, Clark 2013 and Anon 2014).

8   Josephine Dolan (2016) observes that the purchasing power of the pension and the grey pound inadvertently makes its way into the narratives of these films targeted at older people, and usually results in narratives that are deeply neo-colonialist, heteronormative and postfeminist.

9   See Twigg and Martin 2015a and 2015b on cultural gerontology.

10 For other psychoanalytic approaches towards old age see de Beauvoir 1997, Woodward 1991 and Gullette 2004.

11 See also Segers 2007, Anderson 2010, Van Gorp and Vercruysse 2012, Cohen-Shalev 2012, Cohen-Shalev and Marcus 2012, Gravagne 2013, Wearing 2013, Chivers 2015 and Graham 2016.

12 See Rodowick 1997; Bogue 2003; Pisters 2003, 2012, 2015; Powell 2007 and Martin-Jones 2011 for some scholarship on Deleuzian philosophy and cinema.

13 This methodology – treating everything on an equal level of comparison – also bears affinity with certain schools of thought in feminist science studies that do not necessarily agree with metaphors and analogies as an epistemological framework for multi-/inter-/trans-disciplinary consideration of both cultural and science studies. See Barad 2007 for a discussion of an epistemological framework that rejects analogies and representations.

14 See also Adams and Gardiner 2005, Gray 2019 and Hatton 2021 on relational approaches to dementia.

15 This is to also make interdisciplinary work dialogic. Cinema is an audio-visual medium of time. Likewise, time is also an extremely important building block of the gerontological imagination. See Baars 1997, 2007; McFadden and Atchley 2001 and Baars and Visser 2007.

16 See Yoshimoto 2006 and Chen 2010 for such discussions about concepts of 'Asianness' and 'universality'.

1

Performing Time/Performed by Time

In *U Me Aur Hum* (Ajay Devgan, 2008, India), Piya, a 28-year-old woman, is having dinner with her husband, Ajay, when a cake is delivered to their table. Surprised, Piya questions the purpose of the cake and Ajay, thinking Piya is joking, asks her to cut the cake. Her face displays a sense of confusion with the whole situation and she continues to insist that he explains the presence of the cake. Undeterred, Ajay maintains that she is pulling a prank on him and says that they have already discussed the purpose of the dinner yesterday. Piya looks even more confused and, exasperated, Ajay announces that it is their first wedding anniversary. The film cuts to a shot of Piya in close-up. She still looks confused but, immediately, she breaks into laughter and jokes about how Ajay has become the 'perfect scapegoat' for her impeccable performance. It is only when Piya is diagnosed with early onset Alzheimer's disease that Ajay finds out that she had been genuinely confused at that moment, and that she had been engaged in an act of double performance here – performing the action of putting on a performance.

This scene where Piya performs the notion that she knew that one calendrical year has passed since she got married despite actually unable to remember, a performance of conforming to empty, homogeneous time despite clearly being out of it, is a typical scenario in films about dementia. In *A Moment to Remember* (John H. Lee, 2004, South Korea), for instance, Su-jin, a 27-year-old woman who too lives with early onset Alzheimer's disease, goes to the doctor as she has been displaying moments of forgetfulness. In her second visit, the doctor begins by asking her what the date is. Su-jin pauses, slightly bemused, and laughs it off, saying that she always loses track of the date. The doctor immediately chastises her for returning to the follow up appointment a week late. He asks her how many siblings she has and she is able to provide the correct answer. She is, however, unable to state the age of her sibling. At first, Su-jin says twenty. Then she hesitates and says nineteen. She laughs awkwardly and explains that she has always been bad with numbers. The doctor asks her to state her sister's birthday and the film cuts to a Dutch angle shot of her face, cinematographically signposting the confusion and disorientation that she is encountering.

Without giving Su-jin a chance to answer the question, the film cuts immediately to a shot of her beginning the process of a computerised tomography (CT) scan, and the laser beams are focused on her head as she enters the machine. The film cuts back to the doctor's room as he continues with his line of questioning: what is the colour for the walk signal that suggests it is safe for pedestrians to cross? Su-jin retorts indignantly and demands to know why the doctor is asking her these questions, trying to swerve her way out of the uncomfortable situation in the room. The film cuts to a shot of Su-jin entering the CT machine. She is in the background of the shot, out of focus, whilst the foreground is a shot of her brain imaging appearing on the computer screen. As that happens, the line of questioning continues. Significantly, through the aural editing, Su-jin is not given a chance to respond and the audience only hears the barrage of oncoming questions on maths and logic directed at her as she continues to undergo her CT scan.

Like Piya, Su-jin's out-of-timeness is highlighted, not least because she is only given the chance to fail at answering questions specifically related to time (tell the date and remember the age and birthday of her sister). Yet, Su-jin's inability to answer the questions does not stop her from performing in such a manner that attempts to cover up her inability to answer. She deflects and laughs about how she is always bad with numbers and dates although the attempts to pass as being in time do not quite work and the film puts her under the medical gaze of the CT machine after she fails to answer the questions related to time. These attempts to perform as being in time further highlight the idea that she is no longer in sync with the empty, homogeneous time that the diagnostic tests require her to be.

These temporal negotiations/ambivalences displayed by Piya and Su-jin extend beyond the filmic. In analysing the conversational patterns of people living with frontotemporal dementia, Lisa Mikesell notes that people living with dementia often adopt strategies of repetitional response in their everyday conversations, where they would repeat back whatever that was said to them in order to advance the conversation. These ways of speaking, Mikesell notes, are regularly used by people living with dementia in order to appear certain and confident, leading Mikesell to write that people living with dementia, consciously or unconsciously, 'make an effort to present themselves as knowing or capable participants with the ability and rights to assert their autonomy' (Mikesell 2010: 493). Put differently, the speech patterns of people living with dementia, and how they interact in conversational situations, can never be straightforwardly read as a display of cognitive abilities or lack thereof; there is always a quality of ambivalence, and performance, underlying how they appear.

In bringing research about people living with dementia together with the scenes discussed above, two issues are highlighted. Firstly, Piya and Su-jin perform a sense of in-time-ness in order to convince the world around them that they are alright but, in the process of doing so, highlight the ways that their out-of-time-ness is actually performed by the empty, homogeneous time that their societies are subscribed to. It underlines the complex negotiations with multiple temporalities – clock and non-clock – that a person living with dementia negotiates. This being the case, films about dementia offer the potential to challenge the dichotomies of linear/non-linear time and blur the temporal categorisations that so many scholars writing about temporality have identified. Secondly, Piya and Su-jin's performances of in-time-ness raise the question of the agency of people living with dementia. If, as Steven R. Sabat (2001) observes, people living with dementia are socially and culturally positioned as unable to care for themselves or make their own decisions, and are therefore denied their own agency, might the examination of films about dementia through the prism of difference and performance open up ways of re-positioning the lived experiences of people living with dementia?

In exploring the depiction of agency in films about dementia, this chapter develops a model of change so as to understand the more general notion of agency as the constant embodied and performative negotiation between the normative and the anti-normative. I do this by undertaking an analysis of *A Moment to Remember* and *U Me Aur Hum*, both films in which relatively young women are catapulted into the cultural 'old' through early onset Alzheimer's disease, forcing them to rapidly negotiate a radically new way of living. To work through the complexities of change explored in the films, I put forward the concept of 'temporal identification', arguing that a subject is always *performing* time and *performed by* time. Working from a close analysis of each film, I show that Piya and Su-jin (and the characters around them) are in a constant state of agentic becoming and that looking at time through the lens of performance engages with a politics of intersectionality, as one's temporal identification is not merely reduced to one kind of categorisation. In developing 'temporal identification' as an analytic framework, this chapter lays the foundation for the rest of the book to think about the ways that films about dementia encourage a temporally relational worldview.

Dementia and the temporality of agency

In one key scene in *A Moment to Remember,* just before she is officially diagnosed with dementia, Su-jin sits in the living room with Cheol-su, her husband, as she works on her scrapbook. All of a sudden, she stands up and walks to the kitchen. She picks up a pair of rubber cleaning gloves and puts them on before walking to the refrigerator and opens it whilst taking off the gloves. She searches the fridge for something, puts the gloves in the fridge and then closes it again. Then, Su-jin walks to the front door, opens it, and looks out, searching for something. She closes the door, turns around and sees her husband. She exclaims: 'Where were you?' In response, Cheol-su starts laughing and what might be traditionally thought of as non-diegetic guitar music enters the scene. Here, the music is light-hearted and, through the music, Su-jin's behaviour and meander around the house is coded as nothing out of the blue – she is just her usual absent-minded self who has gotten so engrossed in her scrapbooking that she forgot her husband is sat behind her.

Su-jin returns to her scrapbook, picks up the photo that she has been gluing at the beginning of the scene, asks whether Cheol-su has glued it, and continues with her scrapbooking. Cheol-su begins to show signs of concern and asks about the doctor's appointment that was meant to have happened during the day. Su-jin, not realising that she has forgotten about the appointment, answers that the doctor had asked her to come back next week, leading Cheol-su to become even more concerned. Aurally, the music does not stop and the implication that Su-jin might have dementia or any other form of head trauma is alleviated. In this scene, pre-diagnosis, Su-jin's warped temporality is audio-visually coded to be just part and parcel of Su-jin's absent-mindedness, and not of serious concern.

By contrast, after Su-jin is diagnosed with early onset Alzheimer's disease, the same kind of 'absent-mindedness' is coated with a more menacing undertone. Here, Su-jin is cooking a feast for her mother-in-law's birthday. The scene opens with a close-up shot of a kettle boiling on the stove. It cuts to a wide-angle shot of Su-jin chopping some spring onions. The whole kitchen is filled with Post-it notes reminding Su-jin where things are in relation to her. Su-jin is positioned in the centre of the shot; in the background, the kettle is boiling and, in the foreground, the knife that Su-jin uses is prominently positioned. The film then cuts to a close-up shot of the knife chopping some spring onions. Very quickly, then, before the scene even proceeds, the wide-angle shot of Su-jin chopping vegetables is sandwiched by two close-up shots of danger, of potential accidents waiting to happen.

The film cuts to a close-up shot of Su-jin as she continues chopping. She pauses, looks up, and turns her head. Immediately, music enters the film's score. This music is markedly different from the relaxed melodic guitar that the audience has heard before; instead, it is menacing, droning and dissonant, furthering a sense of threat. Then, the film cuts to a point-of-view shot of a calendar. The shot is largely blurred, tunnel-visioned, with the calendar in sharper focus in the middle of the shot. The film cuts back to a reverse shot of Su-jin staring catatonically at the calendar, unable to make sense of it. At that moment, someone knocks on the door and she walks towards the door, still holding the knife in her hand. She opens the door. The film cuts to a close-up of her face, and the audience sees her facial expression change from happiness to displeasure. A reverse shot reveals Su-jin's ex-partner from two years ago at the door. Quickly, Su-jin starts smiling and drags him into the house, asking him to get ready for dinner. Throughout, the knife is prominently placed in the middle of the frame as Su-jin grabs her ex-partner, and the menacing atmosphere continues to permeate the scene.

Unlike pre-diagnosis Su-jin, whose multiple temporalities are dismissed as 'absent-mindedness', post-diagnosis Su-jin's inability to comprehend a calendar and her re-living the past in the present are imbued with a sense of danger, as if the actions carried out by Su-jin do not belong to her, and have the potential to hurt and harm. Consequently, *A Moment to Remember* raises interesting questions regarding Su-jin's agency as a person living with dementia: does dementia remove agency from the person? On the surface, the film would appear to do so, audio-visually coding her actions post diagnosis as not being controlled by her mind, rendering her as having no agency. This view would be affirmed by neurologists Sylvia S. Fong et al. (2017), who, in their examination into the animacy (state of being sentient) and agency (defined as the capacity for intrinsically driven action) of people living with frontotemporal dementia and Alzheimer's disease, suggest that people living with dementia not only display deficits of animacy but also demonstrate a significantly impaired sense of agency. If we were to follow Fong et al., Su-jin's actions would be seen as having no agency.

Conversely, nursing scholar Geraldine Boyle criticises this focus on the brain in discourses of agency and people living with dementia. Instead, Boyle thinks of agency as 'the means by which the subjective self becomes a social self' (Boyle 2017a: 2).[1] Boyle contends that agency should be measured by a person's ability to be reflexive, and she proposes three ways to think about this notion of reflexivity: relational, dialogical and emotional. For Boyle, a person demonstrates agency if they display the ability to interact with people, negotiate their thoughts verbally or non-verbally, or convey their emotions (Boyle 2017b: 4). Agency, then, where people living with dementia are concerned, is embedded 'within relationships of care and mutual dependence', and is a constant process of negotiation with multiple groups of people (Boyle 2017b: 4).

This approach is echoed in the work of other scholars who decentralise brain and cognitive capacity in order to understand the experience of dementia. Julian C. Hughes, for instance, puts forward the concept of the situated embodied-agent (SEA) view of the person living with dementia, and asserts that the person pre-dementia diagnosis and the person post-dementia diagnosis are connected 'by embodiment and by the situatedness that the embodiment entails' (Hughes 2001: 89). Likewise, Hughes and Carmelo Aquilina suggest that the concept of agency brings about the notion of intention into the debate. They maintain that 'the intentional nature of an action can be taken to imply that which the action, being of this type, itself aims at' (Aquilina and Hughes 2006: 156). In turn, this approach shifts the discourse around agency from that of the mind to that of the embodied person living with dementia, where their actions can be read as filled with agency because they are intended to interact with their situated surrounding.[2]

In short, agency, where people living with dementia are concerned, can be thought of in terms of the embodied and the performative. The person living with dementia is embedded within a larger network of care and mutual dependence, and their actions interact with their situated surroundings. In other words, there is a constant push and pull between different groups of people where one's agency is negotiated with other subjects' agencies. Accordingly, Su-jin's actions in *A Moment to Remember* can be read as not losing her agency but as a display of a different form of agency: she is still holding on to the knife throughout the scene because she still intends to chop the vegetables to cook the feast for her mother-in-law's birthday, and she is still holding on to the knife when she is asking her ex-partner to get ready for dinner because she intends to get dinner ready for the both of them. When she first sees her ex-partner, she loses her smile because this is not her husband, but regains it because he is now her current partner, and her emotions are reflexively negotiated with her embodied situation. In a sense, then, Su-jin is moving from one perceived temporality to another. Rather than reading the film's evocation of menace as that which is denying the person living with dementia's agency, my contention – and I articulate this claim more fully in Chapter Five – is that the sense of horror engendered in *A Moment to Remember* works to affectively highlight Su-jin's temporal indeterminacy.

From this viewpoint, agency can be understood 'as a temporally embedded process of social engagement' (Emirbayer and Mische 1998: 963). This perspective evokes the work of Judith Butler, who thinks about agency as a process of signification. She writes:

> The subject is not *determined* by the rules through which it is generated because signification is *not a founding act, but rather a regulated process of repetition* that both conceals itself and enforces its rules precisely through the production of substantializing effects. In a sense, all signification takes place within the orbit of the compulsion to repeat; 'agency', then, is to be located within the possibility of a variation on that repetition. (Butler 1990: 145; emphasis in original)

Here, Butler is interested in the performativity of gender, where a subject's gender identification is constantly performed and repeated. Agency, for Butler, demonstrates an ambivalent and oscillatory relationship to both the past powers that shape it and the future possibilities that may come. In this sense, the Butlerian agency is a 'vacillation between the already-there and the yet-to-come', 'a crossroads that rejoins every step by which it is traversed', and a 'sense of done over, done again, done anew' (Butler 1997: 18). Understood in this way, agency is an ambivalent moment that does not solely exist in the present, which in turn becomes a site for complex negotiations between the past (hegemonic powers) and the future (radical or oppositional potential). Once negotiated, the present moment becomes the past and a new set of negotiations between the past and the future happens through the subject's agency – through their embodied interactions with a present situation.

This focus on the in-betweens as the site of temporal ambivalence that vacillates between the past and the present, Stephanie Clare contends, 'freezes time by formulating becoming as a series of moments or steps' (Clare 2009: 57). For Clare, Butler's ideas ignore the 'becoming of the subject as a continuous (though perhaps uneven) process' where 'agency emerges in the process of becoming, not in the mysterious moments between beings' (Clare 2009: 59). By contrast, Clare argues that it is useful to think about the ways in which the subject and agency is actualised from the virtual to the actual (concepts that I develop further in Chapter Three). For Clare, viewing agency as a process of actualisation rather than realisation means that we can understand agency as 'a process of transformation', where 'virtual power actualizes itself producing a difference' (Clare 2009: 60). That is to say, thinking about agency as a process of actualisation, rather than realisation means that we can think of agency as a constant process of change, of negotiation, of becoming(s). Clare's nuanced re-reading of Butler's theory moves the conversation from the signification of the body to also that of the body as embodied practice. In other words, this is to think of agency as embodied and performative, and as personal and social.

Films about dementia, in part concerned about cinema and in part concerned about dementia, contribute to this discussion of agency and temporality by highlighting and emphasising the complexities of temporal change. As I repeatedly show throughout this book, a constant embodied and performative negotiation between the past, present and future can be read in films about dementia, and such films become a site where multiple times and temporalities meet, collide and/or co-exist in a heightened manner. A debate about the cultural and political implications of this for film, and for cultural production more broadly, runs as a constant undercurrent to the specific analysis in each chapter.

I have pointed to the ways in which this constant state of change is highlighted in *A Moment to Remember*. This state of becoming is also foregrounded in *U Me Aur Hum*. Piya, in one scene, carries her baby to the bath to give him a bath. Whilst walking, she sings the lullaby 'Hush, Little Baby' to the child. This rendition of the lullaby is reverberated, which is a sonic phenomenon caused by multiple soundwaves reflecting off surfaces, where sound continues to persist after it has been produced. Whilst reverberations happen in all kinds of spaces, the reverberated song that the audience hears is heightened and does not match the bedroom and bathroom setting that Piya and her baby are in. In turn, this suggests that the lullaby that the audience hears is neither coming out from her mouth nor is it necessarily relegated to the film's score without an identified source because her lips match with the lyrics. Instead, drawing from Robyn J. Stilwell (2007), this music that is neither here nor there occupies the 'fantastical gap' between the boundaries of diegetic and non-diegetic music, and the song becomes an aural manifestation of the multiple temporalities that the person living with dementia experiences. The sound quality in this scene allows the audience to map the temporal and emotional terrain of both Piya and her surrounding world.

Piya puts the baby in the bath, turns on the tap, and the bath fills up. While waiting, she goes to her bedroom to prepare for the post-bath clean up. All this while, the audience continues to hear the music although Piya has stopped singing – coupled with the visual images of her preparing for the post-bath procedures, the lullaby becomes a suggestion that Piya is still thinking about her baby. Once she is ready, she starts to leave for the bathroom. But, before she is able to, something catches her eye and she stops.

Immediately, the lullaby fades out and is replaced by a fast-paced score music comprising brass and string instruments. Very quickly, the mood of the scene changes from that of haunted sereneness to that of action and danger. Likewise, the editing pattern of the sequence changes pace. As the film cuts to shots of the bath rapidly filling up with the baby still in it, the film moves into a series of shot/reverse shots of Piya, standing completely still, looking at a lizard.

As that happens, Ajay returns home from work. The fast-paced music continues and, through the rapid editing, the stillness of Piya is juxtaposed with the disorder around her (the bathtub is rapidly filling up, the dog is barking frantically, and Ajay is struggling to get into the flat). Amidst all the chaos, the music builds up to a crescendo. As Ajay opens the door and enters the house, the fast-paced non-diegetic music fades out. The film cuts to a close-up of Piya's eyes as she continues to stare at the wall and, at that moment, 'Hush, Little Baby' fades into the film before quickly fading out again. In its place, the score music returns and Ajay runs into the room and past Piya into the bathroom. The film then cuts to a wide-angle shot: Piya is positioned in the centre of the frame, still staring at the lizard, and Ajay, in contrast, is running across the horizontal axis of the frame. At that particular moment, the fast-paced music fades out and the lullaby re-enters the film.

Piya's actions here can still be understood as having agency. In one moment, her actions are intended to interact with her baby; in another moment, her actions are intended to interact with the lizard on the wall. In other words, her actions, like Su-jin's, can be understood as moving through from one temporality to another, and she is in a constant state of change and becoming. As Piya's actions begin to negotiate with the actions of the lizard, the film aurally oscillates between the fast-paced score music and the slow and haunted lullaby. The score music is used to add to the suspense and tension in the outside world of Piya, as the chaos around her builds up, locking the audience into a sense of linear time and temporality as they are encouraged to will Ajay through time to save the baby. The lullaby, on the other hand, is used to give the audience an insight into her inner world, her psyche, as her experiences of multiple times and temporalities manifest aurally. The film's choice to continuously switch between these two modes of music as Piya continues to observe the lizard, therefore, not only adds a certain level of pathos to the film as the baby's vulnerability is highlighted, but it also draws the audience's attention to this constant state of change and becoming. The baby and his bath are still in Piya's mind, and the lizard is also, simultaneously, on her mind too. As such, through the use of music, her agentic actions highlight the constant negotiation between the inside world and the outside world that a person living with dementia experiences.

Piya's agency as a constant state of change and becoming can be seen as a negotiation between different temporalities, as her embodied self and her inner psyche negotiate with the external world of actions: the outside world, and the empty, homogeneous time that accompanies it, performs unto Piya a set of expectations and identifications; the inside world, and the heterogeneous temporalities that accompany it, performs a different kind of expectations and identifications out of Piya. Piya's agency – and agency in a wider sense – as a series of change and becoming can therefore be understood as a performance of time, as she is performing time and performed by time.

The performance of time

To elaborate on the concept of temporal identifications and how they work in these two films, I turn to Henri Bergson's work on time and temporality. For Bergson, the time that the body experiences in the external world is a particular homogenised kind. It is time that is spatialised, where time is reduced to the homogeneity of space. He uses the example of counting to illustrate his ideas. In order to count to the number 50, for instance, we have to firstly imagine that there are 50 individual '1's. Then, we have to put these individual units in succession for fifty times so that we can ultimately arrive at the final outcome. As such, Bergson notes, this gives off the impression that 'we have built up the number in duration and in duration only' (Bergson 1950: 78). However, Bergson suggests that this is not the case, and that we are really counting in space rather in time. This is because we 'involuntarily fix a point in space each of the moments which we count, and it is only on this condition that the abstract units come to form a sum' (Bergson 1950: 79). In other words, for Bergson, the question of how we understand time in the external world is, really, a question of how we understand space; the understanding of time as linear, empty and homogeneous means that we think of number – and, by extension, the material world – as 'a juxtaposition in space' (Bergson 1950: 85).

In contrast, Bergson introduces the notion of pure duration to characterise the way time might work in the inner self. He writes:

> Here we find ourselves confronted by a confused multiplicity of sensations and feelings which analysis alone can distinguish. Their number is identical with the number of the moments which we take up when

> we count them; but these moments, as they can be added to one another, are again points in space. Our final conclusion, therefore is that there are two kinds of multiplicity: that of material objects, to which the conception of number is immediately applicable; and the multiplicity of states of consciousness, which cannot be regarded as numerical without the help of some symbolic representation, in which a necessary element is *space*. (Bergson 1950: 87; emphasis in original)

Time in the external world, or what Bergson describes as homogeneous duration, is a distinct multiplicity where everything is laid out in space and not in time. Everything is clearly and distinctly spatialised. Contrarily, in the inner world of the self, time as pure duration functions in a significantly different manner. For Bergson, the inner world of the self experiences multiple sensations and affects (often simultaneously). However, these experiences are not laid out in a successive and homogeneous manner as that of the outer world. Rather, they coalesce in a heterogeneous manner.

Here, time as a force that affects the inner self is experienced as pure duration, which Bergson defines as 'the form in which the succession of our conscious states assumes when our ego lets itself *live*, when it refrains from separating its present state from its former states' (Bergson 1950: 100; emphasis in original). Put differently, the homogeneous time of the outer world spatialises everything and bastardises the understanding of time. Conversely, as multiple sensory and affective forces are experienced in the inner self, things are not laid out in the same successive manner as the outer world. The inner world's experience of time is that of pure duration, where multiple times and temporalities come together. Unfortunately, Bergson avers, when this inner experience of pure duration is reflected on by the person, the symbolic world immediately shifts that articulation of time from that of pure duration to that of spatialised time.

In thinking about the forces of time, Bergson suggests that we can work through certain issues of identification. For Bergson, the notion of identification

> is the absolute law of our consciousness: it affirms that what is thought is thought at the moment when we think it: and what gives this principle its absolute necessity is that it does not bind the future to the present, but only the present to the present. (Bergson 1950: 207)

That is to say, we need to stop thinking about identification in a causal manner, where the present is affected by the past and the present affects the future. Instead, Bergson suggests thinking of identification as a moment in the present, where time is not only heterogeneously experienced by the inner self but is also negotiated with the homogeneity of spatialised, linear time of the outside material world. This focus on one's identification as that of the present (and not as a casual chain) is significant because it does not separate out the multiple temporalities that are coeval, and we can begin to think of one's temporal identification as always in a state of becoming rather than in a state of being.

Here, drawing from Bergson's analysis of time as a force that affects one's identification in the present, I suggest that it is helpful to think through the ways in which a subject performs time and is performed by time. For Bergson, on the one hand, there are the empty, homogeneous times and temporalities that perform a set of social expectations unto the subject. On the other, there are the heterogeneous times and temporalities that the subject attempts to perform. Expanding on Bergson's ideas through an analysis of films about dementia, I argue that instead of thinking about the self as being performed by homogeneous time and performing heterogeneous times, we can think of the subject's temporal identification as relational, and as a constant negotiation between multiple times and temporalities. In thinking about the person's identifications through the temporal present where multiple temporalities come together, agency is no longer thought of as an ambivalent state of being in the present that vacillates between the past and the future, as that proposed by Butler, but as a constant state of change, of becoming, and of negotiation.

Su-jin and Piya, in drawing attention to the notion of agency as becoming, are case studies that provide an opportunity to think about the malleability of such temporal performances. Su-Jin, for example, in *A Moment to Remember*, is a 27-year-old who is portrayed as an independent woman who navigates her way round the hierarchies of South Korean society. The film begins with her left hanging by a married man whom she is having an affair with and follows her narrative as she actively pursues Cheol-su to go out with her, and then to marry her. She is a successful fashion designer, directs advertising campaigns and clinches business deals. Additionally, she also finds the time to clean the house and to cook for her husband, performing the role of a loving wife on top of a successful careerist.

Yet, all this changes with her diagnosis with early onset Alzheimer's disease. When Su-jin finally goes to the doctor for her follow-up appointment, the doctor delivers the news and, confused, she asks the doctor to explain what that means. As he begins to do so, the film cuts to a wide-angle shot of Su-jin walking amongst group of people in their work-wear, lost and forlorn in the sea of office workers. As the doctor explains the situation to

Figure 1.1 Su-jin lost in a sea of working people in *A Moment to Remember*

her, and she begins to realise the gravity of the whole situation, the film intercuts between the office and the public. Back in the office, the doctor advises her to quit her job; outside, completely devastated, Su-jin leaves the path of working passers-by and goes towards a pillar, leaning against it for support. Here, she is in the foreground of the shot, in sharp focus, whilst the workers are in the background, out of focus, and the two entities are separated by a wooden fence. Su-jin's dementia has caused her to exit working life.

The narrative shifts to the interior of her house as Cheol-su returns home from work. He enters the house and sees Su-jin standing in the kitchen cooking dinner. The film then cuts to Cheol-su in his workshop as he notices that Su-jin is standing there, wearing an apron, holding a tray of fruit for her husband, smiling and beckoning him to take a break. Visually, she is bathed in a pool of warm yellow light, almost angelic, and appears to have comfortably and happily taken on the role of the dutiful and faithful housewife. Quickly, this idea is interjected by a close-up of Su-jin, exposing the deep sadness that is hidden behind that performed happiness, drawing the audience's attention to how her gender performance has shifted upon her dementia diagnosis, and that she is not necessarily comfortable with this new performance. In the previous scene, upon diagnosis, Su-jin breaks down completely and is separated off from the working culture that she used to be a part of. Instead of negotiating a balance between work and domesticity, Su-jin here is moved into the sphere of the domestic interior, where she cooks for and waits on her husband.

Next, the film cuts to Su-jin and Cheol-su cuddling as she asks Cheol-su whether she should quit her job and become a housewife. Cheol-su says that he would love that because it is a man's job to financially provide. In turn, Su-jin announces that she is going to quit immediately, and Cheol-su is concerned, asking Su-jin what has happened. Instead of responding, Su-jin kisses him. She pauses, looks into Cheol-su's eyes, and asks whether he wants a baby. Here, Su-jin's adherence to biological (have children) and domestic roles (do household chores) recalls the notion of chrononormativity as put forward by Elizabeth Freeman, where the 'naked flesh is bound into socially meaningful embodiment through temporal regulation' (Freeman 2010: 3). Chrononormativity, for Freeman, 'is a mode of implantation, a technique by which institutional forces come to seem like somatic facts', where 'people are bound to one another, engrouped, made to feel coherently collective, through particular orchestrations of time' (Freeman 2010: 3). Put differently, empty, homogeneous time not only conditions people to think collectively in a linear way, but it is also a means to maintain the hegemonic ideals of society, becoming a means of controlling and disciplining the desires and fantasies of individuals. Women are, for instance, largely reduced to the temporal rhythms of the body and the domestic, where they are encouraged to get married by a certain age so that they can have children before a certain age, where they are encouraged to stay at home to take care of the children and do household chores, day in day out, temporally conforming to a cyclical pattern of domestic labour; men, conversely, are bound to the hours of capitalist labour time, where they have to leave the house by a certain time to start work in the day and can only come home when work ends.

Borrowing from Freeman, we can think of bodies on film being performed by chrononormativity (or empty, homogeneous time), where a set of social expectations is performed unto the people in a particular society. All the while, these bodies can choose to perform differently, not adhering to the temporal expectations placed upon the bodies by society. A young, middle-class, cis-gendered, able-bodied, white and heterosexual woman choosing not to have children or get married, for example, can be seen as the subject performing her own time in relation to/negotiation with the times that are performed unto her. I caution, however, and maintain that this is only one way to think about one's temporal identification. As I elaborate later, to think of one's temporal identifications is to think of the performance of time as a constant process of negotiation, of becoming, of performing/performed by multiple times and temporalities. That is to say, the subject can be attempting to perform the linearity of empty, homogeneous time but is, instead, performed by the heterogeneous temporalities around them.

Whilst these constant becomings are often minute and not necessarily noticeable in everyday life, films about dementia heighten these temporal negotiations. When Su-jin proposes to quit her job, Cheol-su is unaware that she has just been diagnosed with dementia and that her motivation to quit her job is due to her being performed by the curative time imposed upon her by the doctor. Curative time, for Alison Kafer, assumes that disabilities need to be treated so that (dis)abled people can function and effectively contribute to the progress of society or, failing which, casts these disabled bodies as completely out of time (Kafer 2013: 27–8). Yet, despite the curative time that is performed on Su-jin, where the doctor's recommendation can be read as removing her future (she has to give up her dreams of living a long and successful hegemonic life ahead), Su-jin proposes to have a child with Cheol-su. By quitting her job, she is shifting her temporal rhythms from that of work to domestic time, moving deeper into the seemingly traditional/conservative sphere of gender performance where her role is to stay at home, clean the house and bear children. However, Su-jin's performance of woman's time, of wanting a child, of becoming a stay-at-home mother, can be seen as a defiance of this removal of her futurity.[3] She is performed by curative time, which causes her to move into a gender role that she is not necessarily comfortable with. Yet, paradoxically, in performing her new gender role's temporality, she is in turn performing an imagined futurity that tugs against curative time. Su-jin's temporal identification immediately postdiagnosis, therefore, highlights the relationality within multiple approaches towards time and temporality, as she is simultaneously performed by and performing time, and different temporal rhythms come together.

In other words, from the analysis of *A Moment to Remember*, the performance of time can be understood as intersectional, where one's temporal identification is not merely reduced to one kind of categorisation, where multiple categories of identifications intersect to paint a more nuance understanding of the subject.[4] Like *A Moment to Remember*, *U Me Aur Hum* makes the intersectionality of temporal performances evident. Here, I focus on the moment that the audience comes to realise that Piya is living with dementia. In this scene, Ajay and his friends are driving. It is raining heavily and their visibility is reduced. Whilst driving, Ajay and his friends do not pay much attention to what is on the road but that all comes to a halt as Ajay has to conduct an emergency brake in order to not hit a person on the street. The car screeches to a stop and the film cuts to a close-up of Ajay's face as a look of perplexity and recognition slowly creeps over his face. As that happens, the sound of the heavy rain falling fades out of the film and a high-pitched note enters the film. Concurrently, this high-pitched note is layered with a reverberated track of a woman screaming confusedly.

In a reverse shot, Piya dramatically turns around with a dazed look. Next, the film cuts to a close-up of her as she is completely drenched in the tor-

Figure 1.2 Piya repeatedly refreshed by the rain and the wiper in *U Me Aur Hum*

rential rain, as if she is washed anew by the rain. The camera is positioned in the car as the audience sees the windscreen wipers wiping away the rain on the windscreen, revealing a clearer image of Piya. The film cuts to a series of four jump cuts, each time showing Piya's image being blurred by the rain and wiped afresh by the wipers. At this very moment, then, through the rain, the use of the jump cuts and the wiping metaphor, Piya's performance of her temporal identification is visually coded as a state of becoming and change – there is a different Piya at every single moment that is negotiating with multiple times and temporalities.

Aurally, these temporal negotiations are made even clearer. As she turns around, the sound of a glass shattering enters the mix and, immediately after, the slowed-down sound of water bubbling, an unintelligible voice of a man speaking, and a baby crying enter the sound design. As the film cuts back and forth to Ajay in the car and Piya in the street, the cacophony of sound continues to permeate the film. Finally, Ajay opens the door and steps out of his car. As that happens, this stylised soundscape abruptly stops and the sound of heavy rain returns to the film. As Ajay steps out of the car and approaches Piya, she reveals that she is extremely lost and cannot remember any contact numbers (nor Ajay's name) to call for help. This cacophony of sounds can be read as an aural manifestation of the ways in which Piya is performing time and performed by time, as her subjectivity is negotiating with the multiple times and temporalities – of change happening – as she is visually drenched and constantly washed anew by the heavy rain and the windscreen wipers. Firstly, through the amalgamation of the man's and woman's voices, there is a negotiation between two different kinds of gendered temporalities. Secondly, Piya's role as a mother is also called into question through the sound of the infant crying; as the film reveals later on, Piya is pregnant and her pregnancy is making her condition deteriorate faster.

Thirdly, the sonic melting pot in the scene that explodes as Piya turns her face towards Ajay points towards the presence of crip time. For Kafer, crip time occupies the other end of the temporal spectrum in relation to curative time.[5] Crip time, Kafer argues, embraces the notion that everyone follows different paces of living and that they should not be locked down into a standard understanding of how time functions. A disabled body, for instance, would take longer than an abled body to get somewhere, and crip time recognises and accommodates that. According to Kafer, crip time 'is flex time not just expanded but exploded' and 'it requires reimagining our notions of what can and should happen in time, or recognizing how expectations of "how long things take" are based on very particular minds and bodies' (Kafer 2013: 27). In other words, for Kafer, crip time not only accommodates different paces of life but also challenges the empty, homogeneous clock time (and curative time). This exploded time that accommodates can also be heard in the soundscape as the different sounds all occupy different temporal rhythms: the woman's voice is frantic and high-pitched, the man's voice is slow and low-pitched, the high-pitched screech continues in a single note, the bubbling of water is slowed down, and the baby's cry is looped; and, despite the disparate threads of sound that are put together into this soundscape, none of the sounds are made less prominent for they all occupy different frequencies. In other words, the soundscape is crip time made tangible, times exploded and times embraced.

Fourthly, the sound of the infant crying also draws the audience's attention to the time and temporality of ageing. As I suggested in the Introduction, early onset Alzheimer's disease conceptually catapults a person into the imaginary of the vulnerable 'old'. In *U Me Aur Hum*, as Piya is diagnosed with dementia, she is put under constant supervision by a carer before being moved into a psychiatric ward that is predominantly populated by older people. Cultural notions of care that are mediated by dementia, Chris Gilleard and Paul Higgs note, have come to serve as signifiers of the fourth age, of ageing in the later life (Gilleard and Higgs 2017: 231–5). Piya's early onset Alzheimer's, as mediated through care, therefore culturally pushes her further down her chronological age, into the imaginary of the fourth age and of frailty. Yet, the sound of the infant crying also enacts a different kind of temporal performance as Piya is also linked with the infantile. As the film's narrative progresses, she starts to sheepishly hide behind Ajay, starts to gaze at Ajay with wide-eyed innocence, and starts to follow him around in constant need for guidance, ultimately highlighting the paradox of ageing for people living with dementia as they are both thrust into the category of the cultural 'old' and pulled into the infantile/second childhood.[6]

For ageing studies scholar Margaret Morganroth Gullette, ageing is a cultural process. According to Gullette, there are parallels between the ways we age and the ways in which a child is socialised into a gender. She argues that the gender that children acquire 'is usually like that of one parent, and so a parental "we" includes them' (Gullette 2004: 12).[7] Unlike gender, however, Gullette proposes that acquiring age is slightly more nuanced than that:

> Having an 'age', when separated off by itself, is more puzzling, because subjectively children feel stuck so long at one lowly state quite distinct from the adult: their age changes but their stage of life seem static. Children collect contradictory age-tinged language and revelations about older ages and about getting older in general, often without guidance, from peers, from overhearing adults, from ill-informed educators, haphazard reading, or, more and more, via the mass media. (Gullette 2004: 12)

For Gullette, age is understood as a process of cultural socialisation and this process, understood through a temporal lens, can again be seen as a performance of time. On the one hand, there is the empty, homogeneous time of the outside world performing its temporal expectations onto the body, as the self is aged linearly, and as they are expected to become an 'adult' when they reach eighteen or twenty-one and so on and so forth; on the other, the inner world of the body does not necessarily conform to this chronological notion of ageing and, as such, performs age in a different manner.[8] Through the sound of the baby crying, this paradoxical nature of ageing is heightened and brought to the fore, as Piya has to temporally negotiate the push and pull of both becoming older and younger.

Normativity/anti-normativity

There are at least four different types of intersecting understanding of times and temporalities at work for Piya in this scene, as I have illustrated, and this helps us understand the performance of time as engaged in intersectional politics of identification. In the final portion of the chapter, I discuss how films about dementia, in gesturing towards the ways we are performing and performed by time, encourage a way to think 'through dichotomous concepts rather than through dichotomies' (Deng 2022c: 73). To do so, I turn to a discussion of normativity.

For cultural theorists Robyn Wiegman and Elizabeth Wilson, the concept of anti-normativity is largely predicated on the idea that the normative is 'conceptually and politically limiting', and that norms 'have a readily identifiable outside, are univocally on the side of privilege and conventionality, and should be avoided' (Wiegman and Wilson 2015: 12). This stance, Wiegman and Wilson contend, projects an imaginary of 'stability and immobility onto normativity' that reduces the 'intricate dynamics of norms to a set of rules and coercions that everyone ought, rightly, to contest' (Wiegman and Wilson 2015: 13). This viewpoint on normativity, they argue, glosses over the logic of normativity. Drawing from statistical studies, they observe that statistical understanding of the norm is predicated on the average of a wide range of data from all across cultures and societies, and that for the norm to be generated, the outliers have to be considered too (Wiegman and Wilson 2015: 15). In that sense, the outliers – which some might term as anti-normative – are 'contained in the very heart of the median' (Wiegman and Wilson 2015: 15). In turn, because 'the norm is already generating conditions of differentiation that antinormativity so urgently seeks', Wiegman and Wilson propose to focus on 'relationality that is at the heart of normativity' (Wiegman and Wilson 2015: 16–18).

Following Wiegman and Wilson, I argue that the notion of temporal identifications correlates to this understanding of the normative as relational. Put differently, I am not suggesting that the performance of time is limited to that of being performed by the homogeneous, empty time, and performing heterogeneous non-linear times and temporalities (the Bergsonian model). Rather, I am arguing that one's temporal identification, as a constant state of becoming and change, is always in negotiation with others. Su-jin's and Piya's temporal identifications are predominantly negotiated with their families, husbands and medical institutions, all of which are traditionally understood as associated with more hegemonic/conservative ideologies. By the same token, we can also argue that Cheol-su and Ajay are too in negotiations with intersections of times and temporalities, and that they are also performed by and performing time.

In *U Me Aur Hum*, for instance, when Ajay nearly crashes into Piya, and before the film reveals that it is Piya in front of the car, the camera is trained on the face of Ajay, as a sense of recognition and confusion slowly creeps onto his face. Before the film cuts to Piya, the rich soundscape fades into the film as Ajay is first implicated in this performance of time, before Piya. As Piya is repeatedly wiped clean and refreshed by the windscreen wiper,

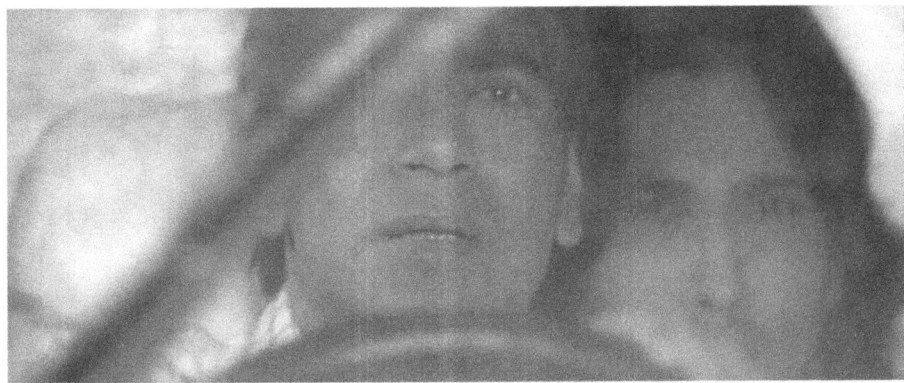

Figure 1.3 Ajay repeatedly refreshed by the rain and the wiper in *U Me Aur Hum*

the film also shows the audience the reverse shot of Ajay, who is also wiped clean and refreshed, too in a state of becoming, too negotiating his times and temporalities with that of Piya's.

Through Piya's dementia, Ajay, a psychiatrist, is thrown into the register of care. His previous temporal identification – oscillating between that of successful work time and that of leisurely pleasure time – is now in direct negotiation with Piya's new and significantly different temporal identification. He is performed by Piya's temporal identification and he, too, has to negotiate his understanding of gendered time, as he returns to the interior world of the domestic home a lot more to help out around the house; has to negotiate becoming a (single) parent as Piya's dementia progresses; and has to question his adherence to curative time and adapt to crip time, as he is forced to confront whether his medical prescriptions for his patients' care are necessarily the best and whether he would follow what he preaches and institutionalise Piya. At every stage, as Piya's temporal performance changes, Ajay's temporal performance changes too – there are no normative/anti-normative dichotomies here but, instead, more of a relational negotiation as both their temporal identifications are interdependent.

A Moment to Remember also makes this relational model towards time and temporality clear. The film begins with Cheol-su sat at the train station with a desolate face. A man at the station asks Cheol-su whether he can borrow a lighter. In response, Cheol-su holds up a letter and announces that the common cultural understanding is that a person's soul and identity are gone when their memories go. In response, the man starts to rant at him for being rude. While that happens, the sound of trains fades into the film and gets increasingly louder as the camera slowly tracks towards the back of Cheol-su and, concurrently, the man's voice becomes increasingly echoed.

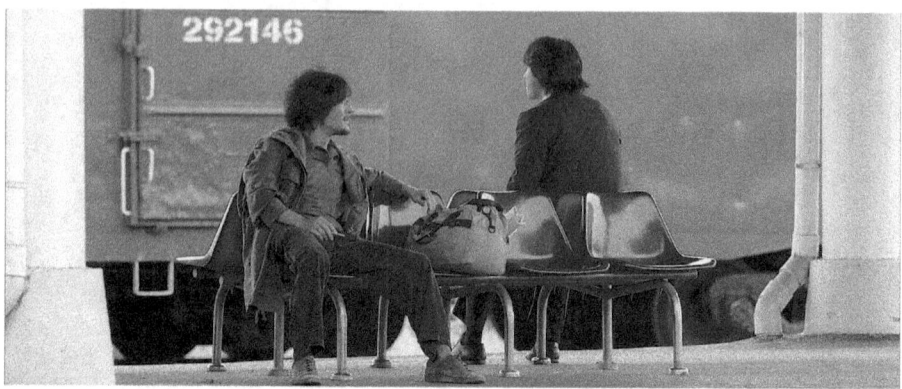

Figure 1.4 Cheol-su and the man at the beginning of *A Moment to Remember*

Almost immediately, the sound of trains cuts out abruptly from the film and the echoed quality of the man's voice disappears. The film cuts back to a shot of the man concluding his rant, as he asks for a lighter again. As he does so, the camera pans to the left, revealing the person that he is speaking to. Instead of Cheol-su, as the audience would expect, Su-jin is sat there, holding on to a pair of train tickets, waiting for the arrival of the man whom she is having an affair with. Ultimately, she realises that she has been abandoned by the man and leaves.

There are multiple layers of narratives and temporal performances at work in these opening moments. Su-jin is waiting – performing her own sense of time – against the backdrop of a train station, which has come to culturally symbolise clock time (the development of empty, homogeneous time is tightly bound up with the development of trains). Viewed in this context, there is a layer of temporal relationality happening: Su-jin is waiting where time drags, whereas the relentless clock time continues to move forward, and it is through this temporal negotiation that Su-jin's temporal identification changes, as she comes to realise that she has been stood up. This, in turn, engenders two new sets of temporal negotiations. Firstly, she is no longer in a relationship with the married man. She is now single, and that allows her to – as the film's narrative progresses – pursue Cheol-su. Secondly, she returns to her parents' home and to an angry father, finding a compromise between familial and independent times.

To elaborate on Cheol-su's presence at the beginning of the film, I take a detour towards the end of the film's narrative. As Su-jin is diagnosed with early onset Alzheimer's disease, Cheol-su initially tries to maintain his life's routine, continuing to go to work, attempting to not let Su-jin's new performance of time be performed on to him. Yet, this does not mean that

Cheol-su's routine is uninterrupted. In one moment, Su-jin calls him by her ex-partner's name and proclaims that she loves him. Despite being devastated, Cheol-su keeps a straight face and acknowledges her words of affection, performing this ambivalent role of being both himself and Su-jin's ex-partner. One day, alone at home, Su-jin remembers this very episode and, horrified, leaves the house and checks herself into a care home.

When Cheol-su returns home in the evening he discovers that Su-jin has left him and he breaks down. Su-jin's decision to leave the house and check into a care home results in her embracing a new temporal identification, and this change in Su-jin significantly affects Cheol-su, as he is finally overwhelmed by the whole situation and is performed by Su-jin's temporalities. Here, in shifting from the normative/anti-normative understanding of time and temporality to that of multiple approaches towards times and temporalities coming together and negotiating – to that of the relational – we can think of Cheol-su's temporal identification not as an unchanging, monolithic normative but as that too which is malleable, as he becomes unable to work even when he goes to work. Likewise, his father-in-law insists that Cheol-su signs the divorce letter so that he can be a single man, free from the burden of caring for and thinking about Su-jin, but he refuses to do this even though he is effectively living the life of an unmarried man.

Instead, Cheol-su begins to spend most of his time melancholically sat at the playground, at home and at the train station. As he sits at the train station, he is approached by the same man at the beginning of the film for a light. As that happens, the film cuts to a wide-angle shot of Cheol-su and the man, revealing that they are sat in the same place and dressed in the same clothes as that in the film's opening sequence. In other words, the very scene that begins the film happens towards the end of the film. Through the editing at the beginning of the film – the use of shot/reverse-shot between Cheol-su and the man and the audio-continuity of the man's rant – Su-jin's temporal negotiations at the beginning of the film, set years before her diagnosis of early onset Alzheimer's disease, are linked to Cheol-su's situation towards the end of the film, whose temporal identification is significantly and noticeably affected by Su-jin's dementia. This not only highlights the relational aspect of one's temporal performances, moving beyond the dichotomised view of linear and non-linear time, but also suggests that temporal performances as a category of analysis has a wider application that affect people who do not live with dementia too.

Films about dementia offer the potential to think about the relational as part of the normative framework, in turn encouraging us to think about how

Figure 1.5 Cheol-su and the man towards the end of *A Moment to Remember*

our temporal identification is always in a state of becoming, of change and of interconnectedness. Rethinking the normative as relational and dialogical, and through the lens of temporality, widens our conception of people living with dementia as being dependent on their carers to that of as being in negotiation with their carers, in turn restoring the agency and personhood of people living with dementia. In this chapter, I have focused on temporality of agency in relation to that of the actions of people living with dementia. In the next chapter, I focus on the narrative agency of people living with dementia, examining the ways in which the narratives of people living with dementia are not prematurely closed but, like people not living with dementia, are continuously engaged in a process of change and creation.

Notes

1 See also Boyle 2013a, 2013b, 2013c, 2014a, 2014b and 2017b.
2 On embodiment and dementia, see Matthews 2006, Hughes 2013, Katz 2013, Kontos and Martin 2013 and Wearing 2013.
3 For (queer and) feminist approaches to time, see Kristeva 1981, Grosz 1995 and 2005, Felski 2000, Cvetkovich 2003 and 2012, Bryson 2007, Love 2007, Berlant 2011, Wiegman 2014 and McBean 2016.
4 For an overview of intersectionality, see Crenshaw 1989 and 1991, Carbado et al. 2013 and Collins and Bilge 2016.
5 Seeing dementia through a (any) model of disability comes with many conceptual issues because the language regularly associated with disability rights cannot be neatly and easily mapped to the discourses and experiences of dementia. See Shakespeare et al. 2019 for a discussion about this challenge and the ways in which thinking about dementia as disability might offer a more profound understanding of the experiences of dementia.

6 See Covey 1993 and Miron et al. 2017 for more on dementia and infantilisation.
7 See scholars like Cowie 1978, Doane 1987 and Stacey 1994 for very different – and more nuanced – approaches towards gender.
8 See Stockton 2009 and Uprichard 2008 on the time and temporality of childhood.

2

The Shape of Dementia Narratives and Deleuze's Third Synthesis of Time

Memories of Tomorrow (Yukihiko Tsutsumi, 2006, Japan) begins in 2010 with Masayuki sat in his wheelchair expressionlessly. He is lit by the warm orange light of the sunset and blends into the dull orange wall behind him. His wife, Emiko, shows him a corkboard full of pictures of people from Masayuki's life but he neither acknowledges her nor the corkboard's presence. She drinks from her cup and puts it back on the table. The film cuts to a close-up shot of the ceramic cup, handle broken off and the word 'Emiko' etched onto it, before cutting to a two-shot of the couple sat on their chairs looking into the sunset. Slowly, the camera moves out of and above the house, providing the audience with a bird's-eye view of the surrounding rural landscape, before dissolving into a shot of a mountain, which time-lapses and cycles through the four seasons. Gradually, the film dissolves to an aerial shot of a busy cityscape. As the camera moves through different portions of the city and then through a window where the film's narrative begins, the buildings in the city begin to deconstruct and disappear. At the beginning of *Memories of Tomorrow*, time is moving backwards as the audience is brought to the narrative's present tense of the spring of 2004, where a younger Masayuki is energetically leading an advertising campaign.

Something similar occurs at the beginning of *Memoir of a Murderer* (Won Shin-yeon, 2017, South Korea). The protagonist, Byeong-soo, walks out of a dark tunnel into a landscape of snowy nothingness. The film cuts to an extreme wide-angle shot from the inside of the dark tunnel as Byeong-soo is positioned within the frame by the arch of the tunnel's exit, as he is visually isolated and enveloped by darkness. His hair is short and grey, and he is wearing his white shoes the wrong way around. His left eye starts to twitch as he begins to look around at his surroundings. Whilst that happens, a menacing low-rumbling drone enters the film's score; concurrently, sounds of people screaming enter the film too. As the air of confusion builds up through the sound and music, the film cuts to the title page. In the theatrical edit of *Memoir of a Murderer*, the film subsequently cuts to a shot of Byeong-soo, with long, black hair, sat at a police station as a police officer asks him whether he has forgotten his address yet again. In the director's version of the film, which is structured significantly differently, the film cuts to a poorly Byeong-soo, with long, grey hair, lying in a hospital bed in a prison cell, as a prosecutor checks Byeong-soo's mental faculties before proceeding to interrogate him about his journal and his life story. Either way, both versions of the film bring the audience back to the beginning of the film's narrative, to the narrative's present tense, as an atmosphere of mystery and thrill slowly builds.

Put differently, both *Memories of Tomorrow* and *Memoir of a Murderer* begin by teasing the audience with a scene from somewhere in time before moving quickly to the film's present tense. For M. Madhava Prasad, this narrative device can be understood as a fragment B, an fB, where 'A and B represent the two principal narrative segments, and fB a fragment that is metonymically linked to B but separated from by segment A' (Prasad 1998: 222). According to Ashish Rajadhyaksha, the fB is 'present not only at the beginning of the film, and hovering over it, but also more commonly right through' (Rajadhyaksha 2013: 74). The fB, then, is 'a kind of commenting track' that is 'embedded in the framing structures of the film', reminding the audience of what is and what will be (Rajadhyaksha 2013: 74). If we were to follow Prasad and Rajadhyaksha, the opening moments in both *Memories of Tomorrow* and *Memoir of a Murderer* can be seen as an fB, as a form of prolepsis, where the pre-determined future of the person living with dementia is shown before the film's primary narrative trajectory – the present – manifests.

For literary scholars Katsura Sako and Sarah Falcus, the opening scene of *Memories of Tomorrow* 'determines the path of the narrative, with the whole film shadowed by this initial image of Masayuki, allowing the viewer to inhabit vicariously the time of prognosis', as the audience is encouraged to see Masayuki's character arc as a journey of decline (Sako and Falcus 2015: 111). Likewise, Philip Gowman, in his review of *Memoir of a Murderer*, observes how the opening shots of the film capture all the 'stress and trauma' of living with dementia, and of the fear that Byeong-soo's 'mind is falling apart and that he will become more dependent on others to look after him' (Gowman 2017). In turn, this understanding of the opening moments in these two films echoes Aagje Swinnen's observation that films about dementia usually 'render the story of a disease in progress that reaches its nadir in the time span of the narrative' (Swinnen 2013: 113). The opening moments of both films signpost an impending decline of the characters' cognitive abilities, and an acknowledgement that these minds are ultimately going to 'lose it' as they battle with dementia. Seen from this perspective, both *Memories of Tomorrow* and *Memoir of a Murderer*, films that largely attempt to narrativise dementia through a first-person subjective viewpoint, are – paradoxically – concerned with the ways the narratives of the characters living with dementia are gradually being closed off.

This chapter comes from a very different viewpoint. I suggest that the opening moments of both films do not ineludibly work as a form of foreshadowing device, where the endpoint of the narrative is already brought to the fore at the beginning of the narrative, where what has passed (the beginning of the film) is used to determine what is to come (the end of the film). Rather, I propose that the opening scenes of *Memories of Tomorrow* and *Memoir of a Murderer* can be understood as expressing the prospect of difference and of change, where the life story of a person living with dementia does not necessarily end with that of decline, and where multiple temporal potentialities are surfaced: Masayuki and Byeong-soo can be seen as not only journeying through a path of decline, but are also simultaneously seen as traversing many other narrative trajectories. As I will discuss below, unlike the tendency amongst many critics to interpret narratives about dementia through the framework of decline and/or continuation, this chapter argues for a shift towards that of narrative creation.

This chapter is concerned with the shape of dementia narratives, and how multiple temporalities manifest and interweave in these story-shapes. Expanding on the argument on temporal performances that I made in the previous chapter, I suggest that the notion of temporal identification, as a framework that is grounded in the complexities of change and becoming, draws our attention to the ways in which our life stories are temporally narrated. Borrowing from Gilles Deleuze's philosophy of difference and difference in itself, I demonstrate that films about dementia are not necessarily invested in the closing off of the life stories and narratives of people living with dementia but, rather, are interested in opening up new and different futures.

Confabulation/hallucination

Central to the focus of the chapter is the conflation of two predominant cultural imaginaries of dementia in cinema, both of which play important roles in the process of narrativising dementia: hallucination and confabulation. Hallucination can be briefly understood as having a sensory experience in the public space that others cannot experience. Separately, confabulation, in medical literature, is broadly defined as the subject incorrectly narrativising the past, present and future worlds around them due to certain faults/distortions of memory. As I demonstrate across the other chapters in this book, the depiction of confabulation and hallucination takes on many forms and functions. For example, in some films, like *The Mimic* (Huh Jung, 2017, South Korea) and *Relic* (Natalie Erika James, 2020, USA/Australia), confabulated hallucinations can be understood as generically furthering the horrors of dementia (see Chapter Five). In other films, like *Summer Snow* (Ann Hui, 1995, Hong Kong) and *3688* (Royston Tan, 2015, Singapore), this trope can be understood as a way in to question and unearth the messy histories of various nations (see Chapter Six).[1] As a starting point, in this chapter, I examine how confabulation/hallucination can be understood as a way in for the audiences to gain an insight into the subjectivities of the person living with dementia.

To elaborate, I turn to one moment in *Memories of Tomorrow*. In this scene, as Masayuki makes his way down his office's narrow corridor just after resigning, the film cuts to a point-of-view shot of him passing through a line of people walking in the other direction. Suddenly, the people start to look at him – into the camera – as the film cuts back to a mid-shot of the upper half of Masayuki, who is trying his best to hide his paranoia/concern that people are staring at him. As that happens, time slows down and everything in the frame proceeds to move in slow motion; a low haunting sound creeps through the score and Masayuki's footsteps become heightened, reverberated and extremely noticeable. Even though the audience is only shown the upper half of Masayuki's body, the texture of the floor becomes clear and, through the sound, the haptic impact of each foot and shoe touching the ground is made palpable.

As he makes his way down the corridor, people continue to stare back into the camera. Unexpectedly, at the end of the line of people, Emiko appears. Free jazz enters the score as Masayuki comes to a standstill and looks directly at Emiko in a confused manner. The film cuts to his point of view as time – slowed down – returns to normal speed again. His echoed footsteps are gone and, in place, the audience hears the usual pattering of the people walking. Emiko continues walking forward whilst gazing directly into the camera – at Masayuki, at the audience – as she chides Masayuki for never being there for the family whenever he goes on 'work trips'. Her voice is also echoed as she walks past Masayuki. Again, time slows down and with every single step she takes, the sound of her heels is heightened, reverberated and made tangible, despite the camera not showing the lower half of her body. Immediately, the film cuts to a shot of Masayuki standing

Figure 2.1 A different kind of textured surface in *Memories of Tomorrow*

in front of a large glass window. He is bewildered and is oscillating from side to side. A bass note drops through the score as a ripple effect vibrates across the frame's *mise en scène*, soaking up the aftermath of the bass note, distorting the audience's understanding of the building's texture and architecture.

Here, as the various characters look directly into the camera, as they directly address the spectator as Masayuki, the audience is not only given an insight into the experiences of living with dementia as Masayuki but *is now Masayuki*. The fourth wall is broken and, borrowing from Tom Brown, this mode of direct address places the audience firmly in the temporal 'present-ness' and 'present tense-ness', creating a sense of immediacy, as what the audience experiences can be taken as what the character is experiencing in the present-tense of the film's diegesis (Brown 2012: 16). In implicating the audience in the experiences of living with dementia, the film engenders and foregrounds a sense of present-ness and present tense-ness, and involves the audience directly in the process of narrativisation as/in place of/alongside the person living with dementia.

Even as Masayuki's world starts to take on many and different sensorial forms and textures, it is not necessarily depicted as wrong to Masayuki. Although Masayuki might appear to look bewildered, paranoid or concerned about his shifting surround, in *Memories of Tomorrow*, Masayuki's confabulated hallucinations – and this moment is one of many – are often born out of the surfacing of his buried memories, secrets, guilts and anxieties, as he attempts to negotiate alien environments that he does not necessarily recognise in the present tense, as his wife appears before him to chide him for cheating during his work trips just as he resigns from his job. That is to say, his interaction with his milieu is affectively tinted by his life course and life story. Because Masayuki's ability to recollect is diminished, the connection between his past and present is made loose and, as Deleuze would describe it, he is literally sinking back into the past, or emerging from it, so as to 'make visible what is concealed even from recollection' (Deleuze 2013b: xi). At this very particular moment, through confabulation/hallucination, the past and the present are brought together into the same temporal plane, and his environment takes on a new and continuously changing narrative shape.

For many medical researchers, this act of confabulation is not seen as conforming to linear chronology and is thus subjected to a medical gaze.[2] However, sociologists Linda Örulv and Lar-Christer Hydén note that rather than seeing confabulation as an act of (unwitting) distortion, it could be understood as a 'result of an active and creative *meaning-making* or *sense-making process*' (Örulv and Hydén 2006: 649; emphasis in original). The person living with dementia, moving in and out of sync with clock time, attempts to make sense of the world around them by narrating their confabulated life experiences in a manner that is as linear as possible. In turn, the act of confabulation achieves three things: first, it allows the person living with dementia to make sense 'of the current situation by organizing one's experiences according to a plot within the scope of a storyline that is familiar'; second, it is important to help one preserve and perform a sense of self 'that is consistent with one's life history and thus has some stability'; and, third, the act of confabulation should not be de-contextualised and seen as the enterprise of a single person, for confabulation as world-building requires an interaction with the people and things in the world around the person living with dementia (Örulv and Hydén 2006: 668). Put differently, confabulation (and self-narrativisation) is a form of creative practice where something new and future-orientated is created.

This act of confabulation/hallucination is also seen in *Memoir of a Murderer*, as Byeong-soo interacts and communicates with his sister, Maria, who is revealed to have committed suicide many years before the narrative of the film. Despite her having died as a teenager, Maria, as experienced by Byeong-soo, is an adult nun living in a convent. The audience is first introduced to Maria as Byeong-soo visits her at the nunnery. As he enters and sits himself on a bench eating his lunch in the foreground of the shot, the audience sees Maria's back in the background of the shot as she hangs up the laundry. She asks Byeong-soo where her niece is and the film cuts to a reverse shot of her, showing the audience her face. Neither Maria nor Byeong-soo look at each other and the audience is shown a series of shot/reverse shots, as Maria continues to do her chores. Byeong-soo reveals to his sister that he is considering checking himself into a care home because he has dementia and this announcement catches Maria by surprise. The film cuts to a shot of her as she, still, closes her eyes and registers a look of despair on her face. She makes the sign of the cross and stifles a cry, unable to verbalise herself in this moment. Then Byeong-soo turns his head slightly, notices that Maria is crying, takes the cue and decides to leave.

Maria, who is revealed to be Byeong-soo's confabulation/hallucination further down the narrative, largely exists in relation to her brother, for Byeong-soo continues to remain in the *mise en scène* despite Maria being the focus of the shot, suggesting that her presence is strongly predicated on having Byeong-soo in the frame. Their interaction is predominantly verbal and even when Maria is crying in silence, Byeong-soo still turns his head slightly to observe her; his confabulation/hallucination is not just sight, but also sound (in a later scene, this extends to touch as Maria hugs him). Byeong-soo is unaware that Maria is no longer alive and continues to narrate her presence into his life story. Yet, in cutting to a shot of Maria making the cross and crying in complete silence before Byeong-soo turns his head to take in the situation, the audience is offered a potential insight into Maria that appears to be not reliant on any sensory interaction/engagement with Byeong-soo, as Maria is allowed to emote independently from her brother (though this instance might still be read as a projection of Byeong-soo). Nonetheless, in this moment, Maria is past and Maria is present (and as we shall see later, Maria is also future); Maria is a crystal-image, which, for Deleuze, 'is time itself, a bit of time in the pure state' (Deleuze 2013b: 85).

Both case study films, with the use of confabulation/hallucination as a formal and narrative approach, pose questions about the ways in which one might understand and narrate their life stories and the life stories of people living with dementia. According to Angela Woods, in medical humanities scholarship, 'narrative is understood to provide privileged access to the subjective experience of illness' and is frequently used by the person living with illness to express their 'changing sense of self and identity, explore new social roles and gain membership of new communities' (Woods 2011: 73). Woods takes a conservative approach and thinks of narrative as 'a specific form of primarily linguistic expression', cautioning against the inclusion of 'virtually all forms of creative self-expression' under this umbrella of narrative (Woods 2011: 74). Claire Charlotte McKechnie, in contrast, suggests that narrative should be thought of in terms of a relationship or a set of rela-

Figure 2.2 Maria crying silently in *Memoir of a Murderer*

tionships between two different worlds, and that 'through reception of the medium, the recipient will make meaning by using narrative' (McKechnie 2014: 120). Explicit in McKechnie's suggestion is the notion of creation, of making, as an intricate part of narrativisation, and, for McKechnie, every time 'we make an effort to produce an expression of suffering' – in whatever means available to us – 'we demand a cognitive engagement that requires the ordering information into narratives [sic]' (McKechnie 2014: 123). In following McKechnie, I think there is merit in moving to think about narratives from a temporal viewpoint. In thinking about narrative as the intermingling of different worlds, we can begin to think of the process of narrativisation as the negotiation between multiple temporal identifications. In other words, the process of narrativisation is deeply embedded in the politics of time, where information is required to be arranged in a temporal order so as to make meaning.

My proposal draws from Paul Ricœur's idea that 'time becomes human to the extent that it is articulated through a narrative mode, and narrative attains its full meaning when it becomes a condition of temporal existence' (Ricœur 1984: 52).³ The circularity of the argument – the way we think about time affects the way we think about narrative *and* the way we think about narrative also affects the way we think about time – works to further the imbricated nature of identification and narrative, where the ways in which one's life story is temporally narrativised furthers our understanding of one's temporal identification, and vice versa. In studying the shape of dementia narratives and teasing out the ways in which events and information are arranged in a temporal order, we become aware of what Jens Brockmeier describes as a process of temporalisation, which in turn challenges the understanding that the ways in which we order events 'in time' is 'a given natural kind' (Brockmeier 2014: 82).

For Brockmeier, when we acknowledge that empty, homogeneous time is the predominant way that 'we think and organize our experiences' and 'not as a given condition under which we live' – that is, when we are aware of the process of temporalisation, we can move beyond looking at how we 'localize ourselves "in time"' to thinking about how we 'localize ourselves in meaningful contexts by – possibly – using temporal assumptions and constructions' (Brockmeier 2014: 82). Writing specifically about dementia, Brockmeier argues that the incessant focus on memory and the declining cognitive functions of people living with dementia alongside the personal and (auto)biographical in everyday culture is myopic. This is because the traditional and dominant medical model of memory and dementia treats memory as a closed-off entity that can not only be measured in a systematic and scientific way but is also the fundamental building block of one's (auto)biography; in other words: no memories of the past, no identification in the present (Brockmeier 2014: 70–4). This medical model rests on the presumption that our life stories have to be structured in a linear and chronological manner, and that any blip in memory would mean that the present identification cannot be properly narrated.

But, as I have repeatedly noted, one's temporal identification – and one's life story – does not just correspond to either linear or non-linear times and temporalities. It is a complex process of temporal negotiation that is always in a state of change and becoming. Filmic narratives of dementia, in aligning with Brockmeier, provide the opportunity to think further about the narrative complexities underneath the performances of time that form the crux of this book, not least because all these different times and temporalities are brought to the fore of our attention. As my analyses of *Memories of Tomorrow* and *Memoir of a Murderer* suggest, the movement towards thinking about narrative and life stories in all its complexities requires a break from the strict chronology to something that embraces all kinds of approaches towards time and temporality, where Maria's presence in the present is both because of Byeong-soo's non-linearity and his attempt to make his life story linear, of him performing time and performed by time.

For social gerontologist Simon Biggs, this effort to fracture the dominance of empty, homogenous time in the structuring of our everyday life is ill-considered. He writes:

> The lifecourse, as a subject of inquiry, is inevitably temporally embedded and must be added to questions of social connect if later life is to

> be more fully understood. Temporal location is a key aspect of aging's originality, its specialness as a lifecourse experience, a source of potential opposition to social norms and helps define its significant horizon. Memory and a connection to the past form a grounding for the self in an uncertain world, a reservoir to draw on for future judgement and an alternative basis on which to make a stand. (Biggs 1999: 216)

Biggs goes even further and rejects postmodern approaches towards narrative, suggesting that the fracturing of narratives and, in turn, identities can be compared to 'a sort of Stalinism for the postmodern mind: a denial of the past as an anchor, as a source of embeddedness for authentic identity' (Biggs 1999: 218). Leaving aside Biggs's claim for there to be an 'authentic identity', a notion which Deleuze rigorously rejected, and a claim which Aleida Assmann (2012) has described as a mark of 'Western exceptionalism', Biggs's suggestion poses significant challenges for understanding the lives and experiences of people living with dementia, who do not necessarily remember and anchor their life course through grounded memories of a seemingly 'objective' past.

By contrast, Amelia DeFalco puts forward an understanding of identifications that embraces a 'belief in multiplicity, in various, even contradictory selves' that 'makes selfhood possible without risking a plunge into the reductive dualism of inner and outer identity, of true cores and social masks' (DeFalco 2010: 29). According to DeFalco, this narrativisation of multiple intersecting identifications – of 'flux, contradiction, and ambivalence' – works the best when the subject becomes increasingly aware that they are 'subjects of time', as time serves as a bridge to breach the divide between the postmodern, discursive subject and their lived experiences in time (DeFalco 2010: 29). For DeFalco, 'narratives of dementia are unavoidably collaborative' (DeFalco 2010: 59). Drawing from Emmanuel Levinas, DeFalco argues that dementia forces the person living with dementia and their responsive witnesses into a Levinasian interaction that subordinates the experiences of the witnesses in relation to the experiences of people living with dementia. In turn, this interaction furthers the sense of uncanniness, where the person living with dementia's 'deteriorated memory produces a frightening strangeness', and where the witnesses also 'comes to recognize [their] own otherness in the process of collaborating with the afflicted' (DeFalco 2010: 60). For DeFalco, then, the construction of narratives is increasingly based on a looser approach to the past, where the multiple pasts from both the person living with dementia and the person not living with dementia are put into negotiation and brought/surfaced/bubbled into the present.

I want to suggest that the proposals put forward by Biggs and DeFalco run into significant conceptual difficulties when the formal and narrative properties of films about dementia are taken into careful consideration, where the actual present tense of both films are not always linked to the past in a manner as described by either Biggs or DeFalco. How might Masayuki's shifting and evolving sensorial engagements with his environment fit into the discourse of decline and/or continuation, for instance? Likewise, the presence of Maria in *Memoir of a Murderer* also raises a few questions on the over-reliance of the past in the process of narrativisation. Maria, as discussed, is a crystal-image of time. Yet, the Maria that exists in the film who is an adult nun does not directly correlate to an image of the past because it is revealed that she killed herself in her teenage years. In other words, Maria here is an invented image from the future, and Byeong-soo's present is more orientated by the future than by the past per se (I will return to nuance this proposition in a little bit). Therefore, the frameworks put forward by Biggs and DeFalco are not able to adequately explain the presence of Maria and her relationship to Byeong-soo's life story and narrative present.

Syntheses of time

This chapter seeks to develop a framework that can account for, beyond that of continuation, the process of making – of creating – that is implicit in and integral to the process of narrativisation. To do so, I return to Deleuze, who puts forward three types of passive syntheses of time that characterise the different negotiations of the past, present and future. The first two syntheses of time draw heavily from Henri Bergson. The first synthesis of time proposes that the past is contracted in the present through the habitual recognition of our body and our soul, where we will expect a clock tick-tocking to continue to tick and to tock. Habit, for Deleuze, 'constitutes our expectation that "it" will continue, that one of the two elements will appear after the other, thereby assuring the perpetuation of our case' (Deleuze 1994: 74). The first synthesis of time, therefore, can be understood as a rather straightforward linear connection between the past and the present that 'constitutes time as a present, but a present which passes' (Deleuze 1994: 79). This comprehension of time coming into the present can be seen articulated in Biggs's argument, where the suggestion is that the present needs to be rooted and connected to a very immediate and grounded past. As I will explain more in Chapter Six, this synthesis of time corresponds to what Deleuze terms the movement-image; crudely put for now, movement-image narratives are primarily linear and are advanced through movement and motion.

The second passive synthesis is related to that of memory. For Deleuze and Bergson, the past is not constituted after the present passes; it is the other way instead. To explain this, Deleuze discusses the four paradoxes of the relationship between the past and the present. First, if a new present needs to arrive before the current present can pass into the past, then there will never be any new presents because the current present does not have a reason for it to pass. Therefore, there must be a past that is contemporaneous with the present so that the present can pass. For Deleuze, this is the first paradox: 'the contemporaneity of the past with the present that it *was*' (Deleuze 1994: 81; emphasis in original). But, for the present to continuously pass as a flow and not a series of individual moments, this past must not be accompanied with only specific points of the present but across the entirety of the present as it passes. This is Deleuze's second paradox: 'the paradox of coexistence' (Deleuze 1994: 81).

Thirdly, for the past to be contemporaneous with the present it cannot be a by-product of the present passing; it must exist before the present does so that the present can pass into it. This is the 'paradox of pre-existence', where an a priori past exists (Deleuze 1994: 82). Lastly, building on from the second and third paradoxes, if the past coexists with the present *and* also pre-exists the present, then the past is not dependent on the present to exist. The second synthesis of time corresponds directly to Bergson's inverted cone of memory where the past itself is a dynamic interplay of virtualities 'in an infinity of diverse degrees of relaxation and contraction at an infinity of levels' and the present is in turn understood as 'the most contracted degree of the past' (Deleuze 1994: 83).

The second synthesis of time can be understood as a contraction of the whole of the past in the present – more of an involuntary memory rather than an active recollection. This synthesis of time corresponds to Deleuze's time-image; time-image narratives, again simply described for now, are advanced less predominantly through movement but more through different versions of the pasts and dreamscapes. This understanding of the past can be seen articulated in DeFalco's argument, where a wider past is shared by both the person living with dementia and the person not living with dementia, and where different pasts interplay and are synthesised into the actual.

However, the presence of Maria in *Memoir of a Murderer* complicates this argument slightly as she, if we were to put her on a temporal plane, belongs to the realm of an invented future where her presence in Byeong-soo's life story is neither that of the past being contracted in the present nor the whole of the pure past surfacing in the present. To work through the nuances of Maria's role and to complicate the approaches towards narrativisation as proposed by Biggs and DeFalco, I turn to an in-depth discussion of two instances in *Memoir of a Murderer*. Here, I try to demonstrate how Maria's presence can be understood as the past *returning differently*. In turn, my argument about Byeong-soo's narrativisation of Maria vis-à-vis his surrounding world offers an alternative way of thinking about the life stories of the person living with dementia as that of continued change and creation.

In the first moment, Byeong-soo wakes up and, in a moment of extreme concern for his daughter Eun-hee, rushes out into the living room where he finds Maria holding a tray of food. Byeong-soo immediately hurries into Eun-hee's room, drags her out of bed, and asks her to momentarily live in the nunnery with her aunt so as to ensure her safety. The film then cuts to a shot of Byeong-soo running out of the house with Eun-hee's suitcase and clothes. As he runs out of the shot, Eun-hee runs into the frame and, at this moment, the camera lingers on her as she looks concernedly. The audience is then shown a reverse shot from over Eun-hee's shoulder, as the audience is shown what she sees (Figure 2.3). In the background of the shot is a black taxi. The taxi driver, in a blue shirt and black waistcoat, closes the boot of his car and walks towards the driver's seat. At this moment, Maria stands right beside the passenger's door and silently looks over the whole situation.

Byeong-soo then runs back towards Eun-hee and drags her towards the car. Just before she enters the car, Eun-hee protests and says '*appa*', calling her father in the hopes of changing his mind. He pushes his daughter into the car, closes the door and throws her scarf in through the taxi's window. Maria opens the front door and enters the taxi. Before she closes the door, Byeong-soo looks directly at her and asks her to take care of her niece for a few days. The film cuts to a reverse shot of Maria looking back at Byeong-soo, again not saying a word, as he closes the door. Upon which, the taxi driver drives off, leaving Byeong-soo alone as he proceeds to complete his 'one last task', to kill Tae-joo, the person whom he has been pursuing throughout the whole film.

In having the camera linger on Eun-hee looking out of the frame at her father before cutting to a reverse shot from behind Eun-hee's shoulder, the sequence is filmed and edited in a way to not only show the audience Byeong-soo's perspective but also Eun-hee's. She is sharing the world and narrative with Byeong-soo, and, in that moment, the taxi, the taxi driver and Maria are all there for both father and daughter. However, later in the film, Byeong-soo discovers a clip of his daughter voicing her support and belief

Dementia Narratives and Deleuze's Third Synthesis of Time **55**

Figure 2.3 Eun-hee's view in *Memoir of a Murderer*

in him on his voice recorder. Registering something, Byeong-soo runs out of the house to try and get a taxi. As he opens the door and exits the house, the film jumps to a shot from a different scene – seemingly from the scene discussed above – of him dragging his daughter towards a vehicle. Almost immediately, the film goes back to Byeong-soo walking out to the streets calling for a taxi. As he mutters for a taxi, the film cuts to another shot of Byeong-soo pushing Eun-hee into the black taxi before returning to the present moment. Once again, as Byeong-soo looks around for a taxi, the film cuts to a shot of him talking to Maria in the black car asking her to take care of her niece for a few days. However, in this shot, whilst the taxi is still black and the driver is still the taxi driver, Maria is not actually in the shot at all. Rather, Byeong-soo is shown looking at an empty space in the passenger seat, talking to his confabulated and hallucinated sister.

The film proceeds to show the present-day Byeong-soo uttering the number eight repeatedly, ostensibly trying to recall the number to call a taxi. As he does so, the film intercuts his attempt to remember with out-of-focus shots of a car plate that slowly pull into focus, revealing the car plate licence number to be 8588. Byeong-soo stops muttering and comes to a standstill, left eye twitching and hands clasping his head, realising and/or registering something different. The film's score, consisting of string instruments strung at an increasingly frantic pace, pauses momentarily as the film cuts to a shot of a silver car. At this moment, Tae-joo exits the car and asks Byeong-soo whether he has called for a taxi; as he does so, the score continues, emphatically imbuing Tae-joo's entrance with a sense of revelation.

The not-present day Byeong-soo then walks to the car boot and puts the suitcase in. He pushes his daughter into the car and puts her scarf into the vehicle. Eun-hee, on the other hand, asks Tae-joo why he is there and proceeds to protest with her father, insisting that she does not want to leave the house. She tries to leave the car but is pushed back by her father. As that discussion occurs, the camera, positioned inside the car in the back seat, pans left to Tae-joo in the driver's seat, who asks Eun-hee to 'pretend' and to 'play along' with his father's whims. The film then cuts to a shot of Byeong-soo speaking to the empty seat in Tae-joo's car – to Maria – telling her to look after Eun-hee for a few days. Next, the film cuts to a mid-shot from over Byeong-soo's shoulders to show Tae-joo looking sinisterly at Byeong-soo, who closes the door. As that happens, the audience is shown a shot of Tae-joo's face in the car's rear-view mirror as he registers a subtle smile on his face. Finally, the scene ends as the film shifts back to present-day Byeong-soo as he continues to mutter 8588.

This is a busy and complex sequence of events with multiple temporalities in negotiation. Seen from Biggs's argument, this sequence might be read as a foreclosure of Byeong-soo's ability to narrativise his life story, as he is losing his cognitive functions to a point where he is unable to make sense of the world around him, hallucinating the presence of Maria and mistaking Tae-joo to be a completely different person (a taxi driver). In turn, the ability of Byeong-soo to protect – let alone be independent of – his daughter is brought into question. Filtered through DeFalco's proposal, the sequence could be read as a continuation of Byeong-soo's life story, as the number eight that he repeatedly mutters triggers a Proustian surfacing of a past, a suppressed/forgotten/misremembered memory, allowing him to realise that he might have put his daughter in harm's way. Indeed, Raquel Medina, drawing from Friedrich Nietzsche, argues that the film aestheticises an eternal return of the same, where his 'repetition of memories always leads him to return to the same starting point' (Medina 2022: 137).

Both readings are grounded on the assumption that this sequence is constructed to be read as Byeong-soo's flashback and this reading relies heavily on the audience's knowledge and recollection of a prior scene where Byeong-soo urgently pushes Eun-hee into a taxi. A flashback, for Maureen Turim, in the most general sense, 'is understood as representing temporal occurrences anterior to those in the images that preceded it' (Turim 1989: 1). For Nitzan Ben Shaul, this rather direct interplay between the cataphora (early cues) and anaphora (the later recall of these cues), where the present-day Byeong-soo's life story is intercut with his flashbacks, can be understood as a way to narratively 'narrow down and block ingrained options so as to impart an apparent sense that the chain of events was predetermined' (Ben Shaul 2012: 41). This is to say, because of the straightforward link between the past and present images through understanding the sequence as Byeong-

Figure 2.4 The mirror from Eun-hee's point of view in *Memoir of a Murderer*

soo's flashback, there is only one way to understand Byeong-soo's dementia in *Memoir of a Murderer* because all other options have been cut off by the film's formal and narrative properties – Byeong-soo's dementia will ultimately cause the foreclosure of his narrative and life story as he no longer is able to remember or continue to remember.

But, as I have proposed earlier, due to the film's cinematography and editing pattern, the earlier scene where Byeong-soo pushes Eun-hee into the taxi does not demarcate the diegesis to only the world of Byeong-soo but is instead a world that is shared and experienced by both father and daughter. Put differently, like Tae-joo's suggestion to just 'play along' (ignoring the derogatory connotation of the phrase), both father and daughter are involved in the process of shared world-building and creation. Through the interaction with Maria's presence, their temporalities continue to entangle as they co-narrativise a life story that is orientated by a sense of futurity. In this sense, reading the later sequence as Byeong-soo's flashback ignores the nuances of the shared world that is created by both Eun-hee and her father.

In addition, positioning the later sequence as that of Byeong-soo's flashback also runs into problems, again due to the film's cinematography and editing pattern. As Byeong-soo closes the door of Tae-joo's car after talking to Maria, the film cuts to a shot of Tae-joo's reflection in a rear-view mirror. If we were to read this image as Byeong-soo's flashback, then the inclusion of this shot would make little sense because of two reasons. Firstly, Byeong-soo has already closed the door and stepped away from the car. Secondly, the shot is captured from inside the car, from the back seat, from Eun-hee's point of view. The moment, however, is also clearly not Eun-hee's flashback because she is not present in the later scene – only Byeong-soo is.

There is, therefore, an impossibility of positions and temporalities in this instance: the cut-away shots of the past do not belong to Byeong-soo's flashback due to the presence of shots that do not come from his viewpoints; this is also not Eun-hee's flashback despite the privileged shot of Tae-joo's face in the rear-view mirror coming from her point of view; Maria, the taxi and the taxi driver are not merely a confabulated hallucination of Byeong-soo's but belong to a world that is also shared and co-created by his daughter; and the past images that return keep changing, keep coming back differently (Eun-hee protests more in one instance than the other, and Byeong-soo throws the scarf in through the window in one past whilst putting the scarf in the car before he closes the door in another, just to name a few).

Demented time

How, then, might we understand this sequence in relation to Byeong-soo's (and Eun-hee's) life story? To do so, I turn to an elaboration of Deleuze's third synthesis of time. For Deleuze, the first two syntheses of time (habit and memory) would only lead to a repetition where nothing changes, where the past contracts in the present and the past is surfaced into the present again. There is a circularity that does not account for the possibility of change in the future or of something new. Yet, things do change, and newness does get actualised. To explain this process of change, Deleuze introduces the third synthesis of time, which he describes as 'time out of joint' or, more fittingly for this book, 'demented time' (Deleuze 1994: 88).[4] For Deleuze, the third synthesis of time introduces a caesura, a cut, a moment 'at which the fracture appears', that breaks the link between the past and the present (Deleuze 1994: 89). Drawing from Fredrich Nietzsche, Deleuze argues that demented time is 'the repetition of the future as eternal return' where time is both linear *and* cyclical (Deleuze 1994: 90). Deleuze writes:

> The eternal return is a force of affirmation, but it affirms everything of the multiple, everything of the different, everything of chance *except* what subordinates them to the One, to the Same, to necessity, every *except* the One, the Same and the Necessary. (Deleuze 1994: 115; emphasis in original)

As I have suggested in the Introduction, Deleuze's philosophy of difference is based on affirmation and not negation. If something is thought of in terms of the Same, then an Idea is reduced to a fixed, unchanging identity, where people and things will be treated as separate entities that are not entangled.

According to Deleuze, if it is the same that repeatedly returns, then nothing will change, and life would become rather nihilistically pointless. Contrarily, Deleuze avers, it is not sameness that returns but instead difference and difference in itself. The eternal return, exemplified by the third synthesis of time, is in other words the death of sameness, where death, Deleuze argues, 'is present in the living in the form of a subjective and differenciated experience' (Deleuze 1994: 112). That is to say, the process of becoming, the process of change, is the dying of fixed ideas. What returns instead is difference in itself – the virtual – that is in turn negotiated differently to form the new. Through the caesura, the dramatic event, time is cut, assembled and reordered. Difference in itself returns and portions of the past are left behind.

Here, I suggest that Deleuze's third synthesis of time, that which is focused on change and creation, is a useful way in to think about the shape of dementia narratives and the ways in which the temporalities experienced by people living with dementia are entangled with the temporalities of people not living with dementia. In *Memoir of a Murderer*, for example, Byeong-soo confabulates and hallucinates the continued existence of Maria into his life story despite her having committed suicide years ago. In turn, Eun-hee performs and is performed by Byeong-soo's world-building, by the (non-)existence of Maria. Her life story and temporal identification becomes entangled and negotiated with her father's, and the presence of Maria becomes a caesura, a dramatic event, that cuts their past from their present.

Consequently, as the temporalities of both Byeong-soo and Eun-hee are cut, assembled and ordered, sameness and fixed ideas in the present pass away – die – whilst difference in itself returns in a different formulation. Everything is forgotten and remembered differently. As Byeong-soo runs out of his house trying to call for a taxi, the barrage of images that return, that come from both his and his daughter's viewpoints, can in turn be understood as the eternal return of difference, as multiple virtual intensities coming back to negotiate with one another differently, creating the possibility of a different future to be actualised – not just for Byeong-soo but also for Eun-hee and everyone in and out of the film. As the film's narrative progresses, Byeong-soo's moment of recognition afforded by the eternal return of difference changes the narrative trajectories of all the characters in the film and the ways in which the audience might have understood the film thus far: Tae-joo is thrust deeper into the realm of the villainous as the audience is encouraged to think that he has kidnapped Eun-hee; Byeong-soo calls his police friend Byeong-man, who then goes off to find Tae-joo, subsequently getting murdered; Eun-hee, in partaking in the world-building with Byeong-soo, is put in harm's way and ends up almost killed in an abandoned house; and, lastly, Byeong-soo is momentarily moved into the realm of vindication, as his perceived suspicions about Tae-joo appear to become completely correct. Understood from this viewpoint, through Deleuze's third synthesis of time, the person living with dementia's narrative is no longer one of foreclosure and decline but that of creation.

This argument regarding *Memoir of a Murderer* is further underpinned by the respective endings of both the theatrical and director's cut of the film. In the theatrical version, after Byeong-soo has successfully killed Tae-joo, the film ends with Byeong-soo stepping out of a dark tunnel into a landscape of snowy nothingness, just like the opening sequence of the film. His left eye starts to twitch and the sounds of people screaming enter the film's score. He reaches into his pocket and takes out a pendant with the face of Tae-joo on it. The film cuts to a mid-shot of Byeong-soo looking up straight ahead. Next, the audience is shown a reverse shot of Tae-joo standing there in the landscape of nothingness looking back at Byeong-soo. Then, the film cuts to an extreme wide-angle shot – this time round, only Byeong-soo is in the film and Tae-joo is no longer in the landscape. Subsequently, the film returns to a close-up shot of Tae-joo looking at Byeong-soo, smiling sinisterly at him. Ultimately, the film concludes with a final reverse shot of Byeong-soo continuing to look ahead with his eyes twitching as his voice-over enters the film, asking the audience to not trust their memories. Rather straightforwardly, the film's ending extends the opening sequence of *Memoir of a Murderer* and continues on with Byeong-soo's narrative, as Tae-joo becomes the new Maria, as he is both here and not here, as the new act of confabulated hallucination opens up the possibility of further narrative developments into Byeong-soo's future.

More complicated, perhaps, is the ending sequence of the director's cut of *Memoir of a Murderer*. After Byeong-soo seems to have successfully killed Tae-joo, he is put under questioning by the police, who want to know how Tae-joo's body has gone missing. Unable to extract a coherent answer out from Byeong-soo, the police release him. The film cuts to Byeong-soo stepping out of a tunnel into a landscape of snowy nothingness, just like above. His eyes start to twitch and, as that happens, a series of images from throughout the film return through a montage sequence. This time, however, instead of framing Tae-joo as the murderer and Byeong-soo as the pursuer of truth, both characters occupy the opposite positions in the montage: Byeong-soo is now the murderer and Tae-joo is now the person trying to pin down the former's crime. By the end of the montage, the film cuts back to a close-up shot of Byeong-soo smiling sinisterly to himself as his voice-over enters the film, asking the audience to not trust their memories. Whereas the theatrical edit introduces Byeong-soo's new confabulated hallucination as the beginning of a new creation and line of flight, the director's version goes beyond that and allows the eternal return of difference in itself. By the end of the film, not only is Byeong-soo unsure of whether he has committed the crime but the audience is also encouraged to question whether it is Byeong-soo or Tae-joo who is the murderer. Consequently, Byeong-soo's continued narrativisation for the future becomes a formal device to further engender a sense of thrill and mystery to the film's atmosphere as the audience is invited to think of the person living with dementia in *Memoir of a Murderer* as either the victim or the perpetuator.

This reading is also equally valid for *Memories of Tomorrow*. Towards the end of the film, Masayuki hallucinates the presence of the younger version of his wife, Emiko. He follows her and wanders into the forest. Throughout the sequence, a haunting low reverberation enters the film score whenever the younger Emiko is in the frame; when the spectre Emiko is not in the frame, the reverberation cuts off, leaving only the natural sounds of the forest in the diegesis. As he wanders deeper into the forest, he comes to where Masayuki and Emiko used to attend pottery classes decades ago when they were still courting. The area is now desolate and crumbling. Masayuki looks around the area and realises that there is no one around. He comes to a standstill and turns his head towards an area. As that happens, the haunting sound fades into the score and the film cuts to a shot of a table with lots of pottery tools on it. The film then goes to a shot of Masayuki sat at the area making a cup. The camera tracks left as he continues to etch the design into the cup whilst, out of frame, Emiko is telling Masayuki the origins of her name. Slowly, Masayuki pauses and looks towards his left. Simultaneously, the camera continues tracking to reveal the younger Emiko sat there talking to Masayuki.

The film cuts to another shot of Masayuki looking and talking to his hallucination. Emiko is sat in the foreground of the frame with her back facing against the camera. The haunting reverberation continues to permeate the score as, suddenly, a sound from off-screen enters, calling Masayuki's attention. The audience is then shown a close-up shot of Masayuki looking up – *sans* Emiko – realising that there is someone. As that happens, the reverberation slowly fades away, leaving only the sounds of crickets chirping in the forest. Then, the film cuts to a reverse shot, revealing the person to be an older version of Masayuki's pottery teacher, who insists on knowing who Masayuki is, claiming that Masayuki is from the nursing home trying to get him back into the care. The pottery teacher notices that Masayuki has made a cup and, together, both of them work to fire the cup.

The entrance and presence of the older pottery teacher is interesting. Even though the communication and interaction between Masayuki and the older pottery teacher appears, on the surface, to not be a hallucination as the haunting sound has faded away, the subtleties of the film's form would suggest otherwise. The audience is first introduced to the pottery teacher not through a shot of his face but, rather, through a shot of Masayuki looking up. In the shot, spectre Emiko is still present in the foreground and the haunting reverberation continues. Unlike the previous moments where the haunting sound cuts out when Masayuki is in the 'real' world of the forest, the reverberation fades off. In addition, before going to a shot of the older pottery teacher, the audience is first shown a close-up shot showing Masayuki's recognition and reaction, taking the audience further into his subjective space before cutting to the reverse shot of what he is seeing. The entrance of the older pottery teacher through the delayed reverse shot, therefore, suggests that he is not necessarily *not* a hallucination, imbuing his presence with a sense of ambiguity and hesitancy that I discuss in the last third of the book.

In addition, the older pottery teacher is semiotically coded to live with dementia for he has escaped the nursing home and wandered into the forest, into his previous work area. He is physically and verbally aggressive and is also unable to recognise Masayuki, claiming that Masayuki is from the nursing home despite being told otherwise. If the presence of the pottery teacher is coded to be something more fantastic, more of a hallucination (or not), the characterisation of the older pottery teacher as a man who lives with dementia and has just escaped the nursing home because it is too dreary takes on an added dimension: Masayuki not only lives with dementia but has, just prior to wandering into the woods, visited a nursing home to potentially check himself into care. Understood from this viewpoint, the older pottery teacher becomes, very much like Maria in *Memoir of a Murderer*, Masayuki's confabulated hallucination that is largely orientated by the future (as the pottery teacher is significantly older and not of the same age as decades ago).

The presence of the older pottery teacher and the important role that he plays in firing the cup that Masayuki is making hence becomes a caesura, an event of change and creation that cuts, assembles and orders time differently. Further down the sequence, both Masayuki and him spend the night together in the woods firing the cup. The old pottery teacher, in a moment of excitement, stands up and starts singing the popular melody 'Tokyo Rhapsody' (1936). As he does so, the film slowly cross-fades from one shot to another, showing him singing from multiple angles. Due to the slow cross-fade, the older pottery teacher from the previous shot often appears in the same frame vis-à-vis the teacher from the incoming shot, as, through the editing pattern, the passing away of the past shot for the future is made visceral.

In the morning, the older pottery teacher is gone, disappeared, and all that remains is the fired cup that has Emiko's name etched into it. Masayuki looks at the cup and holds it dearly to his heart, expressing his care and love for the object, which becomes a symbolic image that 'constitutes the totality of time to the extent that it draws together the caesura, the before and the after' (Deleuze 1994: 89). Consequently, the cup as a symbol of the third synthesis of time at work for Masayuki, as he forgets and remembers differently, becomes extremely significant as the film concludes with a final close-up shot of the hot, steaming cup on a table. This final shot of the ceramic cup is the exact same shot shown in the film's opening scene as Emiko, years later in 2010, sits down in a room with her husband looking at the sunset. Once we accept that the narratives and life stories of Masayuki, like Emiko's, continue to be created through the entangled negotiation of difference in itself, of multiple temporalities, then the opening scene of *Memories of Tomorrow* is no longer one of decline but that where multiple narrative trajectories are embraced and acknowledged.

Memories of Tomorrow, then, as a title becomes extremely apt in encapsulating the notion of Deleuze's third synthesis of time, of demented time, in relation to the person living with dementia. Like *Memoir of a Murderer*, the past returns, forgotten and remembered differently, so that the future can be changed otherwise. This chapter has offered a way of understanding the narrative trajectories of people living with dementia through a framework of difference and change in the present tense, exploring the multifarious performances of time that a person living with dementia experiences in relation to all the other individuals in a wider web of relationality. This discussion of the life stories of people living with dementia is an important companion to the arguments about the agency of the person living with dementia as explored in the previous chapter, where I discussed the agentic actions of people living with dementia through a framework of temporal change. This is because, as Catriona Mackenzie observes, a person's identifications are inexplicably bound up in questions of agency for subjects form identifications and gain agency 'within a community of agents and are constrained by complex networks of social norms, institutions, practices, conventions, expectations, and attitudes' (Mackenzie 2008: 15). If the shape of dementia narratives is primarily predicated through the denial of a future that closes off narratives, then the agency of the person living with dementia is also refused. Conversely, if the narratives of dementia are grounded on the premise of change and creation, then the agency (and identifications) of the person living with dementia becomes difficult to deny.

Hence, to think through the temporal experiences of dementia through the filter of performance is to not just think about questions of identifications but to also examine wider issues of narratives. In considering the process of narrativisation and the temporal performances involved in the continued creation and entanglement of life stories between people living with dementia and people not living with dementia, this chapter appeals itself to recent social sciences research about the future outlooks of people living with dementia, where people living with dementia do not all think of their future as that of lack and decline but 'is something that is fluid and changing' (Ashworth 2019: 18). It bears to note that advocating for a continued creation of narratives does not propel my argument into a good/bad binary that the book is trying to move beyond – the narratives and life stories that are created can be positive or negative, affectively happy or sorry. What is at stake here, instead, is the possibility for a more nuanced form of empathetic engagement between multiple individuals, which is the focus of the next chapter.

Notes

1 See Deng 2022a and Deng 2022b for a further discussion of the politics of dementia in *3688* and *Summer Snow*.
2 See DeLuca 2000, Kopelman 1999 and 2010 and Schnider 2003.
3 See Eakin 2006 and Bitenc 2020 on the performance of identity narratives.
4 The term 'demented' is considered as a derogatory phrase in today's scholarship. Instead, phrases like 'people living with dementia', which is what I use throughout the book, is more commonplace.

3

A Kind of Radical Empathy

Andy Lo's *Happiness* (2016, Hong Kong) begins with images of death. The film opens, in stark black-and-white cinematography, with Kai-yuk sat with his mother's urn by his side as he decides to move from Guangzhou to Hong Kong to reconnect with his estranged father. Kai-yuk's journey to Hong Kong is cross-cut with Aunty Fanny alone in her flat. She walks to the mirror about to tie her hair and discovers, as if for the first time, prominent strands of grey hair on her head. She looks at herself in the mirror, pauses and observes other bits of her face, and leaves. In the next moment, Aunty Fanny is sat in a chair staring into space whilst holding a cigarette – just as she is about to have a drag, she realises that she has left the cigarette for too long, that it is dying, and that she has to extinguish it. Seen together, Aunty Fanny's discovery of her grey hair in the mirror, and therefore her older age, is gently reminiscent of Simone de Beauvoir's much noted repulsion of her own image in the mirror for it reminded her of death and decay (de Beauvoir 1968; 1996).[1] After the opening sequences that are haunted by the spectre of death, colour returns to the film and, through a series of events, Kai-yuk ends up staying with Aunty Fanny, who is then diagnosed with dementia. As complete strangers with no prior understanding of each other's backstories, Kai-yuk and Aunty Fanny start to depend on and support each other, coming to realise that there will be moments of each other's lives that the other will not quite understand.[2]

Not dissimilar to *Happiness*, Naomi Kawase's *The Mourning Forest* (2007, Japan) opens with a montage replete with images of death in a forest that is, by way of contrast, filled with life: an extreme wide angle shot of trees and grass swaying in the wind is juxtaposed with a Buddhist funeral procession that slowly marches across the horizontal axis of the frame; close-up shots of men working together to fell and strip trees so as to make funeral paraphernalia; and sounds of bells and Buddhist prayers that reverberate through the forest are mixed in with the heightened soundscape of wind and wildlife. In doing so, the forest is set up to be a space which, as Erin Schoneveld suggests, 'contains a spirit and life force that cannot be wholly understood', that is, a space where multiple worlds and worldviews come together, differently (Schoneveld 2019: 11). At its core, *The Mourning Forest* is about a narrative of interdependent care between the film's two main characters, Shigeki and Machiko. Machiko, whose son died tragically in an accident prior to the film's present-day, is a younger woman who works as a carer in a retirement home, whereas Shigeki, whose wife passed away thirty-three years ago, is an older man who lives with dementia. The crux of the film sees Shigeki insistently wandering through the forest to visit his wife's grave, with Machiko following him. Throughout the journey not much is said, nor much personal trauma is shared, but at the end of the film, the two characters appear to forge a kind of connection with each other as they both come to terms with their own histories.

Commenting on this caring relationship in *The Mourning Forest*, Kawase says: 'I think the bond between Shigeki and Machiko is empathy. They share something one cannot control: the time they spent with the departed' (Kawase 2007). Kawase's statement, as I read it, highlights two points that are of interest to this chapter. Firstly, the interdependent caring relationship that is formed between the two characters is affectively forged through empathy. And, secondly, these empathetic links do not really link these two characters into the same way of experiencing the world (for death is always encountered variously, differently, and personally), but rather allow these two very different engagements with death to co-exist.[3] Shigeki and Machiko, like Kai-yuk and Aunty Fanny, empathetically understand each other's life stories not through their own lens – not through 'walking a mile in the other person's shoes' – but through forging a connection that is grounded on respecting and acknowledging the other's worldview through that of difference, and this idea of empathy through difference is the key focus here.

This chapter engages with the notion of radical empathy as put forward by Matthew Ratcliffe. Radical empathy, as proposed by Ratcliffe, 'involves engaging with someone else's experiences, rather than one's own, while at the same time suspending the usual assumption that both parties share the same space of possibilities' (Ratcliffe 2015: 242). Such an understanding of empathy through that of difference, as I detail below, is very different from the approach towards empathy that is predicated on sameness or simulation, and it offers a more nuanced understanding of living with dementia that does not Other the person living with dementia. In the previous two chapters I discuss the agentic actions and narratives of people living with dementia through a framework of temporal change. In this chapter, I tie the arguments put forward in those two chapters through an analysis of *Happiness* and *The Mourning Forest*, two films about a stranger caring for, and becoming family with, a person living with dementia. In examining the complexities of both films, the chapter suggests that the proposed temporal framework of change unlocks the possibility for a more nuanced form of empathetic engagement between multiple individuals, articulating a kind of radical empathy that celebrates differences rather than sameness, where to empathise is to come to realise how another person understands the world differently.

Empathy as erasing differences

A way to understand the concept of empathy, as suggested by Suzanne Keen, is to think of it as 'a vicarious sharing of affect', as 'the spontaneous, responsive sharing of an appropriate feeling' (Keen 2007: 4). In experiencing empathy, Keen proposes, in experiencing 'a spontaneous sharing of feelings, including physical sensations in the body, provoked by witnessing or hearing about another's condition' (Keen 2007: xx), a person might start to develop more complex 'feelings *for* another' (Keen 2007: 5; emphasis in original). Put differently, when, say, I (believe I) feel what you feel, I might begin to have a more complex feeling about your situation, shaped by pity or by a need to support. In this sense, it is through an empathetic response that I might start to care for you.

Keen's definition of empathy is influential in the contemporary scholarship on cultural approaches towards dementia, and is engaged with at some length by literary scholars such as Sarah Falcus, Katsura Sako and Rebecca A. Bitenc. Falcus and Sako, for instance, argue that literary narratives of dementia 'bring us, as readers, into an encounter with the other and elicit affective, emotional and cognitive responses that implicate us in caring about those affected with dementia' (Falcus and Sako 2019: 7). This is to say that for them, autobiographical and fictional literary narratives that show the 'inside' of the experience of dementia, might open up forms of responsible and caring reading practices – in other words, caring, to a certain extent, through a Keenian type of empathetic sharing of affect.

Bitenc, in a similar thread, argues that 'both novels and films provide the possibility of experiencing the experience of living with dementia with a particular physical environment and socio-cultural context' (Bitenc 2020: 63). These narratives, she argues, can be understood 'as a form of imaginative phenomenology', that is, the audience/reader can start to imagine 'something of what it feels like to be inside a particular habitus, to experience a world as self-evident' (Bitenc 2020: 63; and George Butte quoted in Bitenc 2020: 63). She makes the argument by comparing and contrasting the ways in which literary and filmic narratives about dementia might encourage such a form of empathy. Writing about the film *Still Alice* (Richard Glatzer and Wash Westmoreland, 2014, USA/UK/France), Bitenc argues that there is 'no obvious one-to-one method of transposing the novel's "inside view" to film' (Bitenc 2020: 68). In place of the assumed inability to foster a first-person viewpoint in cinema, Bitenc contends that *Still Alice* allows the audience an insight into the subjectivities of Alice, the person living with dementia, and the people around her, by asking us to 'read her mind and emotions through close scrutiny of her body language, facial expression, or tone of voice' in 'the same way as we read other people's thoughts, intentions, or emotions in real life' (Bitenc 2020: 68). Bitenc develops this point by recourse to research on mirror neurons and mimicry as forms of empathetic sharing and suggests that, through the use of close-ups, the audience is able to scrutinise the emotions of the characters on screen, and then begin to feel how they feel (Bitenc 2020: 68). Through Bitenc's analysis, the filmic medium comes across in comparison to the novel as less effective and efficient in allowing the audience an empathetic insight into how characters feel. Even when Bitenc praises the strength of the filmic version of *Still Alice*, she talks about the narrative rather than the way the film form works, and one could argue that these scenes she is excited about could just as easily be textually included in the novel.

It would seem harsh of me to be so critical of Bitenc's argument here because she is, primarily, a scholar of literary texts rather than a film studies scholar, but I think it is useful to highlight a few points of disagreement that I have with her argument, as it will serve to demonstrate how I reach a different conclusion regarding empathy and films about dementia. To a certain extent, Bitenc's approach of comparing and contrasting the novel and film versions of *Still Alice* largely falls into the trap of aesthetic value judgement and fidelity evaluation, and does not really focus on the film form itself.[4] When she does talk about various techniques that the film employs, Bitenc is less familiar with the language of film technique. For instance, when discussing a scene where Alice gets disorientated while running, Bitenc refers to the moment as the camera going out-of-focus to convey a sense of feeling lost – however, the cinematography here is not out-of-focus but is rather, in shallow focus, with the foreground of the frame remaining in sharp focus (Bitenc 2020: 68). In turn, her suggestion that this moment is more akin to vertigo than disorientation becomes a little strenuous – not least because vertigo in cinema is regularly portrayed through the use of dolly zooms.

In her examination of the close-up, Bitenc's explanation, through the frame of mirror neurons – that is, when we see someone looking sad, we might also feel the sadness because we mimic their state of being – rests on gaining an insight to the characters via that of sameness, of making the audience's emotions the same as the character on screen. Bitenc's analysis of the close-up rests on an understanding of the shot as something that transparently offers the audience a surface to identify, where the face always gives away one's emotions that the audience can read and can somehow physically attach to. Such an argument is reminiscent of the early work on close-ups done by Béla Balázs (1970), Gilles Deleuze (2013a) and Jean Epstein (1977), where the close-up is treated as an autonomous entity that gives the audience an unadulterated insight into a character's subjectivity.

This consideration of the close-up as independently transparent, and therefore a vehicle for empathy, has more recently been subjected to close scrutiny by Mary Ann Doane and Dimitris Eleftheriotis. According to Eleftheriotis, the face should be thought of as opaque, as always in a state of performance to be interpreted by the audience (Eleftheriotis 2016: 212–13). Separately, for Doane, this attitude to the close-up is 'an attempt to reassert the corporeality of the classically disembodied spectator' (Doane 2003: 108), where the 'cinematic spectator clings to the fragment of a partial reality – a fragment that mimics the effect of a self-sufficient totality' (Doane 2003: 109). Synthesising Eleftheriotis and Doane, when seen as such, Bitenc's approach towards empathy through close-ups becomes a way of the audience forcing what they think onto the characters on screen. In essence, Bitenc's argument can be understood, borrowing from Paul Bloom, as 'the act of coming to experience the world as you think someone else does' (Bloom 2016: 16).[5]

Contrary to Bitenc, I would suggest that films about dementia consistently work to wrong-foot our assumptions of what we think we know the person living with dementia is experiencing, and instead encourage us to embrace the possibility of precisely not knowing the inner subjectivity of the person living with dementia. This in turn allows us to encounter a kind of radical empathy, where to empathise is to realise that the world is shared differently by everything and everyone. To elaborate, I turn to an example from *The Mourning Forest*. The scene begins, at dawn, with both Machiko and Shigeki asleep on the forest bed. All of a sudden the sound of strong wind enters the film, even though the surrounding greenery and the

Figure 3.1 Not necessarily a point-of-view shot in *The Mourning Forest*

smoke from the smouldering campfire remain still. This gust – sonic and/or spiritual – wakes Shigeki up. He notices something to the left of the screen, stands up, and leaves the frame. The film then cuts to a handheld shot that slowly creeps forward as we are shown a woman wearing a white blouse and a teal skirt, with her hair tied up with a brown clip. The audience has already been introduced to this character wearing the same outfit earlier in the film, as she is shown to be Mako, the wife of Shigeki who passed away thirty-three years previously. Mako, like Maria in *Memoirs of a Murderer*, can be understood as a confabulation/hallucination, and she has previously appeared in the film to play the piano with Shigeki. In turn, through the presence of Mako and the handheld shot which slowly moves forward, juxtaposed with the previous shot of Shigeki leaving the frame, the audience is invited to think of this moment as a point-of-view shot that offers one an insight into Shigeki's inner subjectivity.

However, part way through the moving shot, Shigeki enters the *mise en scène* from the left side of the frame. Mako is standing still with her back against the camera and Shigeki. He moves tentatively towards her, pauses, and looks at her from behind. He walks to her front, stretches his hands out to tenderly touch and caress her face. She stops him and holds his hands. Together, they start waltzing in circles, smiling, humming the tune that they played on the piano earlier in the film. The film cuts to a shot of Machiko, awake and looking at the direction that Shigeki has wandered to. As this happens the sound of Mako's voice slowly fades away and we are left with Shigeki humming. The scene ends with the camera lingering on the face of

Machiko as Shigeki continues to hum and dance, off-screen, through the foliage on the ground in the forest.

The editing pattern of this sequence is of interest to my discussion of radical empathy. After seeing Machiko looking at Shigeki, the audience is not offered the reverse shot of him dancing. Because we do not see the reverse shot of what Machiko is seeing, we are never allowed to know whether Shigeki is dancing by himself or dancing with Mako. Mako becomes Schrödinger's Mako: she is both here and not here, and her presence in this very particular moment is not pinned down by the editing pattern. This reading is furthered by the aural editing of the sequence. Even after the film cuts to the shot of Machiko looking at Shigeki, the sound of Mako's humming still persists: it lingers for a moment before fading out completely. As we the audience train our attention on Machiko, we are also encouraged to hold Shigeki's perspective in the same frame. In this sense, the audience is neither denied the subjectivity of Shigeki nor that of Machiko.

Beyond that, questions are also raised as to whether the audience is even encouraged to watch the film from the viewpoints of both Machiko and Shigeki at all. As the above analysis demonstrates, the film wrong-foots our assumption that we are seeing Mako from Shigeki's point of view. If the shot of the handheld camera tracking forward towards Mako is not Shigeki's, it is also not from Machiko because, for one, she does not move from where she is throughout the sequence and, for another, she is possibly still asleep at this moment. In turn, there is another reading of this camera moving, that we are seeing this through the forest's spiritual – animist, even – point of view, and this interpretation is backed up by the presence of the unusually high volume of the gust that does not affect the surrounding (this is also a forest, as seen from the film's opening sequence, that is full of spiritual life). Through the sequence, we are invited to hold multiple worldviews together so as to come to a more complex understanding of the interdependent and caring relationship between Shigeki and Machiko (and beyond). Such a suggestion, Anne Whitehead would argue, is one where we 'hold in balance [more than] two different orientations towards the world' (Whitehead 2017: 53). To radically empathise here then, is to come to an understanding that everyone – and, as I elaborate in the next chapter, everything – shares the same world differently, and films about dementia, with their foregrounding of multiple temporalities that intertwine, encourage us to approach the entangled world through the frame of difference in and of itself.

Entangled worlds and difference in itself

The Keenian empathetic sharing of affect, Whitehead argues, is often understood by many as 'an attribute that needs to be cultivated' so as to help understand the other person better (Whitehead 2017: 7). For Whitehead, in thinking about empathy as a 'model of perspective taking' – like Bitenc's argument above – boundaries and binaries continue to be set up so as to be crossed (Whitehead 2017: 9). A perspective-taking model of empathy, therefore, might mean that a person not living with dementia needs to be able to culture a sense of empathy so as to understand a person living with dementia. However, this approach is predicated on the process of othering, and the person living with dementia is not allowed to empathise with people not living with dementia. In medical research, for example, people living with dementia are regularly characterised as losing or lacking empathy, and such a presumed loss of empathy is used as a diagnostic criterion for frontotemporal dementia. Neuropsychologists Sandra Baez et al., writing about using empathy as a diagnostic tool for dementia, note that empathy 'is essential for human social interaction' and comprises 'the capacity to share and understand the subjective experience of others in reference to oneself' (Baez et al. 2014: 1). Seen in this context, not only does the statement from Baez et al. not allow for people living with dementia to be empathetic, but it also dehumanises this demographic of people. Put differently, this comprehension of empathy relies on a perpetuation of prevailing power structures to function effectively.[6]

Furthermore, as Ratcliffe explains, this kind of empathy assumes 'that both parties find themselves in the *same world*' (Ratcliffe 2012: 478; emphasis in original). This is to say that the perspective-taking approach insists on trying to find similarities between groups of people, and to find common viewpoints so that empathy can happen. Where dementia is concerned, this notion of living in the same world – and note here that this is different from a world that is shared differently – is regularly compromised. For some, like psychologist Mark Freeman, a person's dementia, with its inevitable cognitive deterioration, causes them to move 'into a mode of being shorn of any sense of [their] own history and story, of past and future, indeed, of [their] very identity' (Freeman 2011: 18). According to Freeman, given that the person living with dementia 'has only the most minimal sense of the future', it is difficult to 'imagine what it is that [they] might live *for*, if by "for" we are referring to some purpose, some motivating source of meaning and value' (Freeman 2011: 13; emphasis in original). Subsequently, because of this a person living with dementia leaves narrative behind, and this means that it is up to the carers to help find ways to make the life of the person living with dementia 'dignified and worthwhile' (Freeman 2011: 18). However, this exercise in compassion is not for the person living with dementia because they 'will not be the one to look back on the trajectory of [their] late life to discern its value and worth' but, instead, it will be *us*, the carers (Freeman 2011: 18).

As a response to Freeman and Baez et al., I have already addressed how we might think of the narratives of people living with dementia as those involving change and creation in the previous chapter. In this chapter I focus on the ontological assumption that underpins their ideas: both the arguments put forward by Freeman and Baez et al., I think, propagate the notion that people living with dementia and people not living with dementia are closed-off, separate entities, where the responsibility to reopen/continue the narratives of people living with dementia falls to the burden of people not living with it. Such an approach is based on an empathetic understanding that everyone is living in the same world, and the experiences of people in this world are the same, largely the same, or can be made the same. In contrast to this form of empathy, Ratcliffe puts forward an account of – as he describes it – radical empathy, which acknowledges that everyone undergoes 'shifts in the form of experience from time to time' (Ratcliffe 2012: 486). Building on philosopher Edith Stein, radical empathy, for Ratcliffe, 'is a way of engaging with others' experiences that involves suspending the usual assumption that both parties share the same modal space' (Ratcliffe 2012: 483). It is an account of empathy 'that can encompass how we relate *differently and variously* to our world in common' (Whitehead 2017: 9; emphasis in original). In other words, radical empathy is a kind of empathy that celebrates differences rather than sameness, and that to empathise with someone else is to come to realise and understand how another person understands the world differently and that this sense of difference is underpinned by the complexities of change and becoming.

In the previous two chapters, I have already made the argument that the temporal identifications and narratives of the characters in films about dementia are deeply entangled, where entanglement, borrowing from Karen Barad, does not simply connote 'to be intertwined with another, as in the joining of separate entities, but to a lack of independent, self-contained existence' (Barad 2007: ix). To develop this suggestion, unlike Freeman's and Baez et al.'s formulations, I propose that multiple temporalities are shared – differently – between the person living with dementia and the person not living with dementia, on-screen and off-screen, negotiating and enveloping one another to actualise into individual temporal identifications that shift and ebb.

Here, I point to an example from *Happiness* to clarify this claim. After Aunty Fanny is diagnosed with dementia, she insists on going home by herself and loses her sense of bearing. Signalling the start of her confusion, the sequence begins with a long shot from across the street that slowly zooms in to Aunty Fanny as she looks around her surroundings in a bemused manner. Then, the film cuts to a low angle shot of her, off-centre, walking through an underpass alone. The ceiling that looms over her, and engulfs her, is painted in a dirty yellow, and the walls that surround her are layered with white and green rectangular tiles. The underpass is lit with fluorescent lights that create a diffused, claustrophobic and sickly atmosphere that envelops Aunty Fanny. She takes a piece of tissue and wipes the sweat off her face and, as she walks, her echoed footsteps are heard in the diegesis, even though we do not see her feet, further highlighting the contained nature of her environment.

Finally, Aunty Fanny makes her way out of the tunnel, but she is completely disorientated and does not know where to go. As she stands by a busy crossroad, surrounded by building sites, she calls Kai-yuk for help. She tries to explain where she is but her voice is slightly drowned out by the cacophony of noise that overwhelms her: all kinds of vehicles driving very close to her on a busy crossroad; the sound of concrete being drilled into; and piles driven into the ground by heavy machinery. Other than the vehicles on the road, we do not see the construction equipment being used in the *mise en scène*. Aunty Fanny continues wandering and ends up standing in a walkway. The film cuts to a long shot of her stood in the middle of the frame and the walkway. The right side of the frame is cordoned off with sheets of corrugated iron; the bottom of the frame is covered with concrete pavement; and the top and the right portions of the shot are filled iron pillars that form the arches of the walkway. Aunty Fanny is framed within the frame by a tunnel of grey. As the vehicles on the right move past the walkway they block off sunlight and create square silhouettes that constantly move forward and swallow Aunty Fanny, reminiscent of the tunnel sequences from *2001: A Space Odyssey* (Stanley Kubrick, 1968, USA) and *Solaris* (Andrei Tarkovsky, 1972, Soviet Union).

While Aunty Fanny is disorientated by her environment Kai-yuk also makes his way through the same spaces to look for her. In contrast, Kai-yuk is not captured through a low-angle shot as he walks through the walkway, the yellow ceiling is not diminishing his presence from above him, and he occupies a more central position in the frame. As he walks through the building sites, the sound of busy traffic does not feature in the score and the drilling noises fade off after a while. Just when he is about to find Aunty Fanny, the audience is shown a shot of her looking at the walkway. She is in the fore-

Figure 3.2 Aunty Fanny's environment as out of focus in *Happiness*

ground of the shot, in shallow focus, while everything in the background is blurred (this is the same technique used to convey the sense of disorientation from the scene in *Still Alice* that Bitenc rejects, as discussed above). As Kai-yuk sees her and calls out to her, she turns around and the film cuts to a long shot of the walkway that is now occupied by both characters. The environment is neither out of focus nor tunnel-like. The road by the walkway is more visible and sunlight streams brightly and evenly into the frame. In this short sequence, then, the person living with dementia and the person not living with dementia both experience the same environment through different intensities, drawing our attention to an individualised experience of the world, echoing Ratcliffe's claim that 'the world is presupposed by the *modalities* of experience and judgment' (Ratcliffe 2015: 19; emphasis in original).

Through the manipulation of sight and sound, the atmospheres of the environment are brought to the fore, as the audience is given an insight into the subjectivities of Aunty Fanny, whose surroundings are made alien, and Kai-yuk, whose surroundings are experienced in a less forceful manner. Beyond the filmic, I would suggest that the audience negotiates these intensities in a different way. Vivian Sobchack, writing about sensory cinema and the cinesthetic subject, argues that the audience:

> both touches and is touched by the screen – able to commute seeing to touching and back again *without a thought* and, through sensual and cross-modal activity, able to experience the movie as both here and there rather than clearly locating the site of cinematic experience as onscreen or offscreen. (Sobchack 2004: 71; emphasis in original)

For Sobchack, through synaesthesia – where the stimulation of one sense causes a cross-modal transference to another sense, where the colour yellow, for instance, might be experienced by a subject as the taste of iron – and coenaesthesia – where the different aspects of the sensorium are variously heightened and diminished – the cinesthetic subject can understand what is seen and heard vis-à-vis their other senses: they also smell, taste and feel the film. In other words, the audience is variably touched by the film.

Yet, as the audience cannot 'literally touch, smell or taste the particular figure on the screen that solicits [the] sensual desire', the body of the cinesthetic subject 'will *reverse its direction* to locate its partially frustrated sensual grasp on something more literally accessible' (Sobchack 2004: 76; emphasis in original). Even though I do not see Aunty Fanny's shoes, in hearing her footsteps as she walks through the underpass, for example, I become conscious of the haptic impact of the foot and shoe touching the floor in the film's diegesis; simultaneously, I am also aware of my own foot touching the texture of my shoe, and, as that happens, the intentionality of my body towards the aural aspects of *Happiness* allows my foot to feel, in an intensified manner, Aunty Fanny's walk. As such, following Sobchack, not only am I touched by the film but the film is also touched by me. Due to this never-ending loop of touching, the on-screen/off-screen space is blurred, and the audience is positioned both in the cinema and in the film; put differently, the person living with dementia's sensory and subjective interaction with the film's diegesis is shared and negotiated with the audience's embodied experience beyond the diegetic world.

For Sobchack, this phenomenological engagement with the film happens in the present tense of film watching, as the audience's film-watching experience becomes a process of becoming, a constant process of negotiation between the on-screen and the off-screen space. Consequently, the narrativisation of dementia in *Happiness* becomes a project that concerns both the on-screen and the off-screen, bringing all these different temporal performances into negotiation, amalgamating the sensory realities (I elaborate on this concept below) of both the person living with dementia in the film and the audience watching the film. The on-screen and the off-screen are thus not separate but entangled. For Patricia Pisters, 'screens and the images on our screens are not distinct from the world (as second order representations at distance) but they form an integral part with it' (Pisters 2015: 125). These cinematographic images, Pisters suggests, 'are part of the fabric of the world that is woven between screens, bodies and brains and nonhuman phenomena' (Pisters 2015: 125). In other words, the temporalities performing and performed by the person living with dementia on screen are *also* the temporalities performing and performed by the person off the screen albeit at different levels of intensity.

In proposing that the worlds of the person living with dementia and the person not living with dementia on and off screen are not separate and closed-off entities, I maintain that the multiple temporalities of individuals are entangled and in a constant state of negotiation. To elaborate, I turn to Deleuze's concept of difference and difference in itself. Difference, he writes, cannot be thought of in terms of negation – the person living with dementia is not the same as the person not living with dementia – because this reduces an Idea into a fixed, distinct and unchanging identity (Deleuze 1994: 30–5). This kind of approach towards difference, Deleuze suggests, promulgates an illusionary approach towards reality that celebrates being rather than becoming, where a subject as a being is disconnected to other beings, and where the process of change and becoming is not accounted for.

In contrast, Deleuze calls for a move towards an affirmative understanding of difference as 'the element, the ultimate unity' (Deleuze 1994: 56). Here, Deleuze proposes we think of difference as preceding an Idea rather than deriving from it so as to combat the notion of a fixed Idea. Instead, an Idea is a multiplicity, a variation, and Ideas are rhizomatically connected, 'each being no more than a difference between differences', open to continuous change and rearticulation (Deleuze 1994: 56). To work through this complex understanding of difference in itself, a difference that comes before an image, Deleuze introduces the notion of the virtual and the actual as both sides of the real. The actual is that which is actualised from the virtual, where multiple virtual intensities negotiate and entangle to become the actual. Deleuze writes:

> Actualisation breaks with resemblance as a process no less than it does with identity as a principle. Actual terms never resemble the singularities they incarnate. In this sense, actualisation or differenciation is always a genuine creation. It does not result from any limitation of a pre-existing possibility. It is contradictory to speak of 'potential', as certain biologists do, and to define differenciation by the simple limitation of a global power, as though this potential were indistinguishable from a logical possibility. For a potential or virtual object, to be actualised is to create divergent lines which corresponds to – without resembling – a virtual multiplicity. (Deleuze 1994: 212)

For Deleuze, the concept of identity, and hence representation, is disagreeable because it moots the Idea as a singular and fixed entity. In thinking of identity as an unchanging behemoth, the real becomes opposed to the possible, where something possible could be realised into the real. This opens up a few conceptual difficulties. First, it assumes that everything that is real must be possible, where the possible is 'retroactively fabricated in the image of what resembles it' (Deleuze 1994: 212). Second, if everything that is real must be possible, how might one explain why that which is possible has not been realised into the real (what is the unreal)? Third, due to the possible as a concept developed in retrospect that occurs after the real has come into existence, we are forced to think of the process of 'realisation' as 'a pure act or leap which always occurs behind our backs and is subject to a law of all or nothing' (Deleuze 1994: 211). This approach towards the possible and the real, thus, poses conceptual difficulties as it does not allow for the process of transformation and change to be considered carefully, and it reinforces difference as negation.

As my analyses of Freeman and Baez et al. suggest, the possible-real approach poses great challenges to understanding the experiences of dementia. It seems that a person living with dementia is no longer going to possibly have a real future because they do not experience time the same way as a person not living with dementia, whose future is possible because they have the memories to ground and organise their life stories. In turn, people living with dementia are also not going to ever understand or empathise with the people around them. They are, in effect, ontologically removed from the world. In contrast to the possible-real approach, Deleuze argues that it is more productive to think of everything as real, as part of the fabric of our reality. He puts forward the virtual and the actual as both sides of the 'reality coin'. The actual, the thing that materialises into existence in the present, no longer has an equalising relationship with the virtual (as compared to the real being always possible). Rather, for Deleuze, the virtual-actual relationship is one of asymmetry, where not all that is virtual will be actualised into the actual. The actual can thus be understood as a process of negotiation between different layers of virtual intensities that unfolds into a particular existence in the present moment. The actual, importantly, is never in a state of being and stasis but, rather, in a constant state of change and becoming. Two actual objects will never be the same at any one particular moment in the present because they were actualised through a negotiation of different levels of virtual intensities – of difference in itself – and these two actual objects are in turn negotiated through a wider network of other actual objects (and the virtual intensities that come before that).

At this moment, we can begin to understand the ever-shifting sense of temporal identification as that of an *actual* which is *actualised* through the negotiations of multiple *virtual* intensities: one's temporal identification is never fixed and stable and is always performing and performed by multiple times and temporalities. A person living with dementia is different to another person living with dementia, a person not living with dementia is different to another person not living with dementia, and a person living with dementia is different to a person not living with dementia. Everyone is almost the same, but not quite. Aunty Fanny's temporal identification predicates on a performance of her own times and temporalities, whilst she is also performed by the times and temporalities of the characters and environments around her on screen. In addition to that, her sense of temporal identification is also performing/performed by the individual temporal identifications of the members of the audience off screen. Put differently, everyone is performing and performed by virtuality, and everyone is entangled in a wider web of virtual performances.

What then does Deleuze mean by the virtual, by difference by itself, if it is not the possible? To begin to address this question, Deleuze returns to Henri Bergson's discussion of pure duration, of time that has not been spatialised (see Chapter One for a discussion of pure duration). According to Deleuze and Bergson, there 'is only one time (monism), although there is an infinity of actual fluxes (generalized pluralism) that necessarily participate in the same virtual whole (limited pluralism)' (Deleuze 1988: 82). In other words, the time that is experienced in the present is intricately connected to the past and the future, and these different aspects of the pure duration, past and future, come together to actualise in the actual present. That is to say, and I elaborate further in Chapter Five, the virtual is not quite here but somewhere there, the actual present is, in turn, an index that is haunted by the virtual past and, by extension, the future.

To explore this further, I turn to an example from *The Mourning Forest*. In the film, Machiko and Shigeki come across a river as they wander through the forest in a storm. It is a shallow river where the waterflow is not rapid. Shigeki starts to make his way across the river but something psychically stops Machiko from doing so. She tries to prevent him from crossing the river but he insists on doing so. As he moves further away from her, Machiko starts to scream in desperation at Shigeki before segueing to apologising profusely. As that happens, the sound of a huge rush of water and something breaking enters the film's source and/or score. Shigeki looks up and the camera whip pans to the right as the film quickly cuts to a new shot of a dam breaking. Machiko's screams heighten as a torrent of water rushes through the structure. As Machiko continues to scream in despair, the film cuts back to a shot of the two characters at the same spot: Shigeki is in the foreground of the shot on one side of the river and Machiko is in the background framed on the other side of the river, crying uncontrollably. The river is still flowing normally as before and is nothing like the rapid flow of water that irrupted into the film. Concerned, Shigeki makes his way back to Machiko and says, in a reassuring tone: 'The water of the river which flows constantly never returns to its source ... never returns to its source ever'. After which, he gets close to her, pats her head and hugs her.

The film then transitions to night-time, as Shigeki lights a campfire to keep both characters warm and so that they can dry off from the earlier storm. They bunch against the fire and Shigeki asks whether Machiko is all right. As time passes, and as Shigeki insists that he is feeling nice and warm, he starts to lose consciousness. Machiko sees this and starts to get very concerned. She takes off both their clothes and huddle together so that they can keep warm, all whilst insisting that everything will be fine. For Rie Karatsu, as we see Machiko watch Shigeki and respond to him, we are reminded that she 'plays the spectator's role, which is to observe' (Karatsu 2009: 178). In turn, this embrace between the two characters by the fire 'is not intimate in a sexual way but highlights a growing connection and human instinct to survive' (Karatsu 2009: 178). Separately, according to Kate E. Taylor-Jones, Machiko's naked contact with Shigeki coupled with her 'increasing understanding of his never-ending love for his long-dead wife allows her to reconnect with her own feelings and begin to let go of the trauma of her son's death' (Taylor-Jones 2013: 163). Both readings of the film position Shigeki, the person living with dementia, as the other for whom Machiko – and in turn the audience – is to empathise with so that she can heal her own traumas.

To a large extent, these two readings are compounded by their understanding of the shot of the river breaking the dam as belonging to Machiko's psyche. As the film makes clear from the beginning, Machiko's child has tragically died in an accident a while back, and her fear of crossing the river and the inserted shot become a hint that her child died in a water-related incident. This interpretation of the shot as belonging to Machiko's worldview is furthered by her screams sonically linking the transitions together. As such, the shot of the river breaking the dam that do not happen in the 'present tense' can be comprehended as a surfacing of the trauma that Machiko has repressed for a long time. Embedded in Karatsu's and Taylor-Jones's proposals, hence, is the implicit claim that Shigeki comforting Machiko by the river becomes a way in for her to heal her own trauma and to, in turn, take better care of him by the campfire and beyond. Both interpretations of the film position Shigeki as the other for whom Machiko and the audience are to empathise with so that she can work through her own problems, and correspond to the earlier discussions of the 'perspective-taking model' of empathy which Whitehead criticises.

However, such an account of a seemingly one-sided empathetic exchange between the two characters glosses over the way the movement towards the inserted shot is motivated by Shigeki. As the sound of water enters the film, Shigeki immediately looks up to the right of the screen, and consequently, the camera whip pans to the right before cutting to the new shot. Because of Shigeki looking up, the notion that the inserted shot is linked to Machiko becomes more hesitant, and we can also understand the shot as belonging to him too, as he too is performed, differently, by the rush of water, and as he is then motivated to comfort her. The water of the river that constantly flows, that never returns to the source – as articulated by Shigeki – becomes a poetic rendition of the process of actualisation, of the pure past actualising into the actual present, and of the process of actualisation as a constant state of change. As Shigeki re-crosses the river to return to Machiko and comfort her, as both characters are completely drenched by the storm, water – the virtual past – becomes a way to entangle them in this world. Both characters are linked together by difference in itself, and it is through the multiple temporalities foregrounded by this film about dementia that a kind of radical empathy is aestheticised.

Being radically empathetic

In foregrounding the complex and multiple temporal negotiations, films about dementia draw our attention to the process of actualisation and invite us to consider the ways that we are all performing and performed by time differently. In turn, we are offered the possibility of being radically empathetic, and to realise that affective and interdependent relationships can still be formed without necessarily needing to know and to identify with the figure of the other. In *The Mourning Forest*, thinking about the relationship between Machiko and Shigeki through the framework of radical empathy nuances our reading of the film and does not ontologically remove the person living with dementia from a world that is shared through difference in itself. Likewise, *Happiness* offers such a suggestion too, as Aunty Fanny and Kai-yuk start to bond and care for each other without knowing much about each other's life course or life story.

In *Happiness*, the moment that concretises the development of their relationship is encapsulated through a montage sequence. In the montage, Aunty Fanny and Kai-yuk help each other out whilst also teasing each other. She covers him in a blanket as he falls asleep on a sofa, she pats his head lovingly, and she makes fun of him in an origami class while he throws a tantrum about it. He changes the lightbulb, buys a new clock, and puts up signs to warn her of the broken window in the flat; and he organises her medication into daily amounts so that they can keep track of whether she has taken her medication. They go grocery shopping, and they watch television together wearing 3D glasses. Throughout the sequence, predominantly, even as they repeat the activities, they are wearing different clothes, and this suggests that time is moving forward or, at the very least, passing. This is a tender moment of growing connection between the characters in the film that is underscored by the cheerful and upbeat music in the film's score.

On the surface this montage can be read as a straightforward and linear compression of time, and by the end of the series of shots, as the sequence fades to black, there is a suggestion that the two characters are in a more secure interdependent relationship than before. Put differently, as Deleuze might describe it, this montage gives us an indirect depiction of time (movement-image) through the movement and the relationship of the images (Deleuze 2013b: 33). However, there are three recurring scenes in the montage itself that complicates this reading a little. First, both the characters are carrying their grocery shopping back home. He is wearing a maroon jumper and her a brown vest, and he is carrying a mop while her a bag of toilet rolls. Second, Aunty Fanny is examined by a doctor while Kai-yuk accompanies her. She is wearing a white turtleneck and a pink coat while he is wearing a black coat. And, third, he is trying to convince her to quit smoking. He is wearing a green jumper and she is wearing a green shirt. As the montage progresses, as the characters do different activities wearing different costumes, these three scenes appear in the montage more than once, in turn complicating the analysis of the montage as a straightforward compression of time in a linear manner.

How might we understand the recurring images of these three moments? If, as Deleuze might have it, the montage is to be read as a linear progression and development of the two characters' relationship – and I think the sequence fulfils this narrative purpose – then these moments that re-irrupt in the montage again can be understood as the past coming into the present to form a new relationship with the audio-visual images in a different manner. In other words, threaded through the montage sequence is the virtual negotiating differently with the images so that a more concrete connection can be formed between Aunty Fanny and Kai-yuk. In this sense, like *The Mourning Forest*, the two characters are formally brought together through difference in itself – through radical empathy – as the characters undergo 'a progressively sophisticated experience of mutual understanding that develops' (Ratcliffe 2014: 277). Indeed, this point is furthered narratively, as at this point in the film, Aunty Fanny and Kai-yuk actually do not know much at all about each other's life course and life story. It is only when they start to care and depend on each other does Aunty Fanny find out about Kai-yuk's troubling relationship with his family, and does he discover that she used to be a successful singer.

The film puts forward what Whitehead would describe as 'a theory of empathy that is located, not in the individual subject, but rather in the world that we share' (Whitehead 2017: 27–8) via the montage. Being radically empathetic, in this sense, is to practise what James Thompson has termed as an 'aesthetics of care', which is 'about a set of values realised in a relational process that emphasise engagements between individuals or groups over time' (Thompson 2020a: 44). Thompson, coming from an applied theatre perspective, argues that interdependent care is aesthetically, affectively and relationally negotiated, and that the '[f]elt, embodied, careful collaborative acts of mutual reliance are the minute building blocks of that more caring, just society' (Thompson 2020b: 218). In paying closer attention to the aesthetics of care, and to the ways films about dementia engender a sense of radical empathy, we are invited to search for what Thompson, borrowing from Judith Butler, describes as a 'sensate democracy', where aesthetic activities can contribute to the political arena and produce 'a democratic arrangement that properly values the full sensory life of different communities' (Thompson 2020b: 216.)

This argument has significant ramifications for the current predominant neuropsychiatric approach to dementia, where dementia is held hostage by the 'amyloid cascade hypothesis' which suggests that the amyloid beta protein is the primary cause for Alzheimer's disease.[7] In the last fifty years, the scientific community had aggressively pursued (with significant failures) the amyloid cascade hypothesis in hope for a cure, and this journey to better understand Alzheimer's disease has been comprehensively criticised by neurobiologist Karl Herrup in his 2021 monograph *How Not to Study a Disease*. In turn, the belief that Alzheimer's disease is caused by the amyloid beta protein started to seep into, and take control over, other cultural imaginations of dementia (Zimmermann 2020). In other words, despite the uncertainty surrounding dementia and the amyloid cascade hypothesis, dementia as a neuropathology became the major, or only, way to think about dementia because the scientific, medical and charitable sectors started to back this as the 'correct' way to understand dementia. For sociologist James R. Fletcher, this advocacy of the amyloid cascade hypothesis can be consequently understood as a kind of colonial psychiatry (Fletcher 2020a) and neuropsychiatric imperialism (Fletcher 2020b) where the sense of Enlightened self continues to be epistemologically and ontologically privileged.

As I have referred to throughout this book, extensive scholarship has been done to decentre the focus on the brain and move towards the embodied when thinking about dementia. Films about dementia, through the foregrounding of multiple temporalities in negotiation, through asking us to be radically empathetic, offer the possibility to realise 'that difference is important *to the self*, and that 'the self exists in a relational position which challenges the contingent centrality of our own story of history', in turn posing a way beyond that which is promoted by the dominant neuropsychiatric approach towards dementia (Martin-Jones 2018: 20; emphasis in original). In this chapter, and the previous chapters, I have detailed the relationality between people living with dementia and people not living with dementia, on and off screen. In the next chapter, I develop this discussion further by taking non-human/more-than-human phenomena into consideration, and argue that everyone and everything is entangled in ecologies of temporal performances.

Notes

1 See Woodward 2016 and Gilleard 2021 for responses to de Beauvoir.
2 See Kittay 1999, Held 2006 and Slote 2007 on care and interdependency.
3 As Sophie Woodward and Kim Woodward argue, death, although universal, is 'always experienced in culturally and relationally specific ways' (Woodward and Woodward 2019: 3)
4 See Naremore 2000 on the pitfalls of such an approach.
5 For Bloom, 'this sort of empathy is biased and parochial; it focuses you on certain people at the expense of others; and it is innumerate, so it distorts our moral and policy decisions in ways that cause suffering instead of relieving it' (Bloom 2016: 36).
6 Junko Kitanaka, in her 2021 article on the lives of the dementia *tōjishas* (people who live with dementia who are also advocates for their own rights) in Japan, shows that such a form of empathy regularly infringes on the rights of people living with dementia. As the carers of the people living with dementia begin to imagine how they might feel as a person living with dementia (unidirectional mode of empathy), carers often start to force people living with dementia to eat and do things that they do not enjoy because it is perceived by their carers to be good for them. As Kitanaka writes: 'In the name of care, they are slowly smothered out of existence' (Kitanaka 2021: 270).
7 See Hardy and Higgins 1992 on the amyloid cascade hypothesis.

4
Ecologies of Temporal Performances

This chapter marks a development beyond the examination of temporal performances between humans to also consider the wider ecologies of temporal performances that a person living with dementia might be in. By 'ecologies of temporal performances', I refer to both the networks of temporal performances and the study of temporal performances in and of itself. The former is concerned with how a person living with dementia is performing and performed by the temporalities of the human and non-human phenomena that they are entangled with, and the latter is concerned with the method of studying these enmeshed temporal performances. This understanding of 'ecology' is drawn from the theatre and performance studies scholar Baz Kershaw, who notes that the word 'fundamentally emphasises the inseparable and reflexive interrelational and interdependent qualities of systems *as* systems' (Kershaw 2007: 16; emphasis in original). In drawing the audience's attention to the multiple temporalities in negotiation, films about dementia not only encourage us to think about how we, humans, are temporally entangled with non-human phenomena, but to also consider how we might methodologically think through this entanglement.

I concentrate on the former in this chapter, and will go on to think through the epistemological concerns in the next chapter. Here, through two case study films, I make the claim that a person living with dementia is embedded in ecologies of temporal performances. These two films are *Pandora's Box* (Yeşim Ustaoğlu, 2008, Turkey/France/Germany/Belgium) and *Happy End* (Michael Haneke, 2017, France/Austria/Germany). In *Pandora's Box*, Nusret, the matriarch of the family, the person living with dementia, lives alone by a mountain near the Black Sea. As her condition deteriorates, her three children bring her back to Istanbul so that she can be cared for by people. In *Happy End*, Georges Laurent, who is living with dementia, is the patriarch of an extremely wealthy French family. As the film progresses, he interacts with different surroundings so as to continually try and commit suicide. These two films, though tonally and narratively dissimilar, draw the audience's attention to the ways that the person living with dementia is not just performed by the temporalities of human beings, but also by the temporalities of other non-human phenomena, underscoring 'how ageing is a temporal process of embodied transformations that engages with other ageings that surround us' (Sawchuk 2019: 217). In so doing, I argue, films about dementia offer the possibilities to (re-)imagine the lives of people living with dementia differently.

From nature to ecology

I start by analysing the opening sequence from *Pandora's Box* so as to explore how films about dementia call for a careful attention to the ways that everyone and everything is virtually entangled. The film begins with a wide angle panoramic shot of a mountain. Rolling slopes envelop the background of the shot while lush, green grass occupy the foreground. Gradually, the camera pans right to show a few houses and some utility poles embedded in the landscape. The soundscape that accompanies the shot is rich and textured, and the audience hears – in a sonically heightened manner – grasshoppers chirping, roosters crowing, dogs barking, an eagle crying, cows mooing, magpies singing, mosquitoes buzzing and cowbells ringing, amongst other sounds of animals. Even though we are not shown any animals, this is a landscape that is bursting with life and each animal, with their different rhythms of living, come together to paint a particularly busy world in a largely still shot. The film then introduces the audience to Nusret as she walks out of her house on to the balcony. When she steps into the open air the audience is offered a close-up shot of her as stops to look at her surroundings, before beginning to sort a bag of red acorns on to a metal tray. While she does so, the sound of an eagle crying enters the film and Nusret immediately glances up before continuing with her task. As she reaches into her bag for more acorns, she looks up and something catches her eyes. She pauses, gazes at her surroundings in a concerned manner, loses her focus, and exits the balcony with her bag.

There is an enigmatic quality conveyed in the opening sequence of the film, in large parts due to its editing pattern. The audience first sees the wide angle shot of the landscape and then the close-up shot of Nusret looking outwards at something. When Nusret leaves the balcony, instead of cutting to the reverse shot of what Nusret is looking at, we are offered a shot of the ground littered with acorns. Although the audience does not see a reverse shot of the mountain, because of the editing of the film, the audience can assume that Nusret is reacting to something that she has seen in the mountain. Such an assumption is confirmed again later in the film (discussed below) as she tells her grandson that someone or something in the mountain told her to walk towards there.

For Amir Cohen-Shalev and Esther-Lee Marcus, Nusret's behaviour is a result of her dementia: the acorns falling out of the bag as she walks back into the house could be understood as 'a visual manifestation of a consciousness falling apart', and her reactions to her surrounding landscape are interpreted as her 'hearing voices' (Cohen-Shalev and Marcus 2012: 80). In this sense, Nusret is pitted against the mountain; the mountain is understood as something that is separate from the mind, and it becomes a way for the audience to understand that Nusret's mental state is deteriorating. Indeed, according to Cohen-Shalev and Marcus, as Nusret 'decisively turns away' from the mountain to leave the balcony, she demonstrates a 'vague but powerful determination' that is 'driven by a sudden change of mind' (Cohen-Shalev and Marcus 2012: 79–80). She rejects the mountain because she has regained her cognitive ability, however momentarily.

Such a reading is furthered developed by Raquel Medina, who argues that the mountain, and the desire to return to the mountain throughout the film, is symbolic of 'a return to Nature from a nostalgic pastoral perspective', and of 'the ultimate home for the human being, the resting place in which Nusret will finally belong to Nature' (Medina 2018: 60–1). In Medina's analysis of the film, human beings have been separated from Nature and that they need to be reintegrated with it, and it is Nusret who will return to it at the end of the day. Medina's use of 'Nature' as an Idea is of interest to me here because it is a concept that is juxtaposed with 'globalisation, modernisation, industrialisation and westernisation' (Medina 2018: 61). In other words, Nature, understood by Medina, is a romantic idea that is juxtaposed against the spoils of western modernity. As I will demonstrate, this is an idea of nature that can be located as the by-product of the modern subject – the cogito, the thinking subject – that was philosophised during the Enlightenment period, and it is therefore of significance that it is Nusret, the person living with dementia, who returns to Nature in such an interpretation.

I read the opening sequence of *Pandora's Box* in a significantly different manner: Nusret is not separate from her surrounding but is, instead, performing and performed by everything in the ecosystem that she is embedded in. To elaborate on this claim, I trace the temporal outlook towards nature that underpins the arguments put forward by Shalev-Cohen, Marcus and Medina, and the implications that come with it. For philosopher Marco Altamirano, the invention of the mechanical clock not only informed 'a popular awareness of time' but that it is this particular notion of time that allowed for a new understanding of nature to be developed in the sixteenth and seventeenth centuries (Altamirano 2016: 35). He writes:

> Just as humans create clocks that run automatically, so God created nature that subsequently runs by mechanical law. To be sure, a purely mechanical world of microscopic cranks and levers might seem devoid of theological sense. But for the mechanists of the late medieval and early modern period, the mechanisation of nature was not only compatible with the Christian idea of a transcendent God, it actually demanded it, like a clock demands a clockmaker. (Altamirano 2016: 31)

Clock time, as I discuss throughout the book, is spatialised and can be easily broken down into measurably identical and interchangeable pieces. Fifteen minutes from an hour can be swapped with another fifteen minutes from another hour, and an hour can be exchanged with another hour. Further, as such an understanding of empty, homogeneous time is intrinsically linked to the mechanical clock, the clock allowed mechanists of that period to envision nature as a clocklike machine, filled with independent parts that run smoothly. If nature is a big machine and everything in nature is cogs that interlocked, 'then the only difference that distinguishes one moment from the next is the material configuration of natural parts' (Altamirano 2016: 33). Consequently, for the mechanists, clock time propagated a metaphysical understanding of nature as one where each unit is equal and in a separate state of being, where 'the successive moments of time, like the material configurations that pass through them, are as homogeneous and infinitely divisible as geometric space itself' (Altamirano 2016: 41).

Through the clock, a spatial understanding of nature as a homogeneous assemblage is engendered. This comprehension proved very fruitful for the philosopher René Descartes, who was interested in the ways to know nature with certainty (the problem of error). A mechanist, Descartes saw no difference between man-made objects (like lightbulbs and bicycles) and natural entities (like flora and fauna) and considered them all part of nature. Instead, he believed that there are two aspects to nature: the physical and the conscious. If everything in nature can be broken into objectively measurable and equal pieces, then we can understand these physical – these corporeal – substances through the primary 'geometrical properties of size, shape, and motion, and those alone' (Garber 1992: 298). Conversely, to understand the different subjective and sensory qualities of these objects like heat and colour, a thinking substance is required. In turn, these secondary qualities of nature, for Descartes, 'belong not in extended substance but in mind and mind alone' (Garber 1992: 298). To understand the primary physical properties of nature as objectively as possible, the cogito – the thinking human – must step out of nature in order to master and understand it. Ultimately, Altamirano argues, such a spatial understanding of nature through clock time results in three major consequences, many of which we are still experiencing today. Firstly, because everything can be broken down into homogeneous units, 'a conception of nature that abstracts entities from their concrete environments' is enabled (Altamirano 2016: 48). Secondly, 'a picture of the human in confrontation with nature, rather than in an ecological relation' is facilitated (Altamirano 2016: 32). And, thirdly, the mind is separated from the body (Altamirano 2016: 48).

We can begin to see how the analyses of *Pandora's Box* put forward by Shalev-Cohen, Marcus and Medina adopt a Cartesian approach to nature that is underscored by the strictures of clock time. Albeit their desires to focus on the personhood of the person living with dementia on screen, their recourse to nature as that which is separated from human unfortunately heightens the mind/body divide that dementia studies scholarship has been trying to move away from.[1] Further, their arguments rely on a disenchantment of nature that renders the environment that Nusret is embedded in void. Indeed, for Cohen-Shalev and Marcus (and Medina refers to the same quote in her writing), the opening shot of the mountainous landscape sets 'a mood of pensive calm and quiet beauty' (Cohen-Shalev and Marcus 2012: 79). On the contrary, I would suggest that the mountain is anything but calm and quiet in the opening sequence. The sounds of the animals permeate the atmosphere in a heightened manner. The buzzing sound of the mosquitoes in the air is heard at roughly the same volume as the mooing of the cows from off-screen, which is also heard at approximately the same volume as the crying of the eagle in the sky. The animals are depicted through intensities that entangle, and the effect that is achieved is one where these animals, in being simultaneously all here in the frame and also not here, take on an acousmatic quality which give them 'the *omnipotence* to act on the situation' (Chion 1994: 127; emphasis in original). Accordingly, drawing from political theorist Jane Bennett, the mountain becomes a heterogeneous assemblage that is imbued with an uncanny vitality that can 'impede or block the will and designs but also to act as quasi agents or forces with trajectories, propensities, or tendencies of their own', and the audience is invited to engage with the liveliness of the mountain (Bennett 2010: viii).

Humanity, in this instance, is not separate from but equally a part of the landscape that emphasises 'the incredible variety of possible interrelations that make up the world' (Harper and Rayner 2010: 17). In the opening shot,

Figure 4.1 A landscape that is sonically buzzing with vitality in *Pandora's Box*

through the pan towards the right, the grass, the soundscape, the houses and the utility poles all share the same shot and the same world while in a state of becoming – as the camera moves, and as different things are heterogeneously connected in frame, the landscape continuously takes on new meanings. Further, as Nusret is laying out the acorns, she reacts to the cry of an eagle by looking up at her environment. From this viewpoint, there is also an argument to be made that Nusret is not 'hearing voices' – instead, more ambiguously, she is temporally performing and performed by the virtual intensities of the mountain and the other phenomena in the ecosystem just before she exits the balcony.[2] At every single moment, there is a new set of relationship that is formed between Nusret, her surroundings and the audience. The opening sequence of *Pandora's Box* therefore constructs a world where human and landscape are not separate but are instead entangled in a state of becoming.

As sociologist Stephen Katz writes:

> The fact that we are surrounded by fascinating and divergent temporal conditions, from the deep time of the earth's geological eras to the micro life spans of cellular species, should inspire us to think of aging as encompassing biological, geological, historical, and cosmic spheres. (Katz 2005: 233)[3]

Increasingly, ecocritical scholars have tried to move away from talking about 'nature' to thinking about 'ecology'. This is because, as Timothy Morton notes, the former concept is still haunted by the ghost of Descartes and is still invested in the human/non-human divisions that I discussed above whereas ecology, on the other hand, 'is profoundly about coexistence' (Morton 2010: 4). Coexistence can take on different forms. Donna J. Haraway, for instance, proposes that we are all compost: 'Critters–humans and not–become-with each other, compose and decompose each other, in every scale and register of time and stuff in sympoietic tangling, in ecological evolutionary developmental earthly worlding and unworlding' (Haraway 2016: 97). Morton, in another example, proposes that human and non-human phenomena are all in the mesh, which 'consists of infinite connections and infinitesimal differences' (Morton 2010: 30). In both Haraway and Morton, three tenets of ecological thought come through. First, every human and non-human phenomena in the ecology is deeply entangled. Secondly, these phenomena are not homogeneously separate but, instead, are always in states of becoming. There is neither start nor end, just constant change. And, thirdly, these connections are all temporally heterogeneous. As Sophie Brunau-Zaragoza notes, to 'think ecologically is to think about the kinds of relationships in which we are enmeshed' (Brunau-Zaragoza 2020: 60).[4]

For Altamirano, this conceptual shift from 'nature' to 'ecology' denotes a movement from a spatial understanding of the world to a temporal one, where we think of all human and non-human phenomena as 'arcs of technically conducted extensive events taking place within a series of other events, which emerge from and transform an intensive manifold of eventualities that produced them' (Altamirano 2016: 163). In the previous three chapters, I have gradually built up a picture of Gilles Deleuze's philosophy of time and approach to the world. Briefly recapped, for Deleuze, the actual, which is always in a state of becoming, is actualised through the negotiation of multiple virtual intensities, and the virtual – difference in itself – can be understood as the pure past that returns. In the context of this chapter, we can begin to see how Deleuze's ideas on time are not too dissimilar to the proposals put forward by ecocritical scholars, and my above analysis of the opening sequence of *Pandora's Box* demonstrates such a temporal approach towards ecological thinking.

I will elaborate on this claim with an example from *Happy End*. In the film, Georges Laurent, who lives with dementia, is constantly trying to find ways to commit suicide. Early on, he deliberately drives a car into a tree. He survives the crash and ends up in a wheelchair for the remainder of the film. Partway through *Happy End*, he leaves the house by himself and tries again. The sequence that captures this attempt is filmed in one long take that tracks left, a shot that is reminiscent of Jean-Luc Godard's *Week-end*

(1967, France). Georges, in a suit, is in the middle plane of the shot as he pushes himself forward in the wheelchair. In the foreground of the *mise en scène* is busy traffic that occasionally obscures Georges from view. In the background of the shot are pedestrians of different ages walking at different speed. Georges catches sight of a group of black men, who are wearing caps and hoodies, walking in the background of the shot. He waves them to a stop and talks to them. Throughout this sequence, the sound of traffic overwhelms the diegesis and the audience is unable to hear what he is saying to the black men. Nonetheless, the implication is clear that Georges is asking them to do something for him (later on in the film, he asks his barber to buy him a gun and ammunition) as he removes his watch from his hand and attempts to give it to one of the men, who rejects it and leaves, effectively ending the scene and Georges's attempt.

During the sequence, Georges is always positioned in the centre of the frame – or as close to the centre as possible – and the camera follows him, stopping when he stops. In turn, through the person living with dementia, the multiple temporalities that are in negotiation are highlighted. Like the opening sequence from *Pandora's Box*, this moment captures an ecology that is in a constant state of becoming. Through the tracking shot, the audience is constantly brought into new relationships with the audio-visual images on screen, which are in motion for the most part of the scene, forging new and differential connections. On one level, Georges, the vehicles and the pedestrians are all moving at different rhythms. The different kinds of vehicles on the road – luxury cars, large trucks, two police motorcycles and a man riding a bicycle – that variously obscure Georges materially draw the audience's attention to different temporal performances within and beyond the screen. For instance, the cars have a glossy shine whereas the trucks are dull and covered with tarpaulin sheets, and one of the cars is towing a small boat. The people who drive these vehicles, although we do not always see them, therefore range from rather rich people to labouring people, all with their own temporalities in their various walks of life. Likewise, the pedestrians in the background are variously performing their times and temporalities onto and performed by the other entities around them. An older woman is strolling with an older man, who is holding a walking stick. A pregnant woman is pushing a pram with a baby in it and walking with her two children. These two groups of people meet on the pavement and do the awkward dance of who should pass first because the path is too small, and the older couple decides to step onto the road to allow the woman to easily pass with her pram. Towards the end of the scene, as Georges flags down a group of black men to help him out with his suicide attempt, his racism and classism is temporally and materially laid bare as he attempts to perform white, capitalist time onto the black men by trying to pay them off with his watch. But, also, as this film is set in Calais and released just after the dismantling of the Calais Jungle (an encampment site for thousands of refugees from 2015 to 2016), this exchange also points to the unseen temporalities of the refugees stuck at the border of France.

Taken together, the scene highlights the 'uneven multiplicity of temporalities that is complicated by the labor arrangements, cultural practices, technological environments, and social spaces that respond to this so-called globalized, speedy world' (Sharma 2014: 9). Human and non-human phenomena are entangled in this busy cityscape that is constantly moving, and the person living with dementia is not separate from it, but very much embedded in it and heterogeneously connected to the different entities. Films about dementia, in encouraging a temporally relational worldview, call for a careful attention to the ways that everyone and everything is virtually entangled. In this sense, borrowing from Katarzyna Paszkiewicz, films about dementia can be understood as ecocritical narratives that 'put us into contact with the world, less to look *after* it than to relate and creatively engage *with* it' (Paszkiewicz 2020: 9; emphasis in original).

The melodies of the polyphonic assemblage

What are the wider implications of such a proposal? As Laura McMahon puts it, the virtual has the 'capacity to gesture to realms beyond biopolitical domination' (McMahon 2019: 26). Contemporary conversations of successful ageing, Joanna Latimer notes, are no longer concerned with just asking people to exercise and stay healthy. Instead, they are also – if not more – interested in asking people to consume, to buy anti-ageing products, to take holidays, and to join pension schemes, amongst other purchases. This strategy of continuous consumption, Latimer argues, 'depends on people responding to the call to master their futures' (Latimer 2018: 844). Consequently, discourses of ageing 'enact what it is to be a full person and a good consumer in late modern capitalism' (Latimer 2018: 841). She writes:

> opening ageing up as a site of enhancement creates opportunities for the enactment of what is most valued and precious in neoliberal forms of modernity – to have a 'future' and be 'ready and available' for whenever the call to do this or that comes along. (Latimer 2018: 841)

Bad ageing, conversely, is 'like poverty' and 'is performed as the *failure* of the individual because of how they fly in the face of contemporary neoliberal agendas' (Latimer 2018: 846; emphasis in original). Seen from this angle, the current 'crisis of dementia', as the exemplar of bad ageing, configures the person living with dementia as 'a subject that bodies forth the figure of someone who has not responded to this call' to master their future through consumption, and thus will cost society a lot of money' (Latimer 2018: 844). Simultaneously, Lucy Burke notes, 'the invocation of a dementia as the locus of an imminent and catastrophic threat also sets the scene for a series of market interventions or speculative investment opportunities in anti-aging research' (Burke 2017: 4). Dementia, as understood by Latimer and Burke, is therefore a victim of late capitalist biopolitics, as the site of both costing too much money and promising a lot of money.

This conception has major ramifications on the lives of people living with dementia, and can very literally mean death. Sharon R. Kaufman, for one, notes that dementia takes on three inflections in hospitals: 'as a rationale for facilitating death, as a contested feature of what matters about the patient's identity, and as a moral-clinical designation of value when a frail life is perceived to hang in the balance' (Kaufman 2006: 23). Margaret Morganroth Gullette, for another, worries that the 'assumption that people who "have" Alzheimer's, or who merely believe they do, will want to die preemptively' is increasingly embedded in 'the American terror and cultural sickness about this disease' (Gullette 2017: 141). In both Kaufman and Gullette, the lives of people with dementia are 'subsumed within a powerful symbolic abstraction that precludes us from imagining life with dementia as a potential site of agency or as the locus for transformative ideas about care, community, and non-instrumentalist conceptions of human value' (Burke 2019: 204).

How can examining the ways a person living with dementia is performing and performed by multiple times and temporalities in an entangled world help? In her ethnography on the Matsutake mushroom, Anna Lowenhaupt Tsing traces the environmental devastations that are wrought by capitalism and examines 'what manages to live despite capitalism' – in her case, the Matsutake mushroom and the stories that are entangled with it (Tsing 2015: vii:). To even notice the things that survive, 'we must evade assumptions that the future is that singular direction ahead' because this merely continues the capitalist narrative of progress and constant development (Tsing 2015: vii). Instead, we ought to imagine the different lines of flight that could be formed in heterogeneous assemblages. To do so, Tsing puts forward the concept of the 'polyphonic assemblage', where 'autonomous melodies intertwine' (Tsing 2015: 23). The polyphonic assemblage, she suggests, is akin to 'virtual particles in a quantum field', where 'multiple futures pop in and out of possibility' (Tsing 2015: vii). Tsing writes:

> When I first learned polyphony, it was a revelation in listening; I was forced to pick out separate, simultaneous melodies *and* to listen for the moments of harmony and dissonance they created together. This kind of noticing is just what is needed to appreciate the multiple temporal rhythms and trajectories of the assemblage. (Tsing 2015: 24; emphasis in original)

A relational ecology that encompasses all kinds of temporal performances finds affinity with Tsing's polyphonic assemblage. Adapting Tsing, I am proposing to not conceive of dementia as a victim of capitalism but, instead, to try and think of it as something that lives in spite of capitalism. In listening carefully to the melodies of the polyphonic assemblage in and through films about dementia, we might be able to start envisioning different concepts of dementia and different ways of living with dementia. As Jacques Rancière would argue, these are 'configurations of experience that create new modes of sense perception and induce novel forms of political subjectivity' (Rancière 2004: 9). In creativity engaging with the heterogeneity of it all, new connections are made sensible. For the rest of this chapter, I will imagine through an analysis of both *Pandora's Box* and *Happy End*.

I turn to an example from *Happy End* to clarify this claim. As I mentioned, throughout the film, Georges is largely focused on finding ways to kill himself. This desire to die is read by many – not all – as partly because of his dementia: according to Jeffrey Berman, Georges wants to die because he is 'now wheelchair bound' and 'suffering from dementia' (Berman 2021: 189); for Ian Freer, Georges is described as 'the now senile founder of a construction business who simply wants to end his life' (Freer 2017); and for Maurice Yacowar, the 'forgetful old man eager to die is the film's emotional and moral center' (Yacowar 2018). All three statements about the film implicitly embed the ideas about dementia and life as discussed above – Georges wants to commit suicide because he is forgetting but even as he is losing his memories, he never forgets his desire to die. If we paid close attention to the ecologies of temporal performances that Georges is embedded in, might we imagine other reasons as to why he wants to die? Perhaps, like the Matsutake mushroom that survives despite capitalism's destruction of the world, Georges wants to die in spite of his dementia?

Towards the end of the film, Georges's granddaughter, Eve, also tries to kill herself by taking a heavy dose of antidepressant. Her father is convinced that she attempted suicide because she found out that he has been exchanging sexual messages with a woman on Facebook and will imminently abandon her. Accordingly, Georges is sent to speak to her in order to understand why she did it. The conversation is underscored by three major beats. Firstly, Georges shows Eve a photo album of her grandmother. He recounts how, towards the end of her life, she was very ill – paralysed, bedridden and non-verbal – and he was the care-giver. After three years of caring for her, he suffocates her. Georges insists that it was the correct decision and that he does not regret it at all. Secondly, Eve recalls how, when she was sent to a summer camp at a younger age, she was given antidepressants to calm herself. Instead of taking the antidepressant, she uses it to spike one of her campmates' meals. The victim, unknowingly taking the pills over a period of time, collapses and is taken to the hospital. Thirdly, Georges details how he saw a bird of prey catch another bird in mid-air and then proceeded to tear it apart in the most vicious way.

The conversation between Georges and Eve takes place in his study. At the start of the scene, Eve is framed in a mid-shot as she stands on the threshold of the door, neither in the room nor out of it. Conversely, Georges is positioned in the centre of a wide angle shot, as he is surrounded by the many objects in his room. Georges tries to get Eve to sit by him so that they can talk but she refuses, meekly entering the room, closing the door and standing by the edge of his world. This shot/reverse shot exchange continues for a bit as Georges keeps asking her to move closer – to no avail – and both grandfather and granddaughter are framed in increasingly tighter shots. It is only when Georges takes out the photo album that Eve agrees to walk towards him. As that happens, the film cuts to a shot with both characters sharing the same frame; she is on the left of the screen, he is on the right, and, in the centre, they are connected – momentarily – by the cover of the photo album. Before returning to the shot/reverse shot editing pattern that I have just described, the sequence is punctuated by a close-up shot of the photographs in the album. The first page consists of black-and-white photos of Georges and his wife when they were younger, and the second page predominantly contains colour photographs of her when she was older.

The proxemics of the scene are of interest to me because the audience sees Eve hovering on and around the liminal edge of the room. As she walks further into the room and closer to her grandfather, both characters are filmed in continuously tighter shots. The intensities of the room as experienced by both characters change relationally, highlighting how they are temporally performing and performed by each other. Beyond that, as they finally share a frame together, they are also performed by the photo album, with its own materially curated temporality of a life course and life story

Figure 4.2 Georges, Eve and the fleeting presence of the album in *Happy End*

(there are no pictures of Georges's wife in the later stages of her life – or, at least, there are no photographs that visibly mark the final stages of her life as described by him).[5] In turn, through the visual qualities of the sequence, an added nuance is layered onto the conversation between Eve and Georges.

The ideas exchanged in the dialogue are ecologically complex. Eve's life story, Georges's life story and the birds' life stories all hold the ideas of violence and death at their core. When he talks of the bird of prey tearing another bird apart, he notes that watching it in 'real life' is very different from watching it through the media. The latter, as he puts it, is just 'nature in action', whereas in the former, his hands trembled. Rather than reading this as an indictment of the ways technology mediates our worldview and desensitises us towards violence, I am imagining this as a discussion of the nature/ecology opposition. When he talks of watching 'nature in action', it is almost as if he is pointing towards a Cartesian divide between the mind and the body and that he, as a human being, can step out of the situation to demystify it. On the contrary, when he witnessed the killing happen in his garden and when he trembled, he is ecologically performed by the times and temporalities of the birds, and his own outlook towards life shifts too. Here, I would suggest that the audience is invited to think of how Georges's desire to die is perhaps not as strong as we are led to think it is. Maybe, then, there is more to his attempts to commit suicide than his dementia – maybe, he is just very tired of his lived environment. Indeed, reading the film as a criticism of globalised neoliberalism, Alex Lykidis suggests that the desire to die in the film (in Georges and in the other characters) is 'an act of self-abnegation' and 'a rejection of the bourgeois lifestyle' (Lykidis 2021: 241). From this viewpoint, it is interesting to note that as Eve walks closer to him in this scene, he (and Eve) is framed in increasingly tighter and more claustrophobic shots, and not in progressively wider shots – they are trapped by the wealth that surround them. Even though the shot/reverse shot editing pattern links the two characters together, this is a connection that is brutally forged.

In this sense, we can also understand Eve's desire to die as her being performed by the times and temporalities of this extremely wealthy household, of which Georges is the patriarch of. *Happy End* starts with a series of videos that Eve livestreams online. These include her observing and anticipating her mother's bedtime routine; her poisoning a hamster with antidepressants and us watching it die, in real time; and her mother gradually overdosing on antidepressants. From the start, the audience learns that Eve's father left them when she was very young and she was brought up by her mother. It is only when her mother is taken to the hospital, and subsequently dying, that she ends up living with her father. Towards the end of the conversation between grandfather and granddaughter in the study, this exchange happens:

> Georges: Why did you do it?
> Eve: What?
> Georges: The pills.
> Eve: I don't know. [She pauses.] I don't know.

On the surface, this conversation is about why Eve took the antidepressants herself and why she spiked her campmate's meals. But, as George's desire to die intersects with hers, Eve's pause just before she says 'I don't know' again takes on a more ambiguous quality. We are, perhaps, asked to also consider whether she poisoned her mother at the start of the film or her mother did it herself. Further, we are also invited to think through the issue of her killing the hamster, and the ethics of us, as audience, being made to watch a hamster get poisoned and dying in real time. All these connections are heterogeneously made as we ecologically embed Eve in many cruel temporal performances, in turn furthering the film's criticism of capitalism.

Moreover, Georges's reference to his wife in this sequence, and the things that he did to her, also opens us up to consider even wider ecologies of temporal performances beyond the film's diegesis. In *Happy End*, Georges is played by Jean-Louis Trintignant, who also plays another Georges Laurent in Haneke's 2012 film *Amour* (Austria/France/Germany) – Haneke regularly names his characters Georges and Anne Laurent – which is a film about an ageing middle-class couple being dependent on each other. In *Amour*, Anne experiences two strokes that leave her with vascular dementia. Anne is paralysed, bed-ridden and rendered non-verbal, and this turns Georges into her primary care-giver, who repeatedly refuses help from anyone and insists on doing the care work by himself. In perhaps the most notorious moment in *Amour*, Anne lies in bed groaning while Georges tries to comfort her. He holds her hand, caresses it gently and lovingly, and starts telling her a story of him refusing to finish his food at summer camp when he was younger. She calms down when he finishes the story. He looks at her, ponders, hesitates, and then proceeds to smother her with a pillow and the weight of his body. The audience hears her gasp for air, sees her legs flail until they stop, and watches her die, all in one long take. Georges then spends the denouement of the film sealing his flat up, catching a pigeon that somehow ended up in the apartment, and writes a letter. In the very last moments of the film, he is lying in bed by himself when, suddenly, the sound of dishes being washed up enters the film. Georges notices the sound and walks, gingerly, to the kitchen where he sees Anne doing the dishes. This appears to be a pre-stroke Anne, who is not wheelchair-bound nor bed-ridden, and who articulates her words clearly. Anne says she is almost finished, and that Georges should put on his shoes to get ready for their walk. Throughout, Georges looks at her intently. He helps Anne put on her coat, and she reminds him to grab his coat. Together, they leave the apartment.

Scholars writing about the depiction of ageing and disability in *Amour* regularly focus on whether Georges's actions are morally justified (debates surrounding euthanasia and homicide) and why professional palliative care does not feature in the film at all. Gullette, for example, argues that *Amour* is a film that expresses the desire to kill off anyone with dementia: 'Only for Haneke is the illness by itself, worsening, sufficient reason to wish for a death' (Gullette 2017: 156). In another instance, Sally Chivers suggests that the film propagates 'a cultural fantasy that care can be downloaded from the state to the family and that, failing that, death is preferable to any form of institutional care' (Chivers 2015: 77). In both Gullette and Chivers, the film's denouement is read as Georges's fantasy that gives 'voice to the fear on the part of a self-abnegating care-giver that he will – or must – go mad finally in order to eliminate his charge and end his own ordeal' (Gullette 2014: 214). In this regard, Georges in *Amour* is also dehumanised by Anne's dementia.

However, following my argument in Chapter Two about demented time as the past returning differently and creatively, we can also interpret the final moments between Georges and Anne before they go for a walk as an entanglement that imagines a different future. *Armour* does depict a professional care-giver who is extremely competent at her job. At the end of her shift, Georges and the care-giver have a conversation about the possibility of more shifts. Separating the two characters is a wad of cash that is intended as her payment. We see the carer take the money and put it into her bag, and just before she leaves, she tells – reassures – Georges that Anne's groans are just 'a reflex'. Put differently, just as the carer takes the money, she dehumanises and essentialises Anne into her illness and disability. This exchange, I suggest, turns *Armour* into a fierce criticism of the state of care in France as one that has become too neoliberalised. From this viewpoint, both Anne and Georges become victims of capitalism. Consequently, rather than reading Georges at the end of *Armour* as committing suicide or as dehumanised, I argue that, through Anne's dementia, the film allows Georges and Anne to live on despite capitalism.

In turn, when Georges in *Happy End* talks about suffocating his wife, the temporalities of *Amour* are intertextually performed unto *Happy End*, and we are further encouraged to think of Georges as wanting to die because of capitalism, and not (necessarily) because of his dementia. In fact, despite his multiple attempts to die, the film pointedly does not let him die. The film ends with the family hosting an opulent lunch party for a large group of white middle-class people, who are all in formal wear. An incident occurs as the group of white middle-class people are brought into encounter with a group of black refugees, who are in casual clothes. This moment, for Lykidis, highlights 'how the liberal instrumentalization of multiculturalism is used to disguise the fact that neoliberal policies are devastating the working class' (Lykidis 2021: 243). Responding to this event, Georges leaves the restaurant and asks Eve to push him down a concrete slope into the sea so that he can – hopefully – drown. The final moments of the film see Georges, in a formal black-and-white suit, half submerged in the liminal space where concrete and sea meet, as his children rush towards him. As Georges sits at the juncture of all these intersecting times and temporalities between the human and non-human phenomena in the film, the film ends. Consequently, Georges survives, in spite of capitalism.

Enchantment

In a similar vein, in drawing our attention to the multiple temporalities in negotiation, *Pandora's Box* also encourages a re-imagination of demen-

Ecologies of Temporal Performances 101

Figure 4.3 Ecologies of temporal performances in the final moments of *Happy End*

tia narratives that is not necessarily predicated on the person living with dementia dying. Towards the end of *Pandora's Box*, Nusret is put into a care home in Istanbul. Her grandson, Murat, smuggles her out of the city and brings her back, by himself, to her home by the mountain. One day, Nusret claims that someone or something is telling her to go to the mountain, and Murat calms her down by asking her not to worry and that the entities are now asking her to sit down. Sometime later, Murat falls asleep and is woken up by the sound of the door creaking. He rushes out of the house and finds his grandmother by herself in the far distance. The audience is shown a close-up shot of Murat looking at the situation. He stands still, grabs his hair, and cries. Then, the film cuts to a reverse wide angle shot of Nusret walking up the mountain. She is at the bottom the frame and is completely engulfed by the greenery around her. Sonically, this shot is linked to Murat's point of view as the sound of him crying continues to permeate the film. Slowly, the camera moves upwards, leaving Nusret behind for the trees that grow on the mountain. Simultaneously, the sound of Murat crying fades out of the diegesis, and the sound of strong wind blowing enters the film instead, signalling the end of the film.

Like the opening moments of *Pandora's Box*, the ending of the film is equally enigmatic. Analysing the film, Cohen-Shalev and Marcus propose that this scene 'calls for a differentiated definition of care' that attends 'to the call of subjective dignity' over 'that of continued communal care' (Cohen-Shalev and Marcus 2012: 84). Their reading, affirmed by Medina, poses that the final moment 'follows the ethical dilemma Murat faces: either letting his

Figure 4.4 The ambiguous final shot of *Pandora's Box*

grandmother go to the mountain and die, or keeping her prisoner in a world to which she no longer belongs' (Medina 2018: 61). In turn, the mountain becomes

> a salvation-in-death, as Nusret asks Murat to let her disappear again into the mountain before utter forgetfulness takes over ('let me go to my mountain, before I forget that too') – her last, telling words in the film, as well as her ultimate, lucid autonomous decision. (Cohen-Shalev and Marcus 2012: 83)

As I mentioned earlier, the analysis put forward by Cohen-Shalev and Marcus has a tendency to disenchant the surrounding world that Nusret is embedded in, rendering them dead. This position is again underlined here as they characterise Nusret's final statement – to let her go back to the mountain before she forgets it – as 'her ultimate, lucid autonomous decision'; embedded in the claim is that the prior moment where Nusret says that someone or something is telling her to go to the mountain is her being delirious (is her dementia). From this viewpoint, the mountain is lacking vitality. Not too different from scholars talking about *Happy End*, then, the discussion of *Pandora's Box* equates dementia with dying.

I am significantly more hesitant about the claim that Nusret is going to die. For both Cohen-Shalev and Marcus, and Medina, the final shot is understood as filtered through Murat's point of view, and the camera, in this moment, 'tilts up', which means that Murat is looking upwards (Cohen-Shalev and Marcus 2012: 84). This claim appears to be initially supported by

Figure 4.5 The enchanting landscape in *Pandora's Box*

the editing sequence (shot/reverse shot of Murat seeing and what he sees) and the sound design (his crying in the diegesis of the final shot). However, as the camera is positioned so far away from Nusret as she climbs the mountain, the slow, upward movement of the camera becomes more ambiguous, and it could just as easily be the camera craning upwards. Further, partway through the final shot, the sound of Murat crying fades out of the film. In its place, the sound of the wind blowing enters the film and, yet, the trees of the mountain remain persistently still. Consequently, the final shot becomes more than just Murat's point of view, and also takes on an animist quality. Altogether, in addition to the audience being positioned as Murat, I propose that we are also asked to consider the liveliness of the mountain, and to not discount the entity that asks Nusret to go to the mountain as her dementia only. Indeed, every time the film cuts to a shot of the mountain, it takes on a quality of becoming that is almost mystical, constantly revealed and concealed by the mist that envelops the landscape (see Figure 4.5). Accordingly, we are invited to be enchanted by her entanglement with the mountain, to think of her as being a part of wider ecologies of temporal performances, and to shift beyond killing her and her dementia.

As films about dementia heighten our engagement with different kinds of temporalities and demand that we pay close attention to the heterogeneity of it all, all lines of temporal flight are engendered. From this perspective, films about dementia take on an ambiguous quality that enchants us, as we are invited to treat the times and temporalities of all human and non-human phenomena on an equal level. Borrowing from Bennett, to be enchanted is to be in a state of 'temporary suspension of chronological time and bodily movement' (Bennett 2001: 5). To be enchanted, in other words, is to pause and to unfurl time. In the next chapter, I examine how we might methodologically think through these heterogeneous temporalities and suggest that we can do this by hesitantly engaging with the world.

Notes

1. See Fuchs 2020 and Katz 2013.
2. See Pitches 2020 on mountains and performance.
3. See Edensor et al. 2020 on the temporalities of the more-than-human world.
4. Similarly, Arne Næss also puts forward the idea of the 'relational-total field' in deep ecology. See Næss 1973 and Valera 2018.
5. These photographs can be understood as part of Georges's convoy of material support, which is understood by David J. Ekerdt as 'a persistent and dynamic body of belongings that accompanies people across their changing lives' (Ekerdt 2019: 31). For Ekerdt, the ageing process 'lays down a residue of belongings that become biographically meaningful by virtue of their duration' (Ekerdt 2019: 31).

5

Reading the Digital Index in a Hesitant Way

In *The Taking of Deborah Logan* (Adam Robitel, 2014, USA), doctoral student Mia is making a research documentary about Deborah, who lives with Alzheimer's disease. Deborah constantly mends the telephone switchboard locked up in the attic and claims to see a dark figure from her past. Her daughter asserts that Deborah's behaviour is nothing concerning – she is simply (re-)living the past in the present, as she worked as a switchboard operator for the most of her adult life. As the documentary-within-the-film progresses, the film-makers come to realise that the behaviour displayed by Deborah is not characteristic of people living with dementia. Deborah exhibits extremely violent and aggressive tendencies, her skin sheds like a snake, and her mouth is able to open wide enough to swallow the entire head of a young girl. In turn, both Mia and the audience discover that Deborah, who is characterised as slowly emptied of her personality and presence because of her dementia, is actually possessed by a man whom she had murdered years ago. In other words, in *The Taking of Deborah Logan*, through the lens of horror, the negotiations between the past and the present as experienced by the person living with dementia, are surfaced and made visible.

In a similar vein, *The Visit* (M. Night Shyamalan, 2015, USA) sees teenagers Becca and Tyler visit their grandparents for the first time as their mother goes on a holiday. Becca, who loves cinema and wants to perfect the art of film, decides to document the whole visit with both her digital video camera and her Digital Single-Lens Reflex (DSLR) camera. The teenagers find that their bedtime is unusually early, and that they are instructed not to leave their room after 9.30pm. They soon find out why: when night falls, their grandmother goes into a maniacal fury and charges around the house naked scratching at doors. Throughout, though the film is shot to strongly evoke a supernatural film, with specific allusions to films such as *Paranormal Activity* (Oren Peli, 2007, USA) and *Ringu* (Hideo Nakata, 1998, Japan) amongst other horror films, the affect of horror really comes from the idea that the grandparents are old and that the grandmother lives with dementia.

As Shyamalan repeatedly asserts in interviews: 'The subject of the piece is our fear of getting old, which is a variation on our fear of dying' (Shyamalan in Blum 2015). The fear of old age, Shyamalan insists, is a 'primal thing' (Shyamalan in Blum 2015). When informed about their grandparents' behaviour, the teenagers' mother dismisses it as older age; when confronted, their grandfather explains that their grandmother behaves this way because she lives with sundown syndrome, which is a possible symptom of dementia that causes increased confusion and agitation when the sun sets. Although the specific causes of sundown syndrome are still unclear, scientists suggest that sundowning occurs in part due to the body's circadian rhythm – the internal body clock – clashing with the temporality of the outside world.[1] Again, like *The Taking of Deborah Logan*, the horror stems not from the suggestion of supernatural hauntings but from the multiple temporalities experienced by the person living with dementia.

These horrifying portrayals of people living with dementia extend from the silver(ing) screen to wider imaginaries of dementia. People living with dementia have, for instance, been described as zombies and the living dead on multiple occasions, highlighting the ways in which the fear of people living with dementia relate to the fear of experiencing temporalities that do not correspond to the linearity of empty, clock time, where the person living with dementia gestures towards the blurred boundaries between the past and the present (Behuniak 2011; and Aquilina and Hughes 2006). Consequently, people living with dementia become a cultural shorthand 'for something that is incredibly frightening', for 'a complex, unknowable world of doom, ageing, and a fate worse than death' (Zeilig 2013: 262). Both *The Taking of Deborah Logan* and *The Visit*, however, are films that explicitly relay the lives of people living with dementia through the horror genre. Semantically, these two films feature the monstrous body: the aged person living with dementia. Syntactically, these 'monsters' are placed in diametric opposition to that of the 'intellectual' and 'rational' minds (a doctoral student in *The Taking* and a teenager who thinks about cinema through technical jargon in *The Visit*), and that of younger people who are full of life. In both films, through the aesthetics of the found footage horror, the person living with dementia becomes an index of multiple temporalities in the present, and their dementia becomes a horrifying threat that surfaces and directs at the ways in which these multiples temporalities are coeval.

As understood by Charles Sanders Peirce, the index is a sign that shows 'something about things, on account of their being physically connected with them' (Peirce 1998: 5). A footprint in the sand, for example, is an indexical sign that points towards the presence of someone having passed by. Yet, by merely looking at the sign, we are unable to necessarily glean the most insightful conclusion about the nature of the person (who was the person, what were they doing while walking, what colour were their shoes, and so on), consequently leading Mary Ann Doane to write that indexical signs 'provide no insight into the nature of their objects; they have no cognitive value, but simply indicate that something is "there"' (Doane 2007b: 135). In turn, through its semiotic function as that of the pure assurance of a prior existence in the present tense, the index, Mary Ann Doane writes, 'more insistently than any other type of sign, is haunted by its object' (Doane 2007b: 134).

This object that haunts the index, borrowing from Gilles Deleuze, is understood here as a virtual object. As Deleuze writes, the virtual object

> is past as the contemporary of the present which it is, in a frozen present; as though lacking on the one hand the part which, on the other hand, it is at the same time; as though displaced while still in place. This is why virtual objects exist only as fragments of themselves: they are found only as lost; they exist only as recovered. Loss or forgetting here are not determinations which must be overcome; rather, they refer to the objective nature of that which are recovered, as lost, at the heart of forgetting. (Deleuze 1994: 102)

This is to say, firstly, the virtual object that haunts exists as 'shreds of pure past' that are incorporated into the actual object (Deleuze 1994: 101). Secondly, the index – the actual – is a sign that embalms time and captures the relationship between the past and the present. Thirdly, the index, in gesturing towards the virtual object as that of loss *and* recovery, highlights the uneven process of actualisation where not everything in the virtual is actualised into the actual. As such, to attempt to recover – to trace – the virtual past that haunts in the index is to discover a wider map of temporal negotiations and to open up the possibilities for different kinds of temporal performances.

This chapter is interested in the (often uneasy) relationship between the past and the present as manifest in people living with dementia's experiences of time through the framework of generic horror. These experiences of horror, Stephen Prince would argue, reside in the 'confrontation with uncertainty, with the "unnatural," with a violation of the ontological categories on which being and culture reside' (Prince 2004: 2). In both *The Taking of Deborah Logan* and *The Visit*, the presence of the person living with dementia always threatens to hesitantly uproot the 'normal' and 'universal' understanding of time as linear and homogeneous, and always confronts these understandings by strongly hinting at multiple and different ways of conceiving time. Building on the argument that I developed in the previous chapters, where I suggest that everyone and everything is entangled in ecologies of temporal performances, this chapter argues that the found footage horror aesthetics, as employed in both the case study films to narrativise the experiences of dementia, offer the possibility of thinking of the indexical in film as painting a rhizomatic map of temporal performances.

The blurred lines between the past and the present

In both case study films, the relationship between the past and the present is volatile, where the past is always at the edge of horrifying irruption into the present. In one scene in *The Visit*, for instance, Becca hears the grandmother in the next room laughing at a woman yodelling. Thinking her grandmother is watching television, Becca takes the opportunity to interview her. Holding the camera, Becca slowly creeps into the room and she finds her grandmother at the far end of the room. The room is dimly lit by the setting sunlight, and the grandmother is sat in her armchair in the only spot in the room where the sunlight hits, laughing maniacally whilst facing the wall. As Becca and the camera slowly creep up to the grandmother, the sound of the floorboard creaking from the rocking armchair is clearly audible alongside the sound of a woman slow yodelling, and, very quickly, an atmosphere of dread punctuates the room.

Figure 5.1 The grandmother in her armchair at the far end of the room in *The Visit*

As the grandmother sees Becca, she monotonously greets her before announcing that she has the 'deep darkies'. She slowly unties her headscarf and begins strangling herself with it. When stopped, the grandmother responds by saying: 'You have to laugh to keep the deep darkies in the cave'. As she is sat in the only sunlit spot in the room, the darkest secrets that threaten to engulf her are rendered visible through the scene's lighting. In this moment, the grandmother's agitated attempts to suppress her memories seem entirely unprovoked by anyone; instead, her behaviour is coded to be a result of her sundowning, as her dementia horrifyingly surfaces and gestures towards the presence of the multiple temporalities coexisting in her present.

Equally, this irruption and eruption of the past in(to) the present is very much alive in *The Taking of Deborah Logan* as Sarah, the daughter of Deborah, and the documentary team discover Deborah sat in the dark attic by her switchboard. Deborah, who is completely naked, hugs herself whilst sobbing uncontrollably for help. Suddenly, she goes quiet and becomes motionless. Gradually, she lets out a series of unintelligible growls, slowly and menacingly raises her hands to the switchboard, and then proceeds to furiously plug and unplug a telephone cable into the switchboard. This is not the usual vulnerable Deborah and the voice that comes out from this body is also not hers; at this moment, the audience, like Sarah and the documentary team, witness the highly aggressive Deborah being haunted by and possessed by, as everyone will soon comprehend, a death from her past. Yet, importantly, neither Sarah nor the camera crew understands that Deborah is possessed by a supernatural being. Narratively, all of Deborah's behaviour has been explained away rationally, perpetuating, as Andrea Capstick, John Chatwin and Katherine Ludwin argue, 'the biomedical orthodoxy that everything a person with dementia says or does is "a symptom of the disease"' (Capstick et al. 2015: 229). A dangerous threat is clearly registered by the film as Deborah – the person living with dementia – becomes a vehicle to volatilise the relationship between the past and the present.

The scene does not end, and Deborah's violent assault on the switchboard continues, resulting in the switchboard combusting. Sparks fly out from the back of the machine and light up the whole attic as the camera crew goes into a panic. Amidst all the chaos, as Sarah runs towards her mother, as the film crew tries to make sense of the whole situation, and as the room oscillates between extreme darkness and brightness, the film cuts to an extremely brief shot of a man (dead and/or alive) staring into the camera with his mouth wide open – like that of a snake – followed by a quick

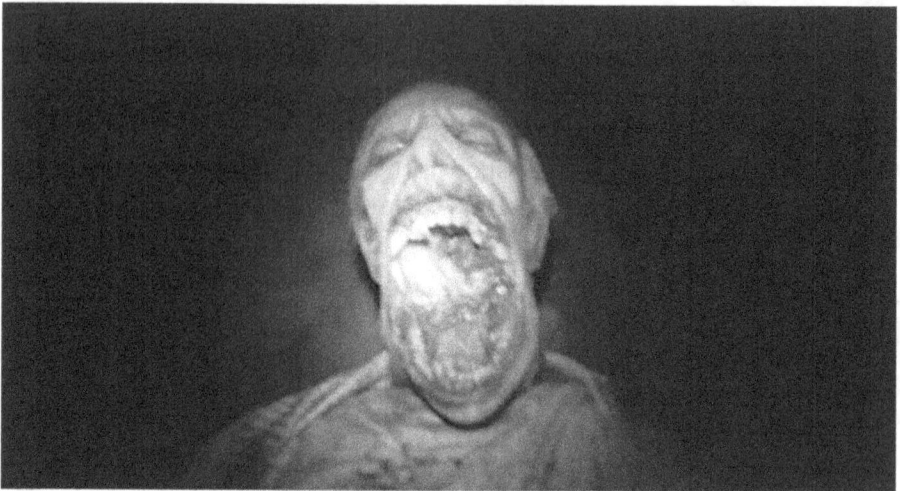

Figure 5.2 The visual irruption of a man in *The Taking of Deborah Logan*

negative black-and-green version of the same shot. Aurally, nothing changes and the audience continues to hear the chaos in the film's diegesis. After this fleeting visual interruption, the film cuts back to Mia and Sarah tending to the unconscious Deborah. The scene ends, and nobody in the film acknowledges this brief interlude.

Writing about this scene, Agnieszka Kotwasińska reads it as an example of a transageing narrative that moves 'beyond the diachronic limitations of linearity' and explores 'transtemporal embodiments in order to resist melancholia's paralysis' (Kotwasińska 2018: 188). As the audience will realise later, the image that appears on screen is the man whom Deborah murdered when she was younger and, in this scene, for Kotwasińska, the roles that Deborah has embodied and performed throughout her life (single mother, businesswoman, murderer and older woman) 'are not temporally disengaged with from each other, but form one vibrant mesh that Deborah experiences simultaneously through her body memory', highlighting the multiple and changing temporal performances throughout Deborah's life course (Kotwasińska 2018: 188).

Yet, on its own, this analysis is tenuous for it goes against the internal logic of the found footage horror, which rarely offers nor privileges the subjective experience of the filmed subject unless the subject takes over control of the filmic apparatus. Conversely, I suggest, the blink-and-you-miss-it shots, watched in relation to the scene, can be read as a technical glitch experienced by the digital camera that is caused by the cameraman's frantic movements and the sudden changes in the amount of light in the

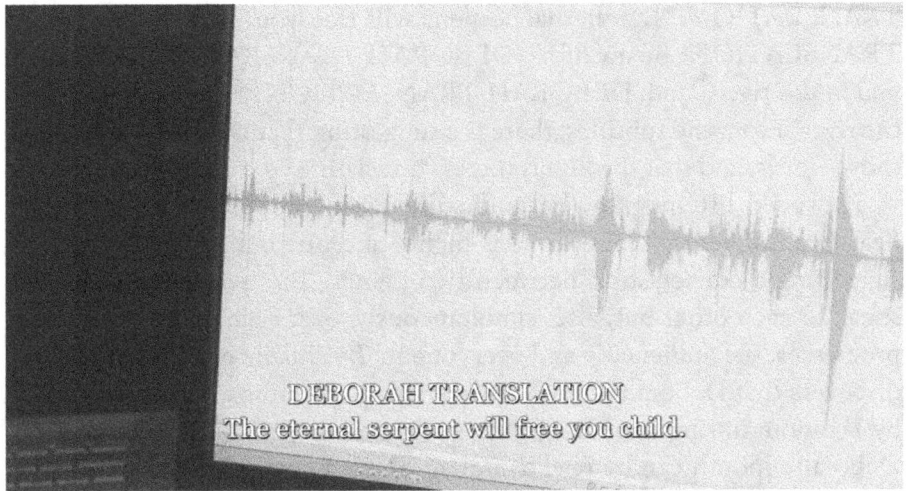

Figure 5.3 Subtitling Deborah's prosopopoeia in *The Taking of Deborah Logan*

room. As Deborah comes into the frame with her heightened experiences of multiple temporalities, the uneasy coexistence between the present and the past, that cinema as a medium tries to translate, explode. Through the technical glitch, cinema's present is haunted by the presence of the past, and this digital glitch also works as a way in to the subjective experiences of Deborah. Through dementia, the indexical dispositions of Deborah and cinema as time embalmed are highlighted, underscoring the oxymoronic nature of the index, which Doane describes as 'this was once the present moment' (Doane 2007b: 140). The index, put differently, is a site that uneasily alludes to the presence of two (or more) temporalities in negotiation.

The idea of temporal negotiation can be seen as a form of prosopopoeia, that is, the communication between the living and the dead. Research has shown that people living with dementia who are bilingual frequently switch back to conversing in their first language, or 'use the wrong language for the setting or interlocutor or produce what appears to be an inappropriate mixture of their two languages' (Paradis 2008: 219). Similarly, in *The Taking of Deborah Logan*, Deborah utters French as she violently assaults the switchboard, a language that is linked to her past. In a later scene, the film crew extracts the audio file of Deborah's speech from the camera, modulates the inflection digitally, and puts it through an online translation programme. The camera zooms into the computer screen (which displays the digitised soundwaves of Deborah) and the crew plays the audio file. Everyone hears the (slightly clearer) French, and subtitles that translate what is being spoken appear on the screen. Visually, the subtitles read: 'DEBORAH

TRANSLATION: The eternal serpent will free you child'; 'DEBORAH TRANSLATION: Be my fifth'; 'DEBORAH TRANSLATION: I will wash you in the river'; and 'DEBORAH TRANSLATION: Your blood will feed the river'. From the subtitles, there is a suggestion that Deborah is saying all those words, and that the film is merely translating.

However, listening to the audio file itself, the audience can clearly hear two different pitches – one is higher and one is significantly lower – suggesting a conversation between two beings. The two different pitches speak to each other but, also, simultaneously, over each other. As the film progresses, the audience – and everyone in *The Taking of Deborah Logan* – discovers that Deborah is haunted by Henry Desjardins, a murderer killed by Deborah during her younger days. In turn, the words that come out of Deborah's mouth can be read as not so much a conversation nor meeting between the past and the present but, as the two vocal pitches clash with each other, more of a collision between these two entities.

As both the grandmother in *The Visit* and Deborah in *The Taking of Deborah Logan* demonstrate, the person living with dementia as index becomes a heightened site where the past and the present negotiate. For Laura Mulvey, this understanding of the index as a translation of multiple temporalities also works well in relation to cinema. She writes:

> In the cinema organic movement is transformed into its inorganic replica, a series of static, inanimate, images, which, once projected, then become animated to blur the distinctions between the oppositions. The homologies extend: on the one hand, the inanimate, inorganic, still, dead; on the other, organic, animate, moving, alive. It is here, with the blurring of these boundaries, that the uncanny nature of the cinematic image returns most forcefully and, with it, the conceptual space of uncertainty: that is, the difficulty of understanding time and the presence of death in life. (Mulvey 2006: 52–3)

Mulvey's contemplation of the uncanny in cinema here draws from both Sigmund Freud and Wilhelm Jentsch. The former suggests that the uncanny arises from the fear of the past whereas the latter argues that the uncanny stems from the new and unfamiliar (future). Mulvey notes that although the arguments put forward by Freud and Jentsch are dissimilar, the two theorists agree on one thing: the uncanny occurs 'whenever the animate and the inmate becomes confused' (Mulvey 2006: 38). Effectively, 'the uncanny nature of the cinematic image' that Mulvey discusses can thus be seen as a kind of *trompe-l'œil*, an audio-visual illusion of something of the real, and this notion of the 'real' and the 'realistic' (which is very much linked to cinema's connection with the index) is created by cinema's complex relationship with time. For Mulvey, this relationship between the past and the present in cinema is extremely porous, which results in the difficulty of separating the two types of temporalities into two coherent subsets; she rejects the dead/alive dichotomy and implicitly embraces the idea that cinema encompasses multiple temporalities.

Mulvey's understanding of cinema vis-à-vis the index predicates on an understanding of cinema as a representational practice, where there is a more 'wholesome reality' that cinema is not part of. As I suggest throughout this book, I come from a viewpoint that does not see cinema as secondary to 'real life' but, rather, as equally constituent of reality. Following Richard Rushton, the 'reality of films does not lie behind or beyond them' but, rather, 'the reality of film is what films themselves are' (Rushton 2011: 9). Reality, as such, is understood to be made up of the virtual and the actual, where multiple virtual intensities negotiate and entangle to actualise into the actual (see Chapter Three). As I elaborate in this chapter, this understanding of reality as ecologies of temporal performances, as a process of the virtual unevenly actualising into the actual, has significant implications on our understanding of the index, seeing it as a sign that opens up the possibility of change or, at the very least, provides a map of the multiple intersecting discourses the are entangled in a performance of time.

Temporal negotiation and hesitancy

In my analyses of *The Taking of Deborah Logan* and *The Visit*, I have argued that the index as trace and deixis induces a sense of temporal negotiation and hesitation where the lines between the past and present are seemingly blurred (for instance, the person living with dementia might be burying something, they might be possessed by a spirit and/or they might be living with dementia). Here, I am interested in the ways that this notion of hesitation is a useful approach to think through questions of time. For Tzvetan Todorov, writing about literary fantasy, the 'fantastic is that hesitation experienced by a person who knows only the laws of nature, confronting an apparently supernatural event' (Todorov 1975: 25). To work through his argument, Todorov proposes a highly rigid understanding of fantasy, where the fantastic is wedged firmly between the uncanny, where the narrative can be explained rationally, and the marvellous, where the narrative can be explained away through superstition or other forms of irrational and/or archaic belief. He writes:

> the marvelous corresponds to an unknown phenomenon, never seen as yet, still to come – hence to a future; in the uncanny, on the other hand, we refer the inexplicable to known facts, to a previous experience, and thereby to the past. As for the fantastic itself, the hesitation which characterizes it cannot be situated, by and large, except in the present. (Todorov 1975: 43)

Here, the uncanny-fantastic-marvellous schematic model proposed by Todorov corresponds directly to the past-present-future understanding of time. Conversely, Bliss Cua Lim suggests that Todorov saw the marvellous as a 'placeholder for medievalism, while the uncanny corresponds to Enlightenment or post-Enlightenment skepticism' (Lim 2009: 108–9). Lim's reformulation of Todorov means that the same uncanny-fantastic-marvellous model would instead parallel a future-present-past comprehension of time. Either way the arrangement, following Todorov's logic would mean the politics of temporality in fantasy is grounded in highly linear and disciplined homogeneous time.

Responding to Todorov, Lim forcefully advocates a postcolonial understanding of fantasy as a genre. According to Lim, Todorov's heavy dependence on linear, homogeneous time meant that cultures and societies that do not experience time in a linear way are omitted from the Todorovian fantastic. She writes:

> Modern time consciousness is a means of exercising social, political and economic control over periods of work and leisure; it obscures the ceaselessly changing plurality of our existence in time; and it underwrites a linear, developmental notion of progress that gives rise to ethical problems with regard to cultural and racial difference. (Lim 2009: 11)

Drawing from the works of Henri Bergson and Dipesh Chakrabarty, Lim works to complicate the Todorovian fantastic by questioning the role of aswang narratives – narratives in the Philippines about the shapeshifting creatures that incorporate aspects of a vampire, witch, manananggal and corpse-eater, amongst many other guises – in relation to the fantasy genre and the Philippines' socio-historical context. Lim's argument is that aswang narratives do not just limit themselves to a fictional genre but have glided between history and story in the Philippines since at least the sixteenth century (Lim 2009: 99). As her analysis points out, the aswang is a belief embedded in the living consciousness of the Philippines and is not – as Todorov would argue – confined to something of the past.

In highlighting the temporal limits of Todorov's understanding of hesitancy, Lim proposes an alternative and here the fantastic is defined

> as a narrative that juxtaposes two (or more) radically different worlds. The encounter with a forked world is registered within the narrative as an experience of limits, whether these be limits of epistemological uncertainty, cultural transparency, or historical understanding. Because the unfamiliar world most often takes the form of a supernatural realm in which the linear chronological time of clock and calendar does not hold, the fantastic has a propensity to foreground a sense of temporal discrepancy that cannot be entirely translated into the terms of modern homogeneous time. (Lim 2009: 28)

According to Lim, the worlds are different because of their different attitudes towards temporality and the fantastic happens when immiscible times – times that 'never quite dissolve into the code of modern time consciousness' – come together (Lim 2009: 14). When these temporalities meet in fantasy narratives, a sense of hesitation is engendered, and the audience is confronted with an epistemological and ontological challenge. They are encouraged to rethink what and how they understand something to be and, in this case, review their reliance on homogeneous, linear time.

For Lim, like Bergson, as the hegemony of spatialised time is so overarchingly strong, 'all attempts to articulate pure duration are betrayed by language' (Lim 2009: 17). The Limian fantastic hence works as 'a kind of *mistranslation operating* between two asymmetrically ranked codes' (Lim 2009: 31; emphasis in original). On the one hand, Lim argues, sits the 'universal' homogeneous time that is rooted in Newtonian science and modern historical consciousness. On the other sits the local and archaic heterogeneous times of superstition, supernatural and the popular (Lim 2009: 31). Lim's proposition of fantasy as that where multiple temporalities come together thus relies very heavily on 'a refusal of anachronism, of a past left behind' in order to 'forge a more ethical, less distorting temporal view of otherness' (Lim 2009: 14–16). The Limian hesitancy, therefore, points towards the notion of temporal mistranslation: to hesitate is to be aware of the multiple temporalities in/at translation.

This notion of hesitation allows us to think through the co-existence of the virtual past in the actual present in relation to films about dementia. As far as the treatments of dementia in *The Taking of Deborah Logan* and *The Visit* are concerned, looking at the temporal experiences of both Deborah and the grandmother through the lens of the Limian fantastic, to hesitate is to pause and to unfurl the negotiations of temporalities into its multiple

Figure 5.4 The grandmother by the oven in *The Visit*

intersecting units. This is to say, the experiences of dementia in the two case study films highlight the 'trace of containment and excess', and gesture towards the presence of the past in and alongside the present, confronting the other characters and the members of the audience with a sense of ontological and epistemological uncertainty (Lim 2009: 32).

To elaborate with an example from *The Visit*. Becca first insists on interviewing the grandmother to know more about her past whilst they are washing the dishes together in the kitchen. When asked, the grandmother immediately walks towards the countertop and starts wiping the surface before noticing the oven in the corner of her eye. The grandmother pauses, walks towards the oven and removes the metal shelf from it. Holding the shelf, the grandmother stops and looks at Becca with a blank look. As she does so, the metal shelf leaving the oven makes a clatter that reverberates through the atmosphere, adding tension to the scene. The grandmother asks Becca to clean the oven and she agrees. As she starts cleaning, the grandmother asks Becca to get further and further into the oven, and eventually, the whole of Becca is completely in the oven, à la Hansel and Gretel. As this happens, the grandmother stands right by the oven door watching Becca clean while she fiddles with the tea towel in her hand. When Becca finishes the cleaning process, the grandmother agrees to the interview about her past.

Nothing menacing happens in this scene. Nonetheless, a sense of horror is engendered by the actions of the grandmother. This is further compounded by the deliberate soundscape – the clatter that reverberates, the water slowly dripping from the tap, and the intense scrubbing from inside the oven – that puts the safety of Becca into question. Via horror, the sense of hesitation is highlighted. The audience and Becca never quite know what the grandmother is doing or what her motives might be, in large parts due to her dementia: she could be walking away from the sink so that she does not have to talk about the interview and, by extension, her past; she could be drawn to the oven because she was distracted, or she could be deliberately planning something treacherous in her head. She could be fidgeting with her tea towel whilst watching Becca clean because she is contemplating closing the oven door, trapping Becca in it, be genuinely concerned with Becca's ability to clean the oven properly, or just merely musing on whether she should do the interview to share the rich and hidden/buried/forgotten past she is mistranslating in the present.

As we can see, the temporalities indexed by the person living with dementia are foregrounded. Likewise, as the person living with dementia is rooted in ecologies of temporal performances, the person not living with dementia (and other non-human species and non-living materials and phenomena) performing and performed by time is also an index that embodies multiple entangled temporalities. Here, as Becca precariously agrees to enter the oven to clean it, the audience is also made aware that she is doing so because she is desperately searching for a past about her mother that she does not have access to. Becca too, as an index of multiple temporalities, is haunted by the virtual object, by shreds of the pure past, and through her attempts to recover more of her past, her temporal identifications and narratives are directly joined to the temporal identifications and narratives of the grandmother's.

A rhizomatic worldview

Seen from this perspective, the index, as trace and deixis, enables a rhizomatic worldview that eschews hierarchies. For Deleuze and Félix Guattari, a rhizomatic worldview emphasises the fundamental principles of connection and heterogeneity, where 'any point of a rhizome can be connected to anything other, and must be' (Deleuze and Guattari 1987: 7). The rhizome, they propose, is a map:

> The map is open and connectable in all of its dimensions; it is detachable, reversible, susceptible to constant modification. It can be torn, reversed, adapted to any kind of mounting, reworked by an individual,

group, or social formation. It can be drawn on a wall, conceived of as a work of art, constructed as a political action or as a meditation. Perhaps one of the most important characteristics of the rhizome is that is always has multiple entryways. (Deleuze and Guattari 1987: 12)

In this sense, the person living with dementia is but one index on a map, a rhizome that surfaces all the virtual intensities alongside the actual present, drawing our attention to not only the ways in which they are performing time and performed by time but also opening us up to examine the ways in which everyone and everything else is performed by and performing time. New connections are drawn and made, new lines of actualisation from the virtual to the actual are created, and consequently, new temporal performances are enacted.

Accordingly, thinking of time through the framework of performance and the philosophy of difference is to be aware of the multifarious ways in which all our temporalities are connected, and, more importantly, it is a methodological approach that allows us to start with any one point – any one index – on the rhizomatic map, as we begin to make new connections and embed more indices in the discussion. We can begin by thinking about the temporalities of the person living with dementia on screen, we can begin by thinking about the temporalities of the person not living with dementia on screen, we can begin by thinking about the temporalities of the individual members of the audience that watches the film about dementia, or we can begin by thinking about the temporalities of cinema – we can start the exploration process at any entry point – and, gradually, through linking one index to various other indices, we can begin to tease out a particular intersection of temporalities that is on the rhizomatic map (and more intersections as we make more connections). Thinking about the performances of time, therefore, becomes a way to avoid canonical case studies that gatekeep and (re-)inscribe hierarchical power structures, to avoid tracing everything to one singular source/mythos, and to avoid the temptation to universalise ideas so as to achieve an overarching Grand Theory.

Both *The Taking of Deborah Logan* and *The Visit* audio-visually make this connection between the intersecting temporalities of the film and the temporalities of the surrounding world explicit for they are both found footage horror films that are unable to contain the action within the cinematic frame. As Cecilia Sayad argues, found footage horror cinema 'collapses the boundaries separating the depicted universe from reality, and by extension challenges the ontological status of the fiction film as a self-contained object' (Sayad 2016: 45). For Sayad, the found footage aesthetic works on two levels. Firstly, it draws attention to the cinematic apparatus and absorbs the camera and the screen into the diegesis. Secondly, the handheld shaky camerawork highlights the 'frame's ability to quickly incorporate what is off-screen into the shot, just as it can easily relegate what is in the shot to the off-screen' (Sayad 2016: 58). This mercurial cinematography, for Sayad, reflects the inability of the cinematic frame to contain the actions within the filmic world as the events in the diegesis on screen bleed into the extrafilmic surround, and vice versa.

For example, this is evident in *The Visit* as the teenagers acknowledge the camera's inability to contain their grandmother's night-time antics by hiding their camera on top of the mantelpiece in hope of catching their grandmother in the frame. Night-time: the static camera in the living room captures a quiet living room and kitchen in deep focus as the grandmother wanders into the frame in the kitchen. She walks towards the living room and exits the frame on the right. The living room is empty and the audience hears the off-screen sound of footsteps, inviting them to think that the grandmother is going up the stairs. However, almost immediately, a full close shot of her face appears in front of the camera and she screams into it, a terrifying moment that exploits and plays with the audience's expectations of the off-screen space beyond the frame, emphasising the unreliable nature of the frame in delineating the space beyond the screen.

The grandmother then grabs the camera and starts walking towards the kitchen. As that happens, the stable point of view is disrupted and the shakiness of the handheld camera returns to the film. She grabs a knife and walks up the stairs. As she moves, the action that the teenagers hope to capture – the grandmother's behaviour at night – is barely contained by the camera. Her white dress, made more prominent by the juxtaposition against the dark background, constantly enters and exits the left side of the shot whilst she climbs up the stairs, encouraging the audience to look beyond the screen. As she reaches the top of the stairs, the grandmother drops the camera and walks towards the teenagers' door with the knife. Immediately, the film cuts away to the other side of the room where the teenagers wake up to the sounds of the grandmother banging on the door. Instead of allowing the audience to see what happens, the audience is only allowed to hear what happens, further advancing Sayad's assertion that the action in found footage horror occurs beyond the frame.

This argument is similarly complemented sonically through the use of digital surround sound. Rebecca Coyle writes that the aural aspects in found footage horror films have the 'doubly contrived role of appearing to be natural and spontaneous, while also being carefully constructed to carry much of the affective dimension' (Coyle 2010: 234–5). Both the sound designs in *The Taking of Deborah Logan* and *The Visit*, which were mixed digitally for a surround sound system, fulfil this dual function. On the one hand, the acousmatic thuds, screams and the fingernails scratching at the doors are spatialised through the Dolby Digital 5.1 Mix, giving the audience a 360-degree understanding of where the events are in relation to the on-screen cameras and characters; on the other hand, these sounds are calculated to shock, scare and get under our skin.

Moreover, like the failure of the found footage horror's frame to contain the diegesis, the digital surround soundscape also pushes the sonic space of the found footage film beyond the screen to the audience, placing the viewer simultaneously in the film and the audience. As the grandmother in *The Visit* climbs up the stairs, the audience can distinctly hear the sound of her breathing, which is presented as from behind the camera. In the cinema, this breathing would have come from the speakers positioned behind the audiences. As the grandmother drops the camera and moves towards the door, the sound of the breathing becomes softer as she moves further away from the camera, shifting to the speakers at the front of the cinema. This surround soundscape is always in relation to the camera, in turn positioning the audience as the camera, which, as Sayad argues, has been absorbed into the diegesis by the found footage horror. Once again, as the audience is positioned in relation to, and directly as, the apparatus, the boundary between the diegetic and the extradiegetic space is lost, unable to contain the experiences of dementia to the filmic.[2]

Through the audio-visual blurring of the extra/filmic spaces, the found footage film is 'presented not as mere artefact but as fragment of the real world, and the implication is that its material might well spill over into it' (Sayad 2016: 45). In both *The Taking of Deborah Logan* and *The Visit*, the found footage horror films only lose their ability to contain the action in the frame when the person living with dementia enters the frame, melding the temporalities of the filmic and the extra-filmic together, adding another layer of hesitancy to the film viewing experience (this world, that world, or both worlds), indexing a rhizomatic map of the world within *and* without the film. In approaching dementia and found footage horror cinema via a lens of hesitancy, a map of multiple indices with no fixed centre is created; instead, hesitancy opens up an entangled and relational approach towards the world, where each index is treated as *equally* important and central as the other.

The digitally haunted index

This argument that I have put forward about the experiences of dementia vis-à-vis indexicality needs some qualification. Throughout *The Visit* and *The Taking of Deborah Logan*, the digital technology employed by the filmmakers is ever-present in the films' *mise en scène*. In *The Taking of Deborah Logan*, we see the documentary crew install digital surveillance cameras in every corner of the house. Similarly, the audio file of Deborah that is discussed earlier has also been digitally modulated by the film crew. Equally, in *The Visit*, digital cameras and editing software are continuously visible in the *mise en scène* as both Becca and Tyler document their stay at their grandparents' house. In both films, with the digital technology heavily foregrounded, questions are raised about the films' indexical nature.

As discussed by many scholars, cinema's 'technologically supported indexicality', though present in both celluloid and video mediums, is widely considered to be broken and lost in the digital era (Doane 2007b: 135). For André Bazin, cinema 'embalms time' (Bazin 2005: 14). He writes:

> The film is no longer content to preserve the object, enshrouded as it were in an instant, as the bodies or insects are preserved intact, out of the distant past, in amber. The film delivers baroque art from its convulsive catalepsy. Now, for the first time, the image of things is likewise the image of their duration, change mummified as it were. (Bazin 2005: 14–15)

Unlike the other art forms, cinema captures the dead and makes it come alive through the projected movement. Bazin's idea of cinema as 'change mummified' therefore points towards a tense relationship between the multiple temporalities that cinema experiences and translates, consequently highlighting the indexical nature of the medium. Further, Philip Rosen observes that cinema as change mummified 'rests on a notion of temporality as a threateningly dynamic force, a threat registered especially in the high valuation placed on stabilizing relations between the present and past' (Rosen 2001: xi). On the one hand, the images mechanically produced by the celluloid strip appeal to the idea of preserving the tangible aspects of life, as time is stopped and perceived as actual by the camera. On the other, the actual itself has to be seen as flowing with time, highlighting the paradoxical qualities of trying to preserve reality, as 'that reality in some sense goes against that which motivates the desire to engage it' (Rosen 2001: 28). In other words, the notion of the cinematic index as change mummified draws out attention to the presence of both the virtual and the actual.

Whilst Bazin's arguments referred to the photochemical celluloid film strip, Laura U. Marks argues that this indexical nature of cinema did not diminish when the technology moved from celluloid to video. Marks demonstrates that the video camera electronically inscribes light onto the tape and 'a calculable number of electrons move along a set of common wavelengths all the way from the object to the image' (Marks 2002: 170). For example, when photons with the purple wavelength enter the analogue video camera's photoconducting layer, the lightwaves excite the electrons in the photoconductor, which in turn dislodge the purple photons 'at wavelengths that continue to correspond to the color of the object being recorded' (Marks 2002: 169). In other words, like the way the celluloid strip reacts chemically to the exposure of light, different electrons in the video tape react to different aspects of light – electrons remember, and cinema continues to be materially haunted by its past.

In turn, Doane observes, with digital media and technology coming into play, the index faces 'a certain crisis of legitimation' (Doane 2007a: 1). In contrast to the celluloid film strip and video technology, digital technology configures and stores these data and images into discrete algorithms of ones and zeros through a series of metallic and silicon strips. According to Marks, two steps intervene in digital imaging 'to break the indexical bond: one that approximates analog information to a symbolic number, and one (repeated in every circuit) that obviates the wave-particle relationship' (Marks 2002: 172). Because of this process of conversion, Marks argues, the indexical is broken, or, at the very least, 'quite attenuated' (Marks 2002: 149). For Doane, like Marks and many other critics, what 'is lost in the move to the digital is the imprint of time, the visible degradation of the image' (Doane 2007b: 144). If we were to follow Doane's proclamation, then my argument about the index would be tenuous because the imprint of time – the past haunting the present – is lost in the digital and the index is no longer a site where multiple temporalities interplay.

For Doane, the cinematic index's privileged physical connection to the 'outside world' is completely negated by the digital. She writes that the digital is 'a medium without materiality, of pure abstraction incarnated as a series of 0s and 1s, sheer presence and absence, the code. Even light, the most diaphanous of materialities, is transformed into the numerical form in the digital camera' (Doane 2007b: 142). Doane's claim is two-fold. Firstly, the digital is immaterial because, unlike celluloid or video tape, it does not have any material constraints. Once translated into algorithms, the digitally stored images can be easily transposed wholesale into another digital storage when the strips of metals and silicon that are fundamental in digital technology wear out. Secondly, building on her first point, as digital information lasts longer than the material itself, and as there is no visible degradation of digital images at all in the process of transference, Doane argues that the indexical connection to the film's material is lost.

My views diverge from Doane's. Instead, I propose that the index is still present in digital film-making. Foremost, in responding to Doane's charge that the indexical is no longer present in the digital (it must be acknowledged that her voice is only one out of the many critics here, who largely argue along similar premises), I draw from Martin Lefebvre and Marc Furstenau, who observe that the 'anxious discourse' surrounding the loss of indexicality is surprising because film studies has, for decades, argued that the film image was a 'semiotic construct', in which the images were understood 'to have been intentionally produced according to specific aesthetic and semiotic protocols' (Lefebvre and Furstenau 2002: 91–2).[3] As an example, Lefebvre and Furstenau point to how apparatus theory argued that the world conveyed by the camera has already been filtered through a bourgeois ideology – the image is forced to look like that because of the implicit ideologies imbricated in the apparatus. This argument is similar to Peirce's thoughts on the index, who writes:

> Here is a view of the writer's house; what makes that house to be the object of the view? Surely not the similarity of appearance. There are ten thousand others in the country just like it. No, but the photographer set up the film in such a way that according to the law of optics, the film was forced to receive an image of this house. What the sign virtually has to do in order to indicate its object – and make it its – all it has to do is just to seize its interpreter's eyes and forcibly turn them upon the object meant. (Peirce 1998: 380)

Braxton Soderman extends Peirce's notion that the indexical link is a forced physical connection between the subject and the object into the digital realm. He posits that the law of computational execution suggests that a computer programme that translates a finite set of algorithms into images must always follow the instructions given to it. Pressing the letter 'm' on the keyboard, for instance, will always result in the letter 'm' appearing on the screen if the particular computer programme has programmed it that way. A different computer programme might result in a different end product but, Soderman avers, that is similar to Peirce's idea that the photographer has 'pointed the camera at a different house' (Soderman 2007: 163). Thus, Soderman, drawing from this idea that the index in cinema is always forced, proposes that there 'is a physical connection between the image on a monitor and the code that created it, but this connection is mediated through conventional symbols' (Soderman 2007: 164). In other words, for Soderman, the index – the existential link between the past and the present – is still present in digital technology.

I am in agreement with Soderman's diagnosis and think that it provides a good defence to Doane's first point about the lack of indexicality in digital film-making. Responding to Doane's second point about the digital's immateriality, however, requires a little more work. Doane suggests that the digital is immaterial because films captured with digital technology do not show signs of degradation, which consequently do not remind us of the medium's material constraints. This, for Doane, means that the imprint of time is not evident and therefore the index is gone from the digital. As a counter-proposal, I want to point to two moments in *The Visit* and *The Taking of Deborah Logan* that highlight the material constraints that Doane suggests do not exist in digital technology.

In *The Visit*, Becca and Tyler are playing hide-and-seek in a claustrophobic area directly beneath the house's raised patio. Both Becca and Tyler, holding digital cameras in their hands, crawl into the area and the audience is shown their respective point-of-view shots. Slowly, the sound of a low rumbling non-melodic drone enters the film's score. Becca turns the camera away from her so that she can begin looking for Tyler. As the camera turns, the grandmother appears and starts crawling towards Becca. Becca screams and quickly moves away. As she does this, the frame's *mise en scène* becomes highly shaky. The drone slowly becomes louder and Tyler, in hearing Becca's scream, realises that something is not right. As he calls out for Becca, the grandmother pops into his point-of-view and charges towards him. Tyler, like Becca, begins to furiously crawl away too as the grandmother continues to chase them. Finally, when the teenagers exit the patio, the droning sound in the score stops.

Throughout the scene, a clear threat is registered when the grandmother enters the frame, not least through the slow rumbling drone that sustains the tension that runs throughout the whole chase sequence. When the grandmother, the person who lives with dementia, enters the frame, both Becca and Tyler frantically run away. As they move, the images captured by their digital cameras become at times smeary and at times staccato. What is happening on-screen is interesting. In digital cinematography, sequences become blurry because the camera's shutter speed – the amount of light that is let into the camera before the shutter closes – is too slow. Conversely, if the camera's shutter speed is too fast, not enough movement will be captured before the shutter closes, which results in a slight staccato effect. Therefore,

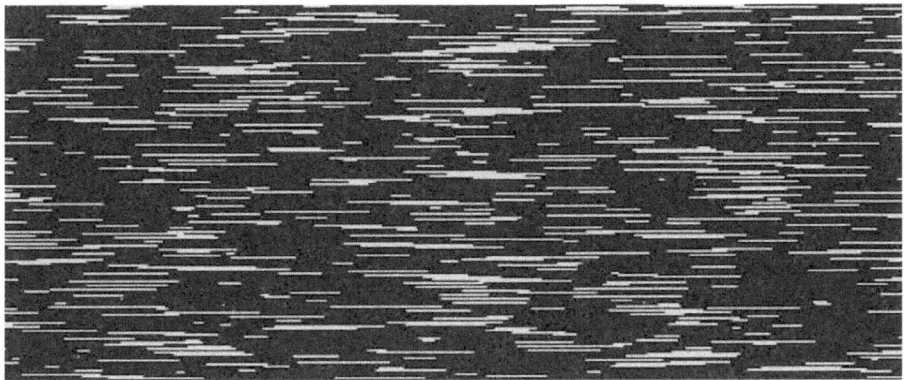

Figure 5.5 Material degradation in *The Taking of Deborah Logan*

in running away frantically from the grandmother, the camera's automatic shutter speed has to adjust very quickly to the surrounding light sources, in turn resulting in this oscillation of shutter speeds. This change occurs when the person living with dementia enters the frame, and her heightened temporal performance not only draws attention to the digital technology's material constraints but also foregrounds the link between the index and digital materiality.

Similarly, *The Taking of Deborah Logan* highlights this material degradation. Towards the end of the film, Deborah kidnaps a young girl from the hospital, brings her to the mines where Desjardins had murdered all his victims, and is about to kill the girl in order to satisfy the ritual that would have given Desjardins eternal life. Mia and Sarah track Deborah down and attempt to save the girl. In one moment, Mia and Sarah creep towards Deborah and the young girl in order to sedate Deborah. Mia holds on to the camera, which is set in night vision mode in order not to notify Deborah of their presence whilst Sarah slowly approaches Deborah with the sedative in her outreached hand. As Sarah gets closer to her mother, Deborah turns around and shouts directly into Sarah's face. The young girl begins to scream and Mia begins to panic. The camera starts to shake about uncontrollably due to Mia's frantic fumbling, and the film jump cuts repeatedly, losing frames in between shots. This chaos is further compounded by the shots of static fuzz that slowly creep into and haunt the sequence as this happens. The night vision mode fails and Mia is forced to turn on the camera's lights, only to be violently attacked by Deborah. The camera and Mia drop to the ground as Deborah continues to assault Mia. At the same time as that happens, zebra lines – signs of a technical glitch – appear on the screen and a loud extended screeching feedback noise enters the audio. Deborah is forcibly removed from Mia and disappears out of the area with the girl. Almost simultaneously, the glitch – visual and aural – disappears from the sequence.

Rosa Menkman writes that the digital glitch 'makes the computer itself suddenly appear unconventionally deep, in contrast to the more banal, predictable surface-level behaviours of "normal" machines and systems' (Menkman 2011: 41). For Menkman, 'glitches announce a crazy and dangerous kind of *moment(um)* instantiated and dictated by the machine itself' (Menkman 2011: 41; emphasis in original). Following Menkman, we can think of the glitch, the visual deterioration of the digital image, as drawing our attention to the workings of the digital, to the strips of metal and silicon, to the ones and zeros passing through the logic gates, to the electrons spinning up and down to create electrical signals, and to the computer programmes that ultimately determine what the images will look like. There is visible degradation in the digital images, and in the case of *The Taking of Deborah Logan*, glitches occur when Deborah, along with the threat to volatilise the relationship between the past and the present, enters the frame, consequently drawing our attention to the continued presence of the index in the digital. Contrary to Doane's claims, then, the indexical nature of cinema is not broken in digital cinematography. Rather, the digitally haunted index exists in a different form of intensity as compared to, say, the index of celluloid cinema, which is engaged in a different kind of temporal performance with the world.

In accounting for the indexical nature of digital technology, the chapter's central claim about the index is refined and nuanced, consequently allowing a mode of hesitant reading to surface. According to David Martin-Jones, the use of hesitancy offers a particular ethics of film analysis, by creating an encounter with a lost past: 'Acknowledging the existence of such lost pasts – histories now recalled only as memories, times, fabulous beings, songs, myths, fables – renders histories previously thought to inform the present, *universally*, now only one amongst many: whether human or non-human' (Martin-Jones 2018: 2; emphasis in original). This mode of hesitant encounter as envisioned by Martin-Jones not only acknowledges the importance of the multiple pasts of all these (non)human phenomena, but also

> encourages us to consider whether we should reorient the informing pathway through the world's memories which shapes our present-day actions and interactions, to question whether we should affirm, or in fact critically reconsider, our faith not with *this world*, but with *this world's history*. (Martin-Jones 2018: 75; emphasis in original)

Martin-Jones argues that reading film via hesitancy opens to an appreciation of a larger, entangled shared worlds and histories, and from this we can work through the ways in which the present day reliance on capitalism, and the repressions that come along with all the multifarious forms of capitalism across the world, might be affected by colonial modernity. Hesitancy highlights the centricity of the Western world as a concept and practice put in place by Europe through its colonial expansions since 1492, and attempts to open up a wider understanding of the multiple histories that have been relegated, as also discussed by Lim. Thus, to encounter various pasts via an ethical analysis that centres hesitation is to decentre this worldview and to allow for a rhizomatic understanding of a map where anywhere can be centre and anywhere can be periphery. This approach, in aligning with Saër Maty Bâ and Will Higbee, 'is about an increasing connectivity within zones of contact' (Bâ and Higbee 2012: 8). Examining the performances of time through a philosophy of difference is a methodology that makes mess and embraces mess.[4]

For Alia Al-Saji, there 'is an unpredictability to hesitating, an interval that it creates, which means that what I make of my hesitations, *or what hesitating makes of me*, is a singular unfurling of time' (Al-Saji 2018: 337; emphasis in original). In hesitantly thinking through the performances of time through the framework of performance and philosophy of difference in relation to films about dementia, as I link the temporalities of one index to another, my own subjectivities are equally implicated in the unfurling of time. The performances of time that I discuss are but one of the many possible performances of time. A different person coming to films about dementia hesitantly thinking through the performances of time would engender a different unpacking of time. In turn, as I discuss in the next chapter, as more unfoldings and foldings of time occur, temporalities past and present thicken, opening up for the possibility of political change.

Notes

1 See Bedrosian and Nelson 2013, Cipriani et al. 2015, Jonghe et al. 2010, Kume et al. 2016, Van Someren et al. 1996 and Zendehbad 2015 on the rhythms of sundowning.
2 This experience becomes more nuanced – but largely similar – when a person is watching the film at home rather than at the cinema. See Klinger 2006 and Kerins 2011 for discussions about the home sound system.
3 See Gunning 2008, Hadjioannou 2012 and Brown 2015 for more discussions about the index and digital culture.
4 See Deng 2022c on the potential for such an approach to decolonise film studies.

6
The Trope of Wandering and the Temporalities of a Nation

In the previous chapters, I laid out the theoretical scaffold to hesitantly think through the temporal identifications of the person living with dementia vis-à-vis the person not living with dementia and other (non-)living phenomena, suggesting that the temporal methodology proposed offers a way to not only think through the ecologies of temporal performances but to also heterogeneously unfurl and surface the 'hidden' and previously neglected aspects of the past in the present. In this chapter, I tie all these threads of argument together through the case study of Singapore and its cinema, and I explore the ways in which the trope of the person living with dementia wandering becomes a way to enter and traverse the nation's discursive sphere of history and historiography.

Singapore and Singapore cinema have been chosen as the chapter's focus because the nation and the nation's cinema take on a particular inflection that results in an architectural environment that has apparently little or no history attached to it. This is an environment in which the nation's revival cinema post-1995 displays a seeming amnesia and aphasia towards its cinematic history and bears little or no resemblance to the 'golden age' of Singapore cinema from 1947 to 1972, where Singapore served as a hub for Malay-language film production in the region.[1] Beyond this, the nation displays a peculiar habit of regularly banning and censoring films made about Singapore by people who live in Singapore because these films do not correlate to the state's sanctioned history, forcing Singapore film-makers to adopt pragmatic film-making strategies to avoid censorship (Khoo 2015). In short, both Singapore and its cinema rely heavily on unstable and often conflicting versions of the past in order to come to a certain understanding of the present.

In this chapter, through the analysis of the short film *Parting* (Boo Junfeng, 2015, Singapore), where the presence of the person living with dementia is integral to the film's narrative, I explore the complexities of memory, of forgetting and of remembering, through the framework of temporal performance. The issues at stake here are twofold. First, this chapter examines the trope of the person living with dementia wandering in relation to the film and puts forward an understanding of wandering as that of both traversing space *and* time. Second, the chapter dissects the ways in which the trope of the person living with dementia wandering in *Parting* works to surface a nation's past(s) in and into the present tense so that it can be remembered again. In this sense, through an analysis of the temporal performances in Singapore and Singapore cinema, this chapter finds its place alongside a growing publication of revisionist history that offers a wider and longer history of Singapore (beyond 1965, the nation's supposed 'Year Zero') that not only considers its colonial histories but also its place as a port island since ninth-century Srivijaya.[2]

The flattening of Singapore's past

Parting is a short film, part of the bigger portmanteau film *7 Letters* which features short film contributions from seven of the most prolific directors working in Singapore. It was released in 2015 as part of Singapore's larger commemoration of its fiftieth year of independence, which was forcefully thrust onto the nation when it was expelled from the Federation of Malaysia in 1965. The film is remarkable in part because it was commissioned and fully funded by the nation's Media Development Authority (MDA) and the Singapore Film Commission (SFC). Like all of the government's arts funding bodies, the MDA and the SFC have a tendency to withdraw their funding for arts projects partway if it were discovered that the projects did not chime with the state's official discourses. Therefore, it is notable that *7 Letters*, which the film critic Maggie Lee describes as not 'being flag-waving government mouthpieces' but 'are by turns argumentative, contemplative, passionate and ironic', was released uncensored and celebrated by the government (Lee 2015).

It is in these contexts that I consider *Parting*. Of particular interest in this chapter is the ways in which The Singapore Story buries and shapes the discourses of the nation's history and historiography, and the ways in which the trope of the person living with dementia wandering in *Parting* might serve as a way to surface and reshape these shreds and layers of hidden past. The Singapore Story, as Kenneth Paul Tan observes, is the Singapore government's official state narrative which focuses 'on national vulnerability, constraints and challenges that transmits and preserves the survivalist mentality well into the present and also harness it for the purpose of justifying' the ruling government's authority (Tan 2016: 236).³ For Thum Pin Tjin, The Singapore Story paraded by the People's Action Party (PAP), the nation's ruling party since its independence in 1965, can be traced back to the nation's British colonial origins, and is used to validate the government's 'intervention into the lives of Singapore's residents; marginalisation of traditional or community sources of socio-political organisations; and expansion of arbitrary executive power' (Thum 2017: 27). In turn, The Singapore Story promotes 'a hegemonic account of an ahistorical middle-class generation that is anxious (even paranoid), materialistic and politically apathetic' (Tan 2016: 236). The Singapore Story, therefore, is a way to foster a national imagination that brings the people together through a discourse of pragmatism. To work through the temporalities of The Singapore Story so as to make my argument about the trope of the person living with dementia wandering in *Parting*, I turn to a discussion of a nation's temporal performances as understood by Homi Bhabha and David Martin-Jones.

According to Bhabha, the nation is 'a contested cultural territory where the people must be thought in a double-time' (Bhabha 2008: 297). For Bhabha, there are two ways in which people are socialised into a nation – pedagogical and performative. On the one hand, the pedagogical approach ensures that national symbols always have pasts (however empty) to ground the present, in turn producing a dominant national narrative that allows the citizens to have an imagined lineage; on the other, Bhabha argues that people's performance of their everyday lives have the potential to catalyse a reconsideration of a nation's past. Drawing from Ernest Renan, Bhabha maintains that the identification of a national people can be made clear through the 'syntax of forgetting' (Bhabha 2008: 310). He writes: 'Being obliged to forget becomes the basis for remembering the nation, peopling it anew, imagining the possibility of other contending and liberating forms of cultural identification' (Bhabha 2008: 311). The nation, hence, relies heavily on the notion of forgetting to remember, on forgetting because there is nothing to remember, and on forgetting in order to remember.

Through this complex syntax of forgetting, the nation's time and temporality do not function in a linear way. Rather, the double-time that Bhabha speaks of works in a cyclical and circuitous manner, where the past is brought into the present through the pedagogical, and the performative brings the present back into the past, reworking the past so as to be brought back into the present again. The national identification engendered by this double-time, I suggest, can also be comprehended through the lens of temporal performance, where a subject's national identification becomes but one aspect of their temporal identification, where the performance of their everyday life has the potential to change the ways in which a national story might be narrated, and the nation's time also affects the performance of the subject's temporal identification. The nation, too, is performing time and performed by time.

For Martin-Jones, this double-time, this constant negotiation between the past and the present, is not too dissimilar to Gilles Deleuze and Félix Guattari's work on deterritorialisation and reterritorialisation. Martin-Jones, working on the way the nation and the national are narrated in cinema, suggests that deterritorialisation 'enables a displacement of narrative into multiple labyrinthine versions' whereas reterritorialisation 'entails a constraining of a narrative into one linear timeline' (Martin-Jones 2006: 4). According to Martin-Jones, reterritorialising narratives are evidenced by the presence of strong movement-images. For Deleuze, the movement-image 'lies in extracting from vehicles or moving bodies the movement which is their common substance, or extracting from movements the mobility which is their essence', and in capturing movement, the cinematic movement-image 'puts bodies, parts, aspects, dimensions, distances and the respective positions of the bodies positions of the bodies which make up a set in the image into variation' (Deleuze 2013a: 27). In movement-images, time passes linearly through movement.

Conversely, deterritorialising narratives point to the presence of strong time-images. In time-images, Deleuze suggests, the sensory-motor connections that chain time in movement-images are broken. In turn, opsigns (pure optical-images) and sonsigns (pure sound-images) arise, bringing the 'objective and subjective, real and imaginary, physical and mental' into constant contact (Deleuze 2013b: 9). In a time-image, we are confronted with not just the actual but also the virtual aspects of time, where various shreds of the pure past are surfaced, no longer secondary and shackled to movement, where 'time is no longer the measure of movement but movement is the perspective of time' (Deleuze 2013b: 22). For Martin-Jones, then, through the process of deterritorialisation and reterritorialisation, and through a complex articulation of remembering and forgetting, the present of the modern nation grows to accommodate and/or appropriate new and updated pasts – in this sense, the constant state of becoming and change is taken into account in this multifarious performance of time.

At this point, we can begin to understand the overwhelming reach of The Singapore Story and the ways this national imagination works to disengage the past from the present tense of the subject's national identification. The PAP government enacts a strict and tight control of the nation's history, at times through violent clampdowns and at times through censorship. In turn, the older generations of people living in Singapore who witnessed or participated in the tumultuous struggle to steer the nation's political direction immediately pre- and post-independence often resort to a form of self-censorship today, refusing to acknowledge their involvement in the turbulent period or buying into the state-sanctioned explanation of 'brainwashing' so as to protect themselves and their families (Loh and Tan 2017: 47). Beyond self-censorship, some people living in Singapore simply do not remember or forget because, due to the complex interplay of state censorship and self-censorship, they were never provided with anything (or very little) to forget to begin with. All in all, then, the temporal performances enacted by The Singapore Story through the process of deterriolisation and reterritorialisation paint a very complex map of cultural aphasia in the nation.

I borrow my understanding of cultural aphasia from Ann Laura Stoler, who suggests that the notion of aphasia 'captures not only the nature of that blockage but also the feature of loss' (Stoler 2016: 128). For Stoler, aphasia

> emphasizes both the loss of access and active dissociation. In aphasia, *an occlusion of knowledge* is the issue. It is not a matter of ignorance or absence. Aphasia is a dismembering, a difficulty in speaking, a *difficulty in generating a vocabulary that associates appropriate words and concepts to appropriate things*. Aphasia in its many forms describes a difficulty in retrieving both conceptual and lexical vocabularies and, most importantly, a difficulty in comprehending what is spoken. (Stoler 2016: 128; emphasis in original)

Unlike amnesia, which suggests that the past is forgotten, the concept of cultural aphasia as proposed by Stoler does not deny the presence of the past in the present. Rather, aphasia highlights the cultural process where people might be denied access to the past because the layered textures of the past has been reshaped so much – for Alia Al-Saji, in cultural aphasia, 'we witness a *flattening* of the past, of the thick material trace of its reconfiguration' (Al-Saji 2018: 345; emphasis in original). This is to say, the flattening process disregards the ways in which the past 'is *differentially weighted by its own duration*' (Al-Saji 2018: 345; emphasis in original). Or, to use a baking analogy (an idea which I revisit below), we can see the past of Singapore as a dough with many layers and folds, and The Singapore Story is a rolling pin that vigorously and violently rolls out the intricacies of this dough through time. In doing so, the textured qualities of the dough of the past are flattened (not removed or forgotten) and the points of entry into the various pasts of Singapore are no longer accessible to the people living in Singapore, and what remains is a particularly shaped dough that most Singaporeans see and know.

The surfacing of Singapore's past

If The Singapore Story overwhelmingly flattens the nation's history and historiography, giving the people living in Singapore little or no way in to the nuances of a more textured past, *Parting*, through the trope of the person living with dementia wandering, makes prominent the shreds of the past in the present tense. The narrative premise of *Parting* is straightforward. Ismail, a man who lives with early stages of dementia, travels to Singapore from Malaysia via the Keretapi Tanah Melayu (KTM) train in the hopes of finding an old sweetheart Swee Choo. Ismail grew up in Singapore but left for Malaysia in 1966, right after Singapore's independence in 1965. For the first time in decades, Ismail returns to a Singapore completely foreign to him; in this city that Ismail has returned to, telephone numbers have one more digit than before, and housing estates have been torn down and replaced with taller ones. The Singapore in *Parting* is what Rem Koolhass describes as 'the truly generic condition of the contemporary city' where 'history has been almost completely blotted out' (Koolhass 1995: 1031). It is also the Singapore that Cherian George describes as possessing 'an unsettling impermanence', in which 'the places you grow up in will not be the places you grow old in, and that you can never go back because what was there then is here no longer' (George 2010: 190). This is not the Singapore that Ismail remembers nor recognises, and this sense of alienation and disorientation is registered and reinforced by the film's editing pattern, where the 180-degree rule that is usually used by film-makers to maintain a cohesive relationship between a character and their surrounding is subtly broken. But – unlike the jump cuts employed by Jean-Luc Godard in *Breathless* (1960, France) or the consistent 360-degree use of space in the films of Yasujirō Ozu – in *Parting*, the editing pattern is still predominantly structured around the 180-degree rule with only a break in this adherence once in a while.

This not-remembering and unfamiliarity with the nation results in Ismail wandering around Singapore, lost, trying to find a fragment of his past. In one instance, Ismail sits on the bus looking out of the window and we are shown a reverse-shot of what he is looking at (the tall buildings of the city and the expressway that he is on). Quickly, the film cuts to various shots of the city, observing and taking in sights of the people living in this country: crowds walk around busily in the Central Business District as tall high-rise

Figure 6.1 Ismail engulfed by the architecture of Chung Cheng High in *Parting*

buildings loom over them, mixed-race families stroll around the city, and two men who may or may not be queer share a cold beverage from the same straw while walking down the street. These shots are not the point-of-view shots of Ismail nor is he present in the frame. Encouraged by Ismail's wander, the film and the camera have gone on their own wander around the city.

In turn, the wandering body, the city and the camera are intimately linked together, recalling Guliana Bruno's claim that 'the modern *flâneur* is the film spectator' (Bruno 1993: 49). For Bruno, cinema 'is the very synthesis of seeing and going – a place where seeing *is* going' (Bruno 2011: 245; emphasis in original). James Tweedie puts forward a similar proposition: 'Like a camera travelling carefully through the city, the body serves as a device for recording the going-ons throughout town. The city is imagined as an extension of the body in motion and the body as an extension of cinema' (Tweedie 2013: 90). Thus, for Bruno and Tweedie, the camera, in following the *flâneur*, the wanderer, gets caught in the act of *flânerie* too. This notion of site-seeing is echoed by *Parting* as Ismail's search for his childhood lover brings Ismail to Chung Cheng High School and the film cuts to an extreme wide-angle shot of Chung Cheng High as Ismail, entirely dwarfed and engulfed by the school's architecture, slowly traverses across the frame.

Here, this concept of the *flânerie* is useful as a starting point to think through the trope of the person living with dementia wandering. For Walter Benjamin, the act of *flânerie*, or the act of wandering, connects the *flâneur* with their past:

> The street conducts the *flâneur* into a vanished time. For him, every street is precipitous. It leads downward – if not to the mythical Mothers, then into a past that can be all the more spellbinding because it is not his own, not private. (Benjamin 2002: 417, M1, 2)

Three things from Benjamin's description of the *flâneur* stand out when filtered through the framework of temporal performances. Firstly, the *flâneur* and their environment are inextricably linked, echoing Tim Ingold's claim that, in the act of walking, 'landscapes are woven into life, and lives are woven into the landscape, in a process that is continuous and never-ending' (Ingold 2004: 333). Second, *flânerie*, here, is seen as an *active* act of wandering as the *flâneur* uses their affective and sensory perception of the streets to create their own narratives. As Lucas Raymond proposes, the *flâneur* writes the city rather than reads it, and their 'spectatorship is an active one', as narratives are created as the *flâneur* wanders along the city streets (Lucas 2008: 171). Similarly, Merlin Coverly suggests that the *flâneur*, who is bound to the developments of the city, 'is a nostalgic figure who, in proclaiming the wonders of urban life, also acknowledges the changes that threaten to make the idle pedestrian redundant' (Coverly 2006: 58). In looking at these two points for the moment, the act of *flânerie* already exhibits a clash of temporalities. On the one hand, there is a tension between the past and the present as the *flâneur* longs for the past whilst simultaneously actively engaging with the present; on the other, there is a cyclical process of inscription, as the times and temporalities of the city work its way into the *flâneur* only to be worked differently back into the environment. Through the act of *flânerie*, both the *flâneur* and the environment are performing and performed by time. In addition to the first two points, Benjamin's description also highlights the notion that these temporalities and narratives that are perceived and written by the act of *flânerie* do not belong to the *flâneur*. These narratives are, as Benjamin argues, 'not private'. Rather, they point to a wider shared and entangled narrative by the people who inhabit the spaces that the *flâneur* wanders. Thus, the *flâneur* can be seen as a wanderer that simultaneously forgets and remembers, and, in the act of wandering, a whole set of histories and pasts can be unearthed and told again, differently.

Seen from this angle, the person living with dementia wandering might be understood as an act of *flânerie*, as the person living with dementia 'goes botanizing on the asphalt' (Benjamin 1997: 36). The *flâneur* is a figure that appears to be, on the surface, wandering aimlessly, allowing their pet turtle to set the pace of the stroll (Benjamin 1997: 54). Yet, beneath the surface, all their senses are at work, traversing space and traversing time, where it is through the movement in time that time is unshackled from movement. Equally, the person living with dementia, whose wandering is often dismissed as aimless and senseless, can be thought of as experiencing 'a form of spatio-temporal disruption' like that of the *flâneur* (Capstick 2015: 211).[4] In turn, from this point of view, the trope of the person living with dementia wandering in films about dementia can be understood to enact a layered performance of time that involves a combination of both movement- and time-images – a process of double-time, a process of reterritorialisation and deterritorialisation, and a process of remembering and forgetting – bringing the film's diegesis, the cinematic apparatus, the audience and the wider rhizomatic world beyond the film together, opening up the possibilities of new narratives and of different lines of flight.

Where Ismail's wander in *Parting* is concerned, it is therefore significant that it is at Chung Cheng High where he learns that Swee Choo has since moved to Australia, thus ending his attempt to reconnect with the Singapore before 1965, the year Singapore gained full independence. Here, borrowing from Mikhail Bakhtin, Chung Cheng High is thought of as a chronotope where 'spatial and temporal indicators are fused into one carefully thought-out, concrete whole' (Bakhtin 2011: 84). Historically, though there were only nine Chinese middle schools in Singapore in the 1950s, and no opportunities for tertiary Chinese-language education, Chinese students were a formidable force in Singapore politics at that time. In turn, Chung Cheng High, the biggest of all these Chinese middle schools, played a significant role in shaping the political course of the nation. C. M. Turnbull describes the Chinese-educated students of the 1950s as idealistic people who 'admired the Beijing regime and eagerly absorbed contraband books and communist propaganda from China' (Turnbull 2016: 252). Kwok Kian-Woon, conversely, argues that this was an unfair label and that whilst there was a 'strong presence of the Chinese-educated in leftist politics' they were not 'the equivalent of either "communist" or "pro-communist" (and pro-China or pro-Chinese Communist party at that)' (Kwok 2001: 497). Nonetheless, the Chinese-educated students and the Chinese middle schools became a fertile playground for the politics of Singapore (from the securing of independence from Britain and the Federation of Malaysia to leaving a complex legacy in the nation's linguistic policies) to play out.

In 1955, a general election was slated to happen for the first time in British colonial Singapore in the hopes of introducing the appetite for self-governance. The PAP put forward candidates to contest four out of the twenty-five available seats. Of the candidates were Lee Kuan Yew and Lim Chin Siong, who were two of the co-founders of PAP. Lee, who was English-educated, had just returned to Singapore after graduating from Cambridge with a law degree, and had a reputation amongst the people living in Singapore as 'a left-wing lawyer' (Turnbull 2016: 252). On the other hand, Lim was viewed as a highly charismatic and effective Chinese-language orator who could rally many Chinese students to fight for the causes of the left. Lim, as described by Clement Mesenas to be 'Lee's bastion in the Chinese community', was not only able to communicate to the Chinese community in Chinese vernaculars but was also able to mobilise a large amount of Chinese middle school students to canvass for the PAP during the campaigning period (Mesenas 2013: 160). As Turnbull notes, the '[a]utomatic registration of voters had increased the electorate from 76,000 to more than 300,000, of whom the majority of voters were working-class Chinese' (Turnbull 2016: 260). This appeal to the Chinese community proved to be successful and the PAP won three out of the four contested seats. Both Lee and Lim were elected onto the assembly and that set the stage for Singapore's independence in 1965.[5]

Singapore gained full internal self-governance from the British in 1959 and the PAP, winning 43 out of the 51 seats, went on to form the government. In 1961, Lim (and the left of the party) was expelled from the PAP as the moderates of the party (which included Lee) lost confidence in the left-leaning members. Lim went on to form the Barisan Sosialis in the same year, which became the second most popular party after the PAP. On 2 February 1963, in the name of national security, the PAP government launched Operation Cold Store in order to detain suspected communists under Singapore's Internal Security Act. More than 100 people were arrested, of which many were Chinese student leaders (Turnbull 2016: 281–2). Lim was one of those arrested during the operation, where he was imprisoned without trial for a long period of time and kept in solitary confinement. During Lim's detainment, Singapore merged with Malaya to form the Federation of Malaysia in 1963 and was then expelled from the Federation on 9 August 1965, with independence forcefully handed to Singapore. Lee Kuan Yew became the Prime Minister of the nation whereas Lim, who was released in 1969, lived a quiet life away from politics until his death in 1996.

The importance of the Chinese middle school students in Singapore's politics should therefore not be underestimated, in part because they played a significant role in getting Lee elected into the assembly in 1955. Yet, today, the students' contributions, like Lim's, have been mostly written out of the nation's official discourse and history, and many of these student campaigners have been politically exiled and described as communists (a derogatory label associated with the ghosts of the Cold War). For instance, when Chung Cheng High was gazetted in 2014 for its architectural significance, *The Straits*

Times – the state-controlled English-language newspaper – described the school as 'a hotbed for the leftish student movement under the influence of the communist underground' (Cheow 2014). Regardless of Chung Cheng High's rich history, its past is largely and consciously erased by the nation, and whatever shreds of the past that remains are in turn framed as a compelling threat to the stability of the nation – in this example, the history and historiography associated with Chung Cheng High is completely shaped by The Singapore Story.

It is therefore significant that in *Parting*, Ismail, having grown up in Singapore in the 1950s and early 1960s, does not recognise the school when he first hears about it, and the school is also where his search for his past ends. Despite Ismail wandering to Chung Cheng High attempting to remember his past, despite being completely overwhelmed and engulfed by the school's architecture, and despite the richness of all the pasts in the school waiting to be unearthed, the film does not allow that to be brought into the present per se – this is because the official narrative of the state does not allow that past to be remembered (and the audience would also probably not remember or know). Seen from this point of view, it could be argued that Ismail's narrative is microcosmic of Singapore's wider issue with forgetfulness, and therefore merely reinforces the inability of the state to remember its past.[6]

The thickening of Singapore's past

However, I argue that in this moment, through the person living with dementia wandering into the school, occupying the space of historical time in the school, *Parting* begins the process of deterritorialising The Singapore Story in preparation for its reterritorialisation. As Ismail comes to realise that Swee Choo has moved to Australia, the film cuts to a mid-shot of him sat in the school processing the fact that he is not going to find Swee Choo in Singapore. As the camera lingers on his face, Swee Choo's voice enters the film, continuing the letter that she wrote to Ismail in 1966. She says, in Malay, 'Something else has changed, Ismail.' Indeed, though Ismail's active search for his past comes to an end in Chung Cheng High, something does change after the encounter in the school. Ismail begins wandering around Singapore again, making his way to the Tanjong Pagar Railway Station in an attempt to take the KTM train to return to Malaysia. Like Chung Cheng High, Tanjong Pagar Railway Station can be thought of as a chronotope that is equally overflowing with historical time as it had been the railway link between Singapore and Malaysia from the early 1920s, where it was the southern terminus for the KTM (Malaysia's main rail operator).

On 1 July 2011, the KTM relocated its southern terminus to another area of Singapore. Before July 2011, the land that the railway station occupied had represented a site of unresolved tension between Singapore and Malaysia for, when Singapore was expelled from Malaysia in 1965, the PAP signed an agreement with the Malaysian government, allowing Malaysia to maintain ownership over the plot of land that the Tanjong Pagar Railway Station was built on. In turn, the railway station became an irregularity in Singapore that was not quite Singapore. Hence, as Liew Kai Khiun et al. observe, the station 'had never been officially legitimized as part of Singapore's past', becoming 'an awkward reminder of the territorial presence of Malaysia on Singapore's soil' (Liew et al. 2014: 765). The station, therefore, becomes an index of Singapore's history pre-1965, a history that Singapore has been consciously trying to control since the removal of history as a subject from the primary school curriculum in 1972 so as to not rouse unpleasant collective memories between the Chinese and the Malays (Lee 2015: 135).

As Ismail enters the station, a group of people dressed up like they are from the 1960s walks out of the station. At that moment, Ismail catches the eye of a young man, who stops, momentarily, as he looks at Ismail with a look of recognition on his face. The sensory-motor schema of the movement-image that has brought Ismail's wander to the Tanjong Pagar Railway Station is broken by the Deleuzian recollection-image. Deleuze writes:

> Here, I abandon the extending of my perception, I cannot extend it. My movements – which are more subtle and of another kind – revert to the object, return to the object, so as to emphasize certain contours and take 'a few characteristic features' from it. And we begin all over again when we want to identify different features and contours, but each time we have to start from scratch. In this case, instead of an addition of distinct objects on the same plane, we see the object remaining *the same*, but passing through *different planes*. (Deleuze 2013b: 45–6; emphasis in original)

As Ismail and the man share a glance, music enters the film's score. Whilst this moment could be seen as a form of hallucination from Ismail's dementia, it could also be read as Ismail's past walking right out of the station to meet him. Through the recollection-image that may or may not be due to the dementia, the man belongs to more than one temporal plane, and the shreds of the virtual past buried in the environment are surfaced and gestured towards. In turn, through the person living with dementia wandering, a sense of temporal indeterminacy – of temporal hesitation – is engendered and encouraged at the railway station, and the relationship between the past and present becomes blurred.

At this moment in the film, seemingly, the sensory-motor schema of Ismail's physical movement through space is broken by the recollection-image that is filtered through his dementia, and a sense of hesitation is generated (see the previous chapter). For Al-Saji, to hesitate is to slow down and modulate temporality. She writes:

> The incompleteness, both of affect and of that to which affect responds, is here felt. To wait is to testify that time makes a difference for experience, that all is not given in the present. To wait, without projection, is not only to be open to a futurity that escapes prediction, but also to a past that can be dynamically transformed through the passage of events, and that grounds the creative potential of events. This breaks with the closure of the past and the predetermination of the future. (Al-Saji 2014: 148)

To hesitate, then, is to unfurl time, as the linearity of the sensory-motor schema is broken, as the present tense is no longer chained by movement to a past that determines the future. Put differently, for Al-Saji, hesitation 'makes possible transformations in habit, and the phenomenological opening that can be utilized and supplemented for such change to take place' (Al-Saji 2014: 149). Seen from this point of view, I suggest that the mode of hesitation as proposed by Al-Saji draws parallel with Deleuze's demented time (see Chapter Two), where the delayed gap induced by hesitation can be understood as the fracture – the caesura – that cuts time, allowing difference in itself to return whilst portions of the past are left behind.

This understanding of the virtual returning to be negotiated differently to form the new through hesitation and demented time is important to my suggestion that thinking of time through the framework of performance allows the past to heterogeneously surface. This is especially significant in relation to Singapore and Singapore cinema, where the past is very consciously and violently suppressed, and where pragmatic practices of self-censorship are adopted by the people living in the nation. As the sense of hesitation is engendered by Ismail's wandering encounter with the man, the film cuts to a shot of a Malay man entering the station walking towards a Chinese woman. This man and woman have been established earlier – through multiple close-up shots of a photograph that Ismail owns – to be the younger version of Ismail and Swee Choo. The young man asks the woman whether she will be following him to Malaysia and she is silent, sobbing, unable to answer his question. Concurrently, the score music continues to play but also, at the same time, the sound of trains running can be heard, giving the impression of this being a busy railway station. All in all, through the sound and music, and the choice of actors, this moment is signposted as Ismail's flashback, where the movement-image narrative has given way to the time-image narrative.

Interestingly, then, while the man and woman look at each other, Ismail walks into the frame, in turn challenging the audience's understanding of this moment as a flashback (and time-image), furthering the notion of temporal indeterminacy brought about by the person living with dementia. It is then revealed that Ismail has actually stumbled on to a camera crew filming a scene, and that the man and woman are merely actors (and not his flashback). As Ismail walks past the camera, the lights, the boom microphone, the production crew and the actors, the self-reflexive moment – driven, once again, by the movement of Ismail's wander – creates a sense of double-time. With the same actors playing both the younger Ismail and Swee Choo, and the actors on the film set, the past is brought into the present to be performed differently, enacting a particular performance of time that pushes and pulls at the deterritorialisation and reterritorialisation processes.

Ismail makes his way to the platform and sits down, waiting for his train – though, of course, the train will never arrive because, as the audience is already reminded at the beginning of *Parting*, Tanjong Pagar Railway Station is no longer the southern terminus for the KTM trains. As he waits in an almost Beckettian manner, the young man and woman walk towards the platform too, taking a break from filming. The man tries to get the woman to say something in Malay and it is revealed that she does not understand a single word of Malay, in direct contrast with the Malay-language voice-over from Swee Choo that the audience has heard throughout the entire film. Though Malay was officiated as Singapore's national language in the Language Policy Act in 1965, Singapore's education system had increasingly moved towards making English the neutral *lingua franca* that allowed all the different racial and ethnic groups in Singapore to communicate (the movement towards English as the preferred language of communication in comparison to other languages like Malay and Chinese played a huge part in erasing the histories of different communities in Singapore). The young woman, then, though dressed in a dress reminiscent of the 1960s, very much represents the Singapore of today and its inability to (re)connect with the past because the nation is too subscribed to The Singapore Story.

Yet, as Swee Choo's voice-over insisted, something has changed through Ismail's wandering. As the woman sits down, Ismail turns and looks at her.

Figure 6.2 Temporal collision between the past and the present in *Parting*

Likewise, the woman turns and looks at Ismail too. A shot/reverse shot ensues as both Ismail and the woman share a smile. On the one hand, this could be read as a polite correspondence. On the other, the look and smile can be read as a queer and knowing exchange that opens up the possibilities for the audience to 'read against the grain' and to renarrativise the temporal identifications of both Ismail and the woman. As they share the glance, the horn of a train arriving enters the film, and, at that moment, the film fades to black, signalling the end of *Parting*. Importantly, before the film draws to a close, in darkness, the sound of the horn continues to linger and permeate the film, consequently imbuing a sense of ambiguity to the final sequence of events.

Through the psychical connection between the two characters, the station comes alive again, and the past – the virtual – is brought into the present, visually and aurally enacting the sense of actualisation as understood by Deleuze. In *Parting*, Ismail's dementia catalyses a wander to Tanjong Pagar Railway Station, and this journey through space and time engenders new lines of actualisation, as shreds of the national past are surfaced differently into the present tense of the film. Moreover, the sound of the train arriving continuing to punctuate the film as the film fades to black can also be read as the various aspects of the present becoming part of the past, consequently reconfiguring the textualities of the past.

Here, I elaborate on this analysis of the final moments of the film by turning to Al-Saji, who, like Henri Bergson and Deleuze, sees the a priori past as co-existing alongside the present. For Al-Saji, as the present passes into the past, as the actual becomes virtual, the present 'magnetizes the whole of the past of which it is a part' (Al-Saji 2018: 342). This present passing, Al-Saji writes, can be understood as a process of virtualisation:

> New relations are woven to the whole of the past; this past shifts as past relations are repeated – confirming and stabilizing them – and as others are diverged from. This shift in relationality means that the past may be redistributed or fragmented; while some 'events' are pulled apart, others come into contact and begin to coalesce. (Al-Saji 2018: 342)

Through the present passing, the past is reconfigured. Using the analogy of a baker handling a piece of dough, Al-Saji sees the process of virtualisation as the stretching out of the past dough and folding it, thickening the dough up again. This argument becomes particularly significant for Singapore and Singapore cinema when we recall that The Singapore Story is a rolling pin that flattens out the layers of Singapore's history and historiography, leaving the people living in Singapore little or no entry points into the intricacies of the past. In the process of virtualisation, the dough is stretched out and folded onto itself, simultaneously fragmenting the past and bringing different and new regions into contact. In turn, Al-Saji notes, 'new relations may form, producing a qualitative change in the relational whole' (Al-Saji 2018: 343). Consequently, through the person living with dementia wandering in *Parting*, as Ismail wanders across a national time, and as the station comes alive again in both the past *and* the present, the film opens up ways to thinking about the past differently, forming fresh links with the now thicker past that was once flat, and providing the characters on screen and the audience avenues into this search for a suppressed past.

In *Parting*, the temporally flattening effects of The Singapore Story are in put in conversation with the temporal performances of the person living with dementia. In attending to the intricacies of these intersecting temporal performances critically and hesitantly, fresh relations with the past are forged, and new and different ways for the past to be remembered in the present are opened up. For Al-Saji, hesitating in a critical manner opens up the opportunity to transform the structures of lived possibility. Firstly, 'hesitation interrupts the embodied past that we live as habit', breaking the sensory-motor schema of the movement-image (Al-Saji 2018: 347). Secondly, 'in the interval that pries open habit, an attentiveness to the present can emerge' (Al-Saji 2018: 347). Thirdly, in pausing, critical hesitation brackets 'the teleology of progress and hope' and suspends 'the logic of utility', allowing 'superfluous and aleatory remnants' to overflow the present (Al-Saji 2018: 347). In critically hesitating, then, movement-image gives way to time-image, allowing the temporalities of the hesitant subject to unfurl and to (re)connect differently with other indexes.

Correspondingly, the trope of the person living with dementia wandering in films about dementia becomes critical hesitation writ large. Through Ismail's wanders, the past thickens, and the people living in Singapore are in turn offered a way in to rhizomatically link their own temporal identifications with the textured layers of Singapore's history and historiography, and to create new narratives from these temporal engagements. This, I believe, is the methodological potential of thinking about time through a philosophy of difference and the prism of performance.

Notes

1 See Millet 2006, Uhde and Uhde 2010, Bin Sa'at 2012 and Lim 2017.
2 See Huang 2006 for a sweep of this revisionist effort/movement. Also see the edited collection *Singapore in Global History* by Aljunied and Heng (2011) for an excellent account of Singapore's transnational history.
3 The term 'The Singapore Story' comes from the eponymous memoirs of Lee Kuan Yew, the first Prime Minister of the country.
4 On dementia and wandering, also see Brittain et al. 2017, Wiersma 2008 and Capstick and Ludwin 2015.
5 For a more comprehensive account of this history regarding the Chinese-language educated students and the formation of the PAP, see Spector 1956, Wee 1999, Stockwell 2009, Yew 2010, Loh et al. 2012, Thum 2012 and Singh 2015.
6 See Deng 2020 on the architectural environment of Singapore as an interesting example of this aphasia.

Coda: My Grandparents

Towards the end of 2017 I returned to Singapore from the UK for a short break, and one of the first things I did was to visit my Ah Ma, my grandmother, who had been diagnosed with vascular dementia the year before. When she saw me walk into the room, my Ah Ma addressed me in Hokkien, a Chinese-language vernacular, and a dialogue between the both of us ensued:

> Ah Ma: You're back from school.
> Me: I am.
> Ah Ma: How was school?
> Me: It was nice. It was cold.

It was a short verbal exchange. My mother, who was in the room with me, got extremely excited with this conversation. For her, my Ah Ma announcing that I am back from school immediately when I entered the room was a sign that my Ah Ma still recognised me.

For my mother, 'You're back from school' is attached with the narrative significance commonly associated with the verbal utterances in films about dementia. In *Still Alice* (Richard Glatzer and Wash Westmoreland, 2014, USA/UK/France), for example, at the end of the film, Alice, who lives with early onset Alzheimer's disease, is sat beside her daughter as she is read a portion of the play *Angels in America*. At the end of the reading, her daughter asks Alice what the play was about. Alice, looking at her daughter, says, 'love'. Very immediately, music enters the score, infusing the final moments of the film with a sense of affective significance. As the music swells, the film cuts to a wide-angle handheld shot of the younger Alice walking on the beach with her daughter. This final image in *Still Alice* is shot on Super 8 film, strongly suggesting that this is a flashback of both Alice's and her daughter's more nostalgic and carefree past.

One understanding of the film's last moments is that Alice, a linguistics professor who no longer has the ability to speak properly due to her early onset familial Alzheimer's disease, is still Alice. She *continues to remember*, and that her enunciation of the word 'love' is imbued with all the audio-visual significance of Alice remembering how much she loves her daughter. This is not an uncommon reading and has been iterated by many critics. Kenneth Hepburn, for instance, writes:

> It allows the viewer to see that Alice, even far into her dementia, is still Alice; her person is still intact though the illness has stripped her of most of the trappings of talent, grace, and skills. She is, echoing lines Lydia reads from *Angels in America*, a soul ascending; she continues to resonate with love. (Hepburn 2015: 329)

Despite Alice being unable to speak, she still has her memories to ground her presence and present, and the final line in the film becomes a way to authenticate her personhood. Through the word, her daughter's relationship with her continues.

My mother's excitement about my conversation with my Ah Ma seemed to stem from the same point of view. In my mother's mind, my Ah Ma announcing that I was back from school was a sign of her recognising that I had returned from Manchester, and that my Ah Ma's memories had not really disappeared. In this way, my mother found some momentary solace and comfort thinking that her mother was still here, and she was still the same mother.

At the risk of coming across as a terrible son, I am more hesitant about my conversation with my Ah Ma than my mother's interpretation. On the one hand, at that moment in time, my Ah Ma could really be referring to me returning from Manchester, acknowledging that I had spent the last six years away from Singapore. On the other hand, the conversation could have been about anything. I could have been my younger self, at the age of six, for example, returning to my Ah Ma's place after nursery (for a lot of my early childhood, I stayed with my grandparents as my parents worked). I could have been my uncle (I look uncannily similar to my uncle) returning from school and wanting to have some food. I could have been my mother, who, after school, usually goes to the cinema to help my Ah Ma out at her stall (my Ah Ma used to work at the cinemas in Orchard Theatres in Singapore, selling sweet treats and snacks to audiences before and after they watched the films). I could have been anyone and we could have been anywhere.

My point is: the verbal exchange between the two of us was so short that it engendered a sense of hesitancy in me which demanded that I pause and think more carefully about the event in the room. Suggesting that my Ah

Ma was definitely addressing me as the prodigal grandson who has finally returned to Singapore only does my relationship (and my mother's) with my Ah Ma a disservice for it flattens the layers of our past and reduces the possibilities for us to carefully think through the entanglements of our life stories. Beyond that, pinpointing my Ah Ma's exclamation to one singular source or explanation becomes a means to further (re)affirm my mother's sadness whenever my Ah Ma does not respond to her questions like 'Do you remember who I am?' and 'Where are you right now?'. For my mother, and the wider family in general, whenever my Ah Ma does not meet the requests that require her to occupy a fixed temporal position, it only serves to prove that her life story is gradually becoming foreclosed.

As I have argued in this book, the person living with dementia, like the person not living with dementia, is always in a state of becoming and change. We are always performing time and performed by time. If we were to insist on asking my Ah Ma to continuously remain on a singular and immobile temporal plane so that she can fulfil our fantasies of a fixed sense of linearity, she can only but be positioned as the threatening Other, as her lived experiences are pitted against our lived experiences. However, if we were to accept that my Ah Ma is experiencing time differently – as we are all experiencing time differently – then we can begin to engage with my Ah Ma and build a shared world together, performing our temporalities onto her and allowing us to be performed by her temporalities. In the same vein, Alice's 'love' does not have to only be read as a reiteration of her love for her daughter; it could be an assemblage of many other things and the final shot of the film could, perhaps, be read as the past returning differently as Alice and her daughter continue with their creation of a collective world, where the life story of Alice is entangled with the life stories of everyone else on and off screen through that of difference.

Years before my Ah Ma's diagnosis with vascular dementia, my Ah Gong, my grandfather, also lived with vascular dementia for a while before he passed away. In one of my visits, my Ah Gong, bed-ridden, had this conversation with me:

Me: Ah Gong.
Ah Gong: (*In Hokkien*) Aeroplane.
Me: Yes.
Ah Gong: (*In Hokkien*) You take care of my daughter.
Me: I will.
Ah Gong: (*In English*) Do not judge, or you too will be judged.
Me: Ah Gong.
Ah Gong: MaoHui.

> Me: Have you eaten?
> Ah Gong: (*In Hokkien*) Ask Ah Ma to make you food.

This exchange took me completely by surprise. In the short moment between my Ah Gong and I, at least three things happened as he performed his intersecting temporalities on to me. Firstly, he addressed me as my father, referring to me as my father's nickname (aeroplane), asking my father to take good care of my mother. Secondly, he asked me to go have food, which was a regular refrain between my grandparents and I. Thirdly, and perhaps the most intriguing of them all, in English, he quoted from the Bible.

My Ah Gong was notoriously opaque as a person. Although he would always go on long bicycle rides by himself whenever his children and grandchildren visited, he would also never fail to make sure that the fridge was filled with his handmade jellies so that we can snack on them. When I mentioned to my uncle that Ah Gong had quoted the Bible in English to me, he just shrugged it off and said that my Ah Gong could actually speak Dutch and English fluently, and could quote the Bible and the Quran at ease. This knowledge was a revelation to me because, growing up, I had never heard my Ah Gong speak any English or Dutch before, let alone have any conversations about religion. It was, as I suggested in the book, a past that had been flattened and was not accessible to me for a variety of reasons, not least because both my Ah Ma and Ah Gong did not really speak about their pasts with me very much.

Yet, through Ah Gong's dementia, shreds of his past and the nation's past are thickened and made available to me. Upon more conversations with my family, I realised that it made perfect sense that my Ah Gong was able to speak so many languages. Ah Gong and Ah Ma grew up in Indonesia as children and subsequently moved to Singapore, which meant that they lived through both the Dutch and British Empires. My Ah Gong had a rather good education and was therefore not only fluent in the languages of both colonisers, but was also familiar with both Christian and Islamic thought. Somewhere along his life course, however, he stopped displaying this knowledge to the people around him, and it meant that I never knew about this aspect of him.

My conversation with my Ah Gong reminded me of *Sandcastle* (Boo Junfeng, 2010, Singapore), a film which follows En as he tries to excavate his late father's involvement with Singapore's student politics in the 1950s and early 1960s (the hidden past that neither his mother nor grandmother wants and/or is able to discuss). In the film, En's grandmother lives with dementia and, when awake, completely refuses to talk about his father's past. Yet, when asleep, she asks her daughter-in-law to persuade her son to admit that he is a communist – no matter the truth – so that he can come back to Singapore and live with the family (En's father is a victim of Operation Cold Store – see Chapter Six – and is living in Malaysia in exile). Yet, despite En hearing his grandmother sleep talk, he is unable to figure out what she is saying.

Nonetheless, again through the grandmother's dementia, the formal properties of *Sandcastle* do allow En (and the audience) a way in to the grandmother's subjectivity in order to have access to this flattened past. Towards the latter half of the film, En brings his grandmother to Malaysia together so that they can visit his father's grave. At the end of the trip, both grandmother and grandson go to a jetty to look at the sea, where, in the far distance, the faint outline of Singapore can be seen. En walks towards the end of the jetty and, as he does so, the film cuts to a mid-shot of the back of En's father taking a picture with his camera. This shot is not filmed from the grandmother's point of view as her head is still in the foreground of the shot, suggesting that this is not necessarily a flashback. En's father turns rounds and smiles at his mother, and the film goes to a reverse shot of the grandmother who slowly looks up and realises that she is seeing her son. A look of surprise overcomes her as the audience is then shown a close-up of two pairs of hands grasping each other. The film then cuts to a shot of the father looking at the grandmother, and back to another shot of hands holding. Finally, the sequence ends with an extreme wide-angle shot of the jetty and the sea, and En is holding his grandmother's hand as they both share a moment.

In this moment, in the close-ups, it is unclear whose hands the grandmother is holding, and she also does not initially realise that her son is standing in front of her. In turn, this suggests that by wandering with his grandmother, En is *also* experiencing this clash of temporalities as he begins to enter and traverse Singapore's history and historiography. Through both the temporal performances of En and his grandmother, the past of Singapore that was flattened by The Singapore Story is thickened. Accordingly, En (and the audience of *Sandcastle*) is hesitantly provided an opening to rhizomatically link his temporal identifications with the intricate layers of the nation's history and historiography in order to create new narratives from these temporal negotiations.

Like En in *Sandcastle*, via the interactions with both my Ah Ma and Ah Gong, I am also provided access to the various shreds of my past that I was never privy to. For my Ah Ma, I had to remind myself that there is perhaps more past to what might be on the surface, as I examined the prospect that maybe she was not addressing me as me per se. For my Ah Gong, I had to ask around for ways to understand this past as I tried to figure out why he was quoting the Bible in English. In both instances, in hesitantly approaching these conversations, in allowing time to unfurl, I am able to slowly piece together bits of the familial and national past that I have been offered, and I am able to form fresh relations with a past that I had not really known was there. In a sense then, in examining the film form vis-à-vis filmic narratives about dementia, this book has – selfishly – become a way for me to work through these personal and hesitant confrontations with my Ah Ma, who lives with dementia, and my Ah Gong, who lived with dementia, as I learnt to orient myself as temporally relational to my grandparents.

Here, I am following Lauren Berlant's suggestion that 'all sorts of narratives are read as autobiographies of collective experience' (Berlant 2008: vii). My interactions with my grandparents or my analyses of films about dementia, however specific and singular, are possibly also – to varying degrees – what many people will encounter now and/or in the near future as the world's population gets increasingly older. The World Health Organization, for one, estimates that there will be about 82 million people living with dementia across the world in 2030, and this figure is projected to rise to 152 million in 2050 (World Health Organization 2019). Alzheimer's Disease International, for another, predicts that there will be about 131 million people living with dementia by 2050, and that for people over the age of 65, the chances of being diagnosed with dementia is 5 per cent whereas for people over the age of 80, the probability increases to 20 per cent (Alzheimer's Disease International 2019). No matter which organisational website or research paper you peruse, whatever the figures they predict, the common underlying agreement is that there will be more people living with dementia.

These numbers on the people who live or will live with dementia in the future, Kathleen Woodward would argue, contribute to the engendering of a sense of statistical panic, where 'fatally, we feel that a certain statistic, which is in fact based on an aggregate and is only a measure of probability, actually represents our very future' (Woodward 1999: 185). Following Woodward, focusing on the number of people living with dementia now and in the future only serves to exacerbate a sense of panic in people regarding ageing in later life. People do not want to be reduced to a mere statistic and would accordingly change their lifestyle to make it 'better' in order to reduce their risk of being diagnosed with dementia.

Instead of proposing the adoption of healthy ageing practices out of a sense of fear and panic, where ageing in later life is again reduced to a good-bad dichotomy, the book offers another way to work through the statistical panic regarding dementia: to understand that everyone and everything is performing and performed by time differently, and to acknowledge that these experiences of time are also underlined by a framework of change and ephemerality. To be clear, I am not saying that we should start drinking jars of lard just because we want to. I am also not saying that we should discount these projections on the people who will possibly live with dementia in the near future. Rather, I am suggesting that in approaching each singular temporal performance carefully and imaginatively, and that in linking each performance of time to more performances of time, we open up a space to further consider the affects of biomedicine, amongst other things, in a world that is gradually growing older. As Berlant writes:

> Aesthetics is not only the place where we rehabituate our sensorium by taking in new material and becoming more refined in relation to it. But it provides metrics for understanding how we pace and space our encounters with things, how we manage the too closeness of the world and also the desire to have an impact on it that has some relation to its impact on us. (Berlant 2011: 12)

From this viewpoint, the understanding of time through the prism of performance – as forms of aesthetics processes – is only but the first step into thinking more carefully about how our life courses and life stories, entangled and relational, are structured by the circulation of personal and general affective forces, and this monograph paves a road for this future research.

Writing this book, I often think about the conversation I had with my Ah Ma in the bedroom that day, and I wonder what she would have said if the dialogue had carried on a little bit longer. Would she, like Ah Gong, have asked me to get some food? Would she have started addressing me as someone specific? Would she have said something completely different? Would the exchange have brought my mother and I joy and excitement? Would it have startled us? Or would it have evoked anger and distress? I do not know but I am always imagining. Maybe we would have a conversation that goes something like this, and maybe, we would all have been able to make perfect non-hesitant sense of it all:

>Ah Ma: You're back from school.
>Me: I am.
>Ah Ma: How was school?
>Me: It was nice. It was cold.
>Ah Ma:
>Me:
>Ah Ma:
>Me:

Bibliography

Adams, Trevor and Paula Gardiner (2005), 'Communication and Interaction within Dementia Care Triads', *Dementia* 4: 2, pp. 185–205.
Aljunied, Syed Muhd Khairudin and Derek Heng (eds) (2011), *Singapore in Global History*, Amsterdam: Amsterdam University Press.
Al-Saji, Alia (2014), 'A Phenomenology of Hesitation: Interrupting Racializing Habits of Seeing', in Emily Lee (ed.), *Living Alterities: Phenomenology, Embodiment, and Race*, Albany: State University of New York Press, pp. 133–72.
Al-Saji, Alia (2018), 'SPEP Co-Director's Address: Hesitation as Philosophical Method – Travel bans, Colonial Durations, and the Affective Weight of the Past', *The Journal of Speculative Philosophy* 32: 3, pp. 331–59.
Altamirano, Marco (2016), *Technology and Environment: An Essay on the Philosophy of Nature*, Edinburgh: Edinburgh University Press.
Alzheimer's Disease International (2019), 'Frequently Asked Questions', https://www.alz.co.uk/info/faq (accessed 17 September 2019).
Anderson, Daniel (2010), 'Love and Hate in Dementia: The Depressive Position in the Film *Iris*', *The International Journal of Psychoanalysis* 91, pp. 1289–97.
Anon (2014), 'Emma Thompson Criticises "Grey Pound" Films for Older Audiences', *BBC News*, 10 April, http://www.bbc.co.uk/news/entertainment-arts-26971676 (accessed 25 April 2016).
Aquilina, Carmelo and Julian C. Hughes (2006), 'The Return of the Living Dead: Agency Lost and Found?', in Julian Hughes, Stephen Louw and Steven R. Sabat (eds), *Dementia: Mind, Meaning, and the Person*, Oxford: Oxford University Press, pp. 143–61.
Ashworth, Rosalie Marie (2019), 'Looking Ahead to a Future with Alzheimer's Disease: Coping with the Unknown', *Ageing and Society*, pp. 1–22, doi: 10.1017/S0144686X19000151.
Assmann, Aleida (2012), 'Authenticity: The Signature of Western Exceptionalism', in Julia Straub (ed.), *Paradoxes of Authenticity: Studies on a Critical Concept*, Bielefeld: transcript Verlag, pp. 33–50.
Bâ, Saër Maty and Will Higbee, 2012. 'Introduction: De-Westernizing Film Studies', in Saër Maty Bâ and Will Higbee (eds), *De-Westernizing Film Studies*, London: Routledge, pp. 1–15.
Baars, Jan (1997), 'Concepts of Time and Narrative Temporality in the Study of Aging', *Journal of Aging Studies* 11: 4, pp. 283–95.
Baars, Jan (2007), 'Introduction – Chronological Time and Chronological Age:

Problems of Temporal Diversity', in Jan Baars and Henk Visser (eds), *Aging and Time: Multidisciplinary Perspectives*, New York: Baywood Publishing, pp. 1–14.

Baars, Jan (2009), 'Problematic Foundation: Theorizing Time, Age, and Aging', in Vern L. Bengston, Merril Silverstein, Norella M. Putney and Daphna Gans (eds), *Handbook of Theories of Aging* (2nd Edition), New York: Springer Publishing Company, pp. 87–100.

Baars, Jan (2017), 'Human Aging, Finite Lives and the Idealization of Clocks', *Biogerontology* 18, pp. 285–92.

Baars, Jan and Henk Visser (eds) (2007), *Aging and Time: Multidisciplinary Perspectives*, New York: Baywood Publishing.

Baez, Sandra, et al. (2014), 'Primary Empathy Deficits in Frontotemporal Dementia', *Frontiers in Aging Neuroscience*, pp. 1–11, DOI: 10.3389/fnagi.2014.00262.

Bakhtin, Mikhail M. (2011), *The Dialogic Imagination: Four Essays*, Austin, TX: University of Texas Press.

Balázs, Béla (1970), *Theory of the Film: Character and Growth of a New Art*, trans. Edith Bone, New York: Dover.

Barad, Karen (2007), *Meeting the Universe Halfway: Quantum Physics and the Entanglement of Matter and Meaning*, Durham, NC: Duke University Press.

Bartky, Ian R. (2000), *One Time Fits All: The Campaign for Global Uniformity*, Stanford, CA: Stanford University Press.

Bazin, André (2005), *What is Cinema? Volume 1*, trans. Hugh Gray, London: University of California Press.

Bedrosian, Tracy A. and Randy J. Nelson (2013), 'Sundowning Syndrome in Aging and Dementia: Research in Mouse Models', *Experimental Neurology* 243, pp. 67–73.

Behuniak, Susan M. (2011), 'The Living Dead? The Construction of People with Alzheimer's Disease as Zombies', *Ageing and Society* 31, pp. 70–92.

Ben Shaul, Nitzan (2012), *Cinema of Choice: Optional Thinking and Narrative Movies*, New York: Berghahn Books.

Benjamin, Walter (1992), *Illuminations*, ed. Hannah Arendt, trans. Harry Zohn, Oxford: Fontana Press.

Benjamin, Walter (1997), *Charles Baudelaire: A Lyric Poet in the Era of High Capitalism*, trans. Harry Zohn, London: Verso.

Benjamin, Walter (2002), *The Arcades Project*, trans. Howard Eiland and Kevin McLaughlin, London: Harvard University Press.

Bennett, Jane (2001), *The Enchantment of Modern Life: Attachments, Crossings, and Ethics*, Princeton, NJ: Princeton University Press.

Bennett, Jane (2010), *Vibrant Matter: A Political Ecology of Things*, Durham, NC: Duke University Press.

Bergson, Henri (1950), *Time and Free Will: An Essay on the Immediate Data of Consciousness*, trans. F. L. Pogson, London: George Allen and Unwin.

Berlant, Lauren (2008), *The Female Complaint: The Unfinished Business of Sentimentality in American Culture*, Durham, NC: Duke University Press.

Berlant, Lauren (2011), *Cruel Optimism*, Durham, NC: Duke University Press.

Berman, Jeffrey (2021), *The Art of Caregiving in Fiction, Film, and Memoir*, London: Bloomsbury Academic.

BFI (2013), *Statistical Yearbook 2013*, http://www.bfi.org.uk/sites/bfi.org.uk/files/downloads/bfi-statistical-yearbook-2013.pdf (accessed 23 June 2016).

BFI (2014), *Statistical Yearbook 2014*, http://www.bfi.org.uk/sites/bfi.org.uk/files/downl oads/bfi-statistical-yearbook-2014.pdf (accessed 23 June 2016).

BFI (2015), *Audiences: BFI Research and Statistics*, http://www.bfi.org.uk/sites/bfi.org.uk /files/downloads/bfi-audiences-2015-11.pdf (accessed 25 April 2016).

Bhabha, Homi K. (2008), 'DissemiNation: Time, Narrative, and the Margins of the Modern Nation', in Homi K. Bhabha (ed.), *Nation and Narration*, London: Routledge, pp. 291–322.

Biggs, Simon (1999), 'The "Blurring" of the Lifecourse: Narrative, Memory and the Question of Authenticity', *Journal of Aging and Identity* 4: 4, pp. 209–21.

Bin Sa'at, Alfian (2012), 'Hinterland, Heartland, Home: Affective Topography in Singapore Films', in Tilman Baumgärtel (ed.), *Southeast Asian Independent Cinema: Essays, Documents, Interviews*, Hong Kong: Hong Kong University Press, pp. 33–50.

Birth, Kevin K. (2012), *Objects of Time: How Things Shape Temporality*, New York: Palgrave Macmillan.

Bitenc, Rebecca (2020) *Reconsidering Dementia Narratives: Empathy, Identity and Care*, Abingdon: Routledge.

Bloom, Paul (2016), *Against Empathy: The Case for Rational Compassion*, London: The Bodley Head.

Blum, Jason (2015), 'M. Night Shyamalan and Jason Blum: *The Visit* Interview', *MoviesOnline*, http://www.moviesonline.ca/2015/09/m-night-shyamalan-jason-bl um-the-visit-interview/ (accessed 8 December 2016).

Bogue, Ronald (2003), *Deleuze on Cinema*, London: Routledge.

Bohn, Linzy, Sheree T. Kwong See and Helene H. Fung (2016), 'Time Perspective and Positivity Effects in Alzheimer's Disease', *Psychology and Aging* 31: 6, pp. 574–82.

Boyle, Geraldine (2013a), 'Still a Woman's job: The Division of Housework in Couples Living with Dementia', *Families, Relationships and Societies* 2: 1, pp. 5–21.

Boyle, Geraldine (2013b), '"She's Usually Quicker than the Calculator": Financial Management and Decision-Making in Couples Living with Dementia', *Health and Social Care in the Community* 21: 5, pp. 554–62.

Boyle, Geraldine (2013c), 'Facilitating Decision-Making by People With Dementia: Is Spousal Support Gendered?", *Journal of Social Welfare and Family Law* 35: 2, pp. 227–43.

Boyle, Geraldine (2014a), '"Can't Cook, Won't Cook": Men's Involvement in Cooking When Their Wives Develop Dementia', *Journal of Gender Studies* 23: 4, pp. 336–50.

Boyle, Geraldine (2014b), 'Recognising the Agency of People with Dementia', *Disability and Society* 29: 7, pp. 1130–44.

Boyle, Geraldine (2017a), 'Revealing Gendered Identity and Agency in Dementia', *Health and Social Care in the Community*, pp. 1–7, doi: https://doi-org.manchester.idm.oclc .org/10.1111/hsc.12452.

Boyle, Geraldine (2017b), 'Showing How They Feel: The Emotional Reflexivity of People with Dementia', *Families, Relationships and Societies* 6: 1, pp. 3–19.

Brittain, Katherine, Cathrine Degnen, Grant Gibson, Claire Dickinson and Louise Robinson (2017), 'When Walking Becomes Wandering: Representing the Fear of the Fourth Age', *Sociology of Health and Illness* 39: 2, pp. 270–84.

Brockmeier, Jens (2014), 'Questions of Meaning: Memory, Dementia, and the Postautobiographical Perspective', in Lars-Christer Hydén, Hilde Lindemann and

Jens Brockmeier (eds), *Beyond Loss, Dementia, Identity, Personhood*, Oxford: Oxford University Press, pp. 69–90.
Brown, Tom (2012), *Breaking the Fourth Wall: Direct Address in the Cinema*, Edinburgh: Edinburgh University Press.
Brown, William (2015), *Supercinema: Film-Philosophy for the Digital Age*, New York: Berghahn.
Brunau-Zaragoza, Sophie (2020), '"Je nous suis dessinées." Towards a Relational Ecology: Remaking the Political Community in Marie Darrieussecq's *Notre vie dans les forêts*', *L'Esprit Créateur* 60: 3, pp. 59–72.
Bruno, Giuliana (1993), *Streetwalking on a Ruined Map: Cultural Theory and the City Films of Elvira Notari*, Princeton, NJ: Princeton University Press.
Bruno, Giuliana (2011), *Atlas of Emotion: Journeys in Art, Architecture, and Film*, New York: Verso.
Bryson, Valerie (2007), *Gender and the Politics of Time: Feminist Theory and Contemporary Debates*, Bristol: The Policy Press.
Burke, Lucy (2017), 'Imagining a Future without Dementia: Fictions of Regeneration and the Crises of Work and Sustainability', *Palgrave Communications* 3: 1, pp. 1–9, DOI: 10.1057/s41599-017-0051-y
Burke, Lucy (2019), 'Dementia and the Paradigm of the Camp: Thinking Beyond Giorgio Agamben's Concept of "Bare Life"', *Bioethical Inquiry* 16, pp. 195–205.
Butler, Judith (1990), *Gender Trouble: Feminism and the Subversion of Identity*, London: Routledge.
Butler, Judith (1997), *The Psychic Life of Power: Theories in Subjection*, Stanford, CA: Stanford University Press.
Capstick, Andrea (2015), 'Rewalking the City: People with Dementia Remember', in Tina Richardson (ed.), *Walking Inside Out: Contemporary British Psychogeography*, London: Rowman and Littlefield International, pp. 211–25.
Capstick, Andrea and Katherine Ludwin (2015), 'Place Memory and Dementia: Findings from Participatory Film-Making in Long-Term Social Care', *Health and Place* 34, pp. 157–63.
Capstick, Andrea, John Chatwin and Katherine Ludwin (2015), 'Challenging Representations of Dementia in Contemporary Western Fiction Film: From Epistemic Injustice to Social Participation', in Aagje Swinnen and Mark Schweda (eds), *Popularizing Dementia: Public Expressions and Representations of Forgetfulness*, Bielefeld: transcript, pp. 229–51.
Carbado, Devon W., Kimberlé Williams Crenshaw, Vickie M. Mays and Barbara Tomlinson (2013), 'Intersectionality: Mapping the Movements of a Theory', *Du Bois Review: Social Science Research on Race* 10: 2, pp. 303–12.
Carlson, Marvin (2003), *Performance: A Critical Introduction* (2nd Edition), London: Routledge.
Carruthers, Lee (2016), *Doing Time: Temporality, Hermeneutics, and Contemporary Cinema*, New York: SUNY Press.
Ceuterick, Maud (2020), *Affirmative Aesthetics and Wilful Women: Gender, Space and Mobility in Contemporary Cinema*, Cham: Palgrave Macmillan.
Chen, Kuan-Hsing (2010), *Asia as Method: Toward Deimperialization*, Durham, NC: Duke University Press.

Cheow, Sue Ann (2014), '8 Things to Know about Chung Cheng High, Singapore's Latest National Monument', *The Straits Times*, 10 July, http://www.straitstimes.com/singapore/8-things-to-know-about-chung-cheng-high-singapores-latest-national-monument-0 (accessed 10 July 2017).
Chion, Michel (1994) *Audio-Vision: Sounds on Screen*, ed. and trans. Claudia Gorbman, New York: Columbia University Press.
Chivers, Sally (2011), *The Silvering Screen: Old Age and Disability in Cinema*, London: University of Toronto Press.
Chivers, Sally (2015), 'Empty Husks: Age, Disability, Care, Death and *Amour*', in Claudia Wassman (ed.), *Therapy and Emotions in Film and Television*, London: Palgrave Macmillan, pp. 72–88.
Cipriani, Gabriele, Claudio Lucetti, Cecilia Carlesi and Angelo Nuti (2015), 'Sundown Syndrome and Dementia', *European Geriatric Medicine* 6: 4, pp. 375–80.
Clare, Stephanie (2009), 'Agency, Signification, and Temporality', *Hypatia* 24: 4, pp. 50–62.
Clark, Nick (2013), 'Rise of the Silver-haired Screen: Older People Take Largest Share of Cinema Audiences', *Independent*, 24 July, http://www.independent.co.uk/arts-entertainment/films/news/rise-of-the-silver-haired-screen-older-people-take-largest-share-of-cinema-audiences-8728982.html (accessed 23 June 2016).
Cohen-Shalev, Amir (2012), *Visions of Aging: Images of the Elderly in Film*, Eastbourne: Sussex Academic Press.
Cohen-Shalev, Amir and Esther-Lee Marcus (2012), 'An Insider's View of Alzheimer: Cinematic Portrayals of the Struggle for Personhood', *International Journal of Ageing and Later Life* 7: 2, pp. 73–96.
Collins, Patricia Hill and Sirma Bilge (2016), *Intersectionality*, Cambridge: Polity Press.
Coverley, Merlin (2006), *Psychogeography*, Harpenden: Pocket Essentials.
Covey, Herbert C. (1993), 'A Return to Infancy: Old Age and the Second Childhood in History', *The International Journal of Aging and Human Development* 36: 2, pp. 81–90.
Cowie, Elizabeth (1978), ' Woman as Sign', *M/F* 1, pp. 49–63.
Cox, David (2012), 'How Older Viewers are Rescuing Cinema', *The Guardian*, 8 March. http://www.theguardian.com/film/2012/mar/08/older-viewers-rescuing-cinema (accessed 23 June 2016).
Coyle, Rebecca (2010), 'Point of Audition: Sound and Music in *Cloverfield*', *Science Fiction Film and Television* 3: 2, pp. 217–37.
Crenshaw, Kimberlé (1989), 'Demarginalizing the Intersection of Race and Sex: A Black Feminist Critique of Antidiscrimination Doctrine, Feminist Theory and Antiracist Policies', *University of Chicago Legal Forum* 1, pp. 139–67.
Crenshaw, Kimberlé (1991), 'Mapping the Margins: Intersectionality, Identity Politics, and Violence Against Women of Color', *Stanford Law Review* 43: 6, pp. 1241–1299.
Crossley, Laura and Austin Fisher (2021), 'Geriaction Cinema: Introduction', *Journal of Popular Film and Television* 49: 3, pp. 130–5.
Cvetkovich, Ann (2003), *An Archive of Feelings: Trauma, Sexuality, and Lesbian Public Cultures*, Durham, NC: Duke University Press.
Cvetkovich, Ann (2012), *Depression: A Public Feeling*, Durham, NC: Duke University Press.
de Beauvoir, Simone (1968), *Force of Circumstance*, London: Penguin.
de Beauvoir, Simone (1977), *Old Age*, trans. Patrick O'Brian, Harmondsworth: Penguin.

de Beauvoir, Simone (1996), *The Coming of Age*, London: W. W. Norton.
DeFalco, Amelia (2010), *Uncanny Subjects: Aging in Contemporary Narrative*, Columbus: Ohio State University Press.
Deleuze, Gilles (1988), *Bergsonism*, trans. Hugh Tomlinson and Barbara Habberjam, New York: Zone Press.
Deleuze, Gilles (1994), *Difference and Repetition*, trans. Paul Patton, London: The Athlone Press.
Deleuze, Gilles (2013a), *Cinema 1: The Movement-Image*, trans. Hugh Tomlinson and Barbara Habberjam, London: Bloomsbury.
Deleuze, Gilles (2013b), *Cinema 2: The Time-Image*, trans. Hugh Tomlinson and Robert Galeta, London: Bloomsbury.
Deleuze, Gilles and Félix Guattari (1987), *A Thousand Plateaus: Capitalism and Schizophrenia*, trans. Brian Massumi, Minneapolis: University of Minnesota Press.
DeLuca, John (2000), 'A Cognitive Neuroscience Perspective on Confabulation', *Neuropsychoanalysis: An Interdisciplinary Journal for Psychoanalysis and the Neurosciences* 2: 2, pp. 119–32.
Deng, MaoHui (2020), 'Singapore as Non-Place: National Cinema through the Lens of Temporal Heterogeneity', *Asian Cinema* 31: 1, pp. 37–53.
Deng, MaoHui (2022a), 'The Temporality and Politics of Language Lost and Found: Cinema, Dementia and the Entangled Histories of Singapore', in Irmela Marei Krüger-Fürhoff, Nina Schmidt and Sue Vice (eds), *The Politics of Dementia: Forgetting and Remembering the Violent Past in Literature, Film and Graphic Narratives*, Berlin: De Gruyter, pp. 189–202.
Deng, MaoHui (2022b), 'Re-Orientating Hesitantly: Approaching the Entangled Temporalities of Cinema, Dementia, and Hong Kong From a Decolonial Viewpoint', in Katsura Sako and Sarah Falcus (eds), *Contemporary Narratives of Ageing, Illness, Care*, Abingdon: Routledge, pp. 104–23.
Deng, MaoHui (2022c), '*Lilting* and the Entangled Temporalities of Europe(an Cinema)', in Gábor Gergely and Susan Hayward (eds), *The Routledge Companion to European Cinema*, Abingdon: Routledge, pp. 67–75.
Diamond, Elin (1996), 'Introduction', in Elin Diamond (ed.), *Performance and Cultural Politics*, London: Routledge, pp. 1–12.
Doane, Mary Ann (1987), *The Desire to Desire: The Woman's Film of the 1940s*, Bloomington: Indiana University Press.
Doane, Mary Ann (2002), *The Emergence of Cinematic Time: Modernity, Contingency, The Archive*, London: Harvard University Press.
Doane, Mary Ann (2003), 'The Close-Up: Scale and Detail in the Cinema', *differences: A Journal of Feminist Cultural Studies* 14: 3, pp. 89–111.
Doane, Mary Ann (2007a), 'Indexicality: Trace and Sign: Introduction', *differences: A Journal of Feminist Cultural Studies* 18: 1, pp. 1–6.
Doane, Mary Ann (2007b), 'The Indexical and the Concept of Medium Specificity', *differences: A Journal of Feminist Cultural Studies* 18: 1, pp. 128–52.
Dolan, Josephine (2016), '"Old Age" Films: Golden Retirement, Dispossession and Disturbance', *Journal of British Cinema and Television* 13: 4, pp. 571–89.
Dudrah, Rajinder (2021), 'The Geri-Actions of the Aging Amitabh Bachchan', *Journal of Popular Film and Television* 49: 3, pp. 136–43.

Eakin, Paul John (2006), 'Narrative Identity and Narrative Imperialism: A Response to Galen Strawson and James Phelan', *Narrative* 14: 2, pp. 180–7.

Edensor, Tim, Lesley Head and Uma Kothari (2020), 'Time, Temporality and Environmental Change', *Geoforum* 108, pp. 255–8.

Ekerdt, David J. (2019), 'Things and Possessions', in Stephen Katz (ed.), *Ageing in Every Life: Materialities and Embodiments*, Bristol: Policy Press, pp. 29–44.

Eleftheriotis, Dimitris (2016), 'Cosmopolitanism, Empathy and the Close-Up', in Yannis Tzioumakis and Claire Molloy (eds), *The Routledge Companion to Cinema and Politics*, London: Routledge, pp. 203–17.

Emirbayer, Mustafa and Ann Mische (1998), 'What is Agency?', *The American Journal of Sociology* 103: 4, pp. 962–1023.

Epstein, Jean (1977), 'Magnification and Other Writings', trans. Stuart Liebman, *October* 3, pp. 9–25.

Falcus, Sarah and Katsura Sako (2019), *Contemporary Narratives of Dementia: Ethics, Ageing, Politics*, London: Routledge.

Felski, Rita (2000), *Doing Time: Feminist Theory and Postmodern Culture*, New York: New York University Press.

Fletcher, James R. (2020a), 'Positioning Ethnicity in Dementia Awareness Research: Does the Use of Senility Risk Ascribing Racialised Knowledge Deficits to Minority Groups?', *Sociology of Health and Illness* 42: 4, pp. 705–23.

Fletcher, James R. (2020b), 'Ethnicity in Dementia Research: Are Social Scientists Complicit in Neuropsychiatric Imperialism?', *Sociology Lens*, 13 February, https://www.sociologylens.net/article-types/opinion/ethnicity-dementia-research-are-social-scientists-complicit-neuropsychiatric-imperialism/28176 (accessed 20 December 2021).

Fong, Sylvia S., Pongsatorn Paholpak, Madelaine Daianu, Mariel B. Deutsch, Brandalyn C. Riedel, Andrew R. Carr, Elvira E. Jimenez, Michelle M. Mather, Paul M. Thompson and Mario F. Mendez (2017), 'The Attribution of Animacy and Agency in Frontotemporal Dementia Versus Alzheimer's Disease', *Behavioural Neurology* 82, pp. 81–94.

Freedman, Morris, Larry Leach, Edith Kaplan, Gordon Winocur, Kenneth I. Shulman and Dean C. Delis (1994), *Clock Drawing: A Neuropsychological Analysis*, Oxford: Oxford University Press.

Freeman, Elizabeth (2010), *Time Binds: Queer Temporalities, Queer Histories*, London: Duke University Press.

Freeman, Mark (2011), 'Narrative Foreclosure in Later Life: Possibilities and Limits', in Gary Kenyon, Ernst Bohlmeijer and William L. Randall (eds), *Storying Later Life: Issues, Investigations, and Interventions in Narrative Gerontology*, Oxford: Oxford University Press, pp. 3–19.

Freer, Ian (2017), '*Happy End* Review', *Empire*, 30 November, https://www.empireonline.com/movies/reviews/happy-end-review/ (accessed 4 January 2022).

Fuchs, Thomas (2020), 'Embodiment and Personal Identity in Dementia', *Medicine, Health Care and Philosophy* 23, pp. 665–76.

Garber, Daniel (1992), 'Descartes' Physics', in John Cottingham (ed.), *The Cambridge Companion to Descartes*, Cambridge: Cambridge University Press, pp. 286–334.

George, Cherian (2010), *Singapore: The Air-Conditioned Nation: Essays on the Politics of Comfort and Control 1990–2000*, Singapore: Landmark Books.

Gibson, Janet (2020), *Dementia, Narrative and Performance: Staging Reality, Reimagining Identities*, Cham: Palgrave Macmillan.
Gilleard, Chris (2021), 'Aging as Otherness: Revisiting Simone de Beauvoir's *The Coming of Age*', *The Gerontologist*, pp. 1–7, DOI: 10.1093/geront/gnab034.
Gilleard, Chris and Paul Higgs (2000), *Cultures of Ageing: Self, Citizen and the Body*, Harlow: Prentice Hall.
Gilleard, Chris and Paul Higgs (2017), 'Enveloping Shadow? The Role of the Nursing Home in the Social Imaginary of the Fourth Age', in Sally Chivers and Ulla Kriebernegg (eds), *Care Home Stories: Aging, Disability, and Long-Term Residential Care*, Bielefeld: transcript Verlag, pp. 229–46.
Glennie, Paul and Nigel Thrift (2009), *Shaping the Day: A History of Timekeeping in England and Wales 1300–1800*, Oxford: Oxford University Press.
Goffman, Erving (1990), *The Presentation of Self in Everyday Life*, New York: Doubleday.
Gowman, Philip (2017), 'Film Review: *Memoir of a Murderer*', https://londonkoreanlinks.net/2017/10/12/film-review-memoir-of-a-murderer/ (accessed 18 October 2018).
Graham, Megan E. (2016), 'The Voices of Iris: Cinematic Representations of the Aged Woman and Alzheimer's Disease in *Iris* (2001)', *Dementia* 15: 5, pp. 1171–83.
Gravagne, Pamela H. (2013), *The Becoming of Age: Cinematic Visions of Mind, Body and Identity in Later Life*, London: McFarland.
Gray, Julia (2019), 'Working within an Aesthetic of Relationality: Theoretical Considerations of Embodiment, Imagination and Foolishness as Part of Theatre Making about Dementia', *Research in Drama Education: The Journal of Applied Theatre and Performance* 24: 1, pp. 6–22.
Grosz, Elizabeth (1995), *Space, Time and Perversion*, London: Routledge.
Grosz, Elizabeth (2005), *Time Travels: Feminism, Nature, Power*, Durham, NC: Duke University Press.
Gullette, Margaret Morganroth (2004), *Aged by Culture*, Chicago: University of Chicago Press.
Gullette, Margaret Morganroth (2014), 'Euthanasia as a Caregiving Fantasy in the Era of the New Longevity', *Age Culture Humanities* 1, pp. 211–19.
Gullette, Margaret Morganroth (2017), *Ending Ageism, or How Not to Shoot Old People*, New Brunswick, NJ: Rutgers University Press.
Gunning, Tom (1993), '"Now You See It, Now You Don't": The Temporality of the Cinema of Attractions', *The Velvet Light Trap* 32, pp. 3–12.
Gunning, Tom (2008), 'What's the Point of an Index?: Or, Faking Photographs', in Karen Beckman and Jean Ma (eds), *Still Moving: Between Cinema and Photography*, Durham, NC: Duke University Press, pp. 23–40.
Hadjioannou, Markos (2012), *From Light to Byte: Toward an Ethics of Digital Cinema*, Minneapolis: University of Minnesota Press.
Haraway, Donna J. (2016), *Staying with the Trouble: Making Kin in the Chthulucene*, Durham, NC: Duke University Press.
Harding, James M. and Cindy Rosenthal (eds) (2011), *The Rise of Performance Studies: Rethinking Richard Schechner's Broad Spectrum*, Basingstoke: Palgrave Macmillan.
Hardy, John A. and Gerald A. Higgins (1992), 'Alzheimer's Disease: The Amyloid Cascade Hypothesis', *Science* 256: 5054, pp. 184–5.

Harper, Graeme and Jonathan Rayner (2010), 'Introduction – Cinema and Landscape', in Graeme Harper and Jonathan Rayner (eds), *Cinema and Landscape*, Chicago: University of Chicago Press, pp. 13–28.
Hassan, Robert (2003), *The Chronoscopic Society: Globalization, Time, and Knowledge in the Network Economy*, New York: Peter Lang.
Hassan, Robert and Ronald E. Purser (eds) (2007), *24/7: Time and Temporality in the Network Society*, Stanford, CA: Stanford University Press.
Hatton, Nicky (2021), *Performance and Dementia: A Cultural Response to Care*, Cham: Palgrave Macmillan.
Hayes, Jills and Sarah Povey (2011), *The Creative Arts in Dementia Care: Practical Person-Centred Approaches and Ideas*, London: Jessica Kingsley Publishers.
Held, Virginia (2006), *The Ethics of Care: Personal, Political, and Global*, Oxford: Oxford University Press.
Hepburn, Kenneth (2015), 'Still Alice', *The Gerontological Society of America* 55: 2, pp. 328–9.
Herrup, Karl (2021), *How Not to Study a Disease: The Story of Alzheimer's Disease*, Cambridge, MA: The MIT Press.
Huang, Jianli (2006), 'Positioning the Student Political Activism of Singapore: Articulation, Contestation and Omission', *Inter-Asia Cultural Studies* 7: 3, pp. 403–30.
Hughes, Julian C. (2001), 'Views of the Person with Dementia', *Journal of Medical Ethics* 27, pp. 86–91.
Hughes, Julian C. (2013), '"Y" Feel Me? How Do We Understand the Person with Dementia?', *Dementia* 12: 3, pp. 348–58.
Ingold, Tim (2004), 'Culture on the Ground: The World Perceived Through the Feet', *Journal of Material Culture* 9: 3, pp. 315–40.
Iwamoto, Yuko and Minoru Hoshiyama (2012), 'Time Orientation During the Day in the Elderly with Dementia', *Physical and Occupational Therapy in Geriatrics* 30: 3, pp. 202–13.
Jonghe, A. De, J. C. Korevaar, B. C. van Munster and S. E. de Rooij (2010), 'Effectiveness of Melatonin Treatment on Circadian Rhythm Disturbances in Dementia. Are There Implications for Delirium? A Systematic Review', *International Journal of Geriatric Psychiatry* 25, pp. 1201–1208.
Kafer, Alison (2013), *Feminist, Queer, Crip*, Bloomington: Indiana University Press.
Kaplan, E. Ann (1999), 'Trauma and Aging: Marlene Dietrich, Melanie Klein, and Marguerite Duras', in Kathleen Woodward (ed.), *Figuring Age: Women, Bodies, Generations*, Bloomington: Indiana University Press, pp. 171–94.
Karatsu, Rie (2009), 'Questions for a Women's Cinema: Fact, Fiction and Memory in the Films of Naomi Kawase', *Visual Anthropology* 22: 2-3, pp. 167–81.
Katz, Stephen (2005), *Cultural Aging: Life Course, Lifestyle, and Senior Worlds*, Toronto: University of Toronto Press.
Katz, Stephen (2013), 'Dementia, Personhood and Embodiment: What Can We Learn from the Medieval History of Memory?', *Dementia* 12: 3, pp. 303–14.
Kaufman, Sharon R. (2006), 'Dementia-Near-Death and "Life Itself"', in Annette Leibing and Lawrence Cohen (eds), *Thinking about Dementia: Culture, Loss, and the Anthropology of Senility*, New Brunswick, NJ: Rutgers University Press, pp. 23–42.
Kawase, Naomi (2007), 'In Competition: "Mogari No Mori" (The Mourning Forest) by

Naomi Kawase', 26 May, https://www.festival-cannes.com/en/73-editions/retrospective/2007/actualites/articles/in-competition-mogari-no-mori-the-mourning-forest-by-naomi-kawase (accessed 19 August 2021).
Keady, John David, et al. (2022), 'Re-Thinking and Re-Positioning "Being in the Moment" within a Continuum of Moments: Introducing a New Conceptual Framework for Dementia Studies', *Ageing and Society* 42, pp. 681–702.
Keen, Suzanne (2007), *Empathy and the Novel*, Oxford: Oxford University Press.
Kerins, Mark (2011), *Beyond Dolby (Stereo): Cinema in the Digital Sound Age*, Bloomington: Indiana University Press.
Kern, Stephen (2003), *The Culture of Time and Space 1880–1918*, Cambridge, MA: Harvard University Press.
Kershaw, Baz (2007), *Theatre Ecology: Environments and Performance Events*, Cambridge: Cambridge University Press.
Khoo, Olivia (2015), 'On the Banning of a Film: Tan Pin Pin's *To Singapore, with Love*', *Senses of Cinema* 76, http://sensesofcinema.com/2015/documentary-in-asia/to-singapore-with-love-documentary/ (accessed 7 July 2017).
Kim, Hoyoung and Jeanyung Chey (2010), 'Effects of Education, Literacy, and Dementia on the Clock Drawing Test Performance', *Journal of the International Neuropsychological Society* 16, pp. 1138–1146.
Kitanaka, Junko (2021), 'Limits of Empathy: The Dementia Tōjisha Movement in Japan', *Journal of The History of Behavioral Science* 57: 3, pp. 266–72.
Kittay, Eva Feder (1999), *Love's Labor: Essays on Women, Equality, and Dependency*, London: Routledge.
Kitwood, Tom (1997), *Dementia Reconsidered: The Person Comes First*, Buckingham: Open University Press.
Klinger, Barbara (2006), *Beyond the Multiplex: Cinema, New Technologies, and the Home*, Berkeley: University of California Press.
Kontos, Pia and Wendy Martin (2013), 'Embodiment and Dementia: Exploring Critical Narratives of Selfhood, Surveillance, and Dementia Care', *Dementia* 12: 3, pp. 288–302.
Kontos, Pia, Karen-Lee Miller and Alexis P. Kontos (2017), 'Relational Citizenship: Supporting Embodied Selfhood and Relationality in Dementia Care', *Sociology of Health and Illness* 39: 2, pp. 182–98.
Koolhass, Rem and Bruce Mau (1995), *Small, Medium, Large, Extra-Large: Office for Metropolitan Architecture*, New York: Monachelli Press.
Kopelman, Michael D. (1999), 'Varieties of False Memory', *Cognitive Neuropsychology* 13: 3–5, pp. 197–214.
Kopelman, Michael D. (2010), 'Varieties of Confabulation and Delusion', *Cognitive Neuropsychiatry* 15: 1, pp. 14–37.
Kotwasińska, Agnieszka (2018), 'Un/re/production of Old Age in *The Taking of Deborah Logan*', *Somatechnics* 8: 2, pp. 178–94.
Kristeva, Julia (1981), 'Women's Time', trans. Alice Jardine and Harry Blake, *Signs* 7:1, pp. 13–35.
Kume, Yu, Ayuto Kodama, Kotara Sato and Satoko Kurosawa (2016), 'Sleep/Awake Status Throughout the Night and Circadian Motor Activity Patterns in Older Nursing-home Residents with or without Dementia, and Older Community-dwelling People without Dementia', *International Psychogeriatrics* 28: 12, doi: 10.1017/S1041610216000910.

Kwok, Kian-Woon (2001), 'Chinese-Educated Intellectuals in Singapore: Marginality, Memory and Modernity', *Asian Journal of Social Science*, 29: 3, pp. 495–519.

Landes, David S. (2000), *Revolution in Time: Clocks and the Making of the Modern World* (2nd Edition), Cambridge, MA: Harvard University Press.

Latimer, Joanna (2018), 'Repelling Neoliberal World-Making? How the Ageing-Dementia Relation is Reassembling the Social', *The Sociological Review Monographs* 66: 4, pp. 832–56.

Le Goff, Jacques (1980), *Time, Work and Culture in the Middle Ages*, Chicago: University of Chicago Press.

Lee, Maggie (2015), 'Film Review: *7 Letters*', *Variety*, 30 September, http://variety.com/2015/film/reviews/film-review-7-letters-1201605259/ (accessed 9 July 2017).

Lee, Michael H. (2015), 'Globalisation and History Education in Singapore', in Joseph Zajda (ed.), *Nation-Building and History Education in a Global Culture*, London: Springer, pp. 131–53.

Lefebvre, Martin and Marc Furstenau (2002), 'Digital Editing and Montage: The Vanishing Celluloid and Beyond', *Cinémas: Journal of Film Studies* 13: 1–2, pp. 69–107.

Levy, Becca R. and Theodore Dreier (1997), 'Preservation of Temporal Skills in Alzheimer's Disease', *Perceptual and Motor Skills* 85: 1, pp. 83–96.

Liew, Kai Khiun, Natalie Pang and Brenda Chan (2014), 'Industrial Railroad to Digital Memory Routes: Remembering the Last Railway in Singapore', *Media, Culture and Society* 36: 6, pp. 761–75.

Lim, Bliss Cua (2009), *Translating Time: Cinema, the Fantastic, and Temporal Critique*, Durham, NC: Duke University Press.

Lim, Edna (2017), 'Singapore Cinema: Connecting the Golden Age and the Revival', in Liew Kai Khiun and Stephen Teo (eds), *Singapore Cinema: New Perspectives*, Abingdon: Routledge, pp. 20–36.

Loh, Kah Seng and Kenneth Paul Tan (2017), 'Convergence and Slippage between Film and History: Reviewing *Invisible City*, *Zahari's 17 Years* and *Sandcastle*', in Liew Kai Khiun and Stephen Teo (eds), *Singapore Cinema: New Perspectives*, Abingdon: Routledge, pp. 37–50.

Loh, Kah Seng, Edgar Liao, Cheng Tju Lim and Guo-Quan Seng (2012), *The University Socialist Club and the Contest for Malaya: Tangled Strands of Modernity*, Amsterdam: Amsterdam University Press.

Love, Heather (2007), *Feeling Backward: Loss, and the Politics of Queer History*, London: Harvard University Press.

Lucas, Raymond (2008), 'Taking a Line for a Walk: Walking as an Aesthetic Practice', in Tim Ingold and Jo Lee Vergurst (eds), *Ways of Walking: Ethnography and Practice on Foot*, Farnham: Ashgate, pp. 169–84.

Lykidis, Alex (2021), *Art Cinema and Neoliberalism*, Cham: Palgrave Macmillan.

Mackenzie, Catriona (2008), 'Introduction: Practical identity and Narrative Agency', in Catriona Mackenzie and Kim Atkins (eds), *Practical Identity and Narrative Agency*, London: Routledge, pp. 1–28.

Marks, Laura U. (2002), *Touch: Sensuous Theory and Multisensory Media*, London: University of Minnesota Press.

Martin-Jones, David (2006), *Deleuze, Cinema and National Identity: Narrative Time in National Contexts*, Edinburgh: Edinburgh University Press.

Martin-Jones, David (2011), *Deleuze and World Cinema*, London: Continuum.
Martin-Jones, David (2018), *Cinema Against Doublethink: Ethical Encounters with the Lost Pasts of World History*, Abingdon: Routledge.
Matthews, Eric (2006), 'Dementia and the Identity of the Person', in Julian Hughes, Stephen Louw and Steven R. Sabat (eds), *Dementia: Mind, Meaning, and the Person*, Oxford: Oxford University Press, pp. 163–77.
Mc Parland, Patricia, Fiona Kelly and Anthea Innes (2017), 'Dichotomising Dementia: Is There Another Way?', *Sociology of Health and Illness* 39: 2, pp. 258–69.
McBean, Sam (2016), *Feminism's Queer Temporalities*, Abingdon: Routledge.
McFadden, Susan H. and Robert C. Atchley (eds) (2001), *Aging and the Meaning of Time: A Multidisciplinary Exploration*, New York: Springer Publishing Company.
McKechnie, Claire Charlotte (2014), 'Anxieties of Communication: The Limits of Narrative in the Medical Humanities', *Medical Humanities* 40, pp. 119–24.
McMahon, Laura (2019), *Animal Worlds: Film, Philosophy and Time*, Edinburgh: Edinburgh University Press.
Medina, Raquel (2018), *Cinematic Representations of Alzheimer's Disease*, London: Palgrave Macmillan.
Medina, Raquel (2022), 'Writing the Past to Fight Alzheimer's Disease: Masculinity, Temporality, and Agency in *Memoir of a Murderer*', in Heike Hartung, Rüdiger Kunow and Matthew Sweney (eds), *Ageing Masculinities, Alzheimer's and Dementia Narratives*, London: Bloomsbury, pp. 125–41.
Menkman, Rosa (2011), *The Glitch Moment(um)*, Amsterdam: Institute of Network Cultures.
Mesenas, Clement (2013), *Dissident Voices: Personalities in Singapore's Political History*, Singapore: Marshall Cavendish.
Mikesell, Lisa (2010), 'Repetitional Responses in Frontotemporal Dementia Discourse: Asserting Agency or Demonstrating Confusion?', *Discourse Studies* 12: 4, pp. 465–500.
Millet, Raphaël (2006), *Singapore Cinema*, Singapore: Editions Didier Millet.
Miron, Anca M., Susan H. McFadden, Amanda S. Nazario and Jennifer Buelow (2017), 'Perspective Taking, Empathic Concern, and Perceived Humanness of People with Dementia', *Educational Gerontology* 43: 9, pp. 468–79.
Morton, Timothy (2010), *The Ecological Thought*, London: Harvard University Press.
Mroz, Matilda (2012), *Temporality and Film Analysis*, Edinburgh: Edinburgh University Press.
Mulvey, Laura (2006), *Death 24x a Second: Stillness and the Moving Image*, London: Reaktion Books.
Næss, Arne (1973), 'The Shallow and the Deep, Long-Range Ecology Movement. A Summary', *Inquiry* 16: 1– 4, pp. 95–100.
Nanni, Giordano (2012), *The Colonisation of Time: Ritual, Routine and Resistance in the British Empire*, Manchester: Manchester University Press.
Napper, Lawrence (2017), *Silent Cinema: Before the Pictures Got Small*, London: Wallflower.
Naremore, James (2000), 'Introduction: Film and the Reign of Adaptation', in James Naremore (ed.), *Film Adaptation*, London: The Athlone Press, pp. 1–16.
Nolan, Mike, Tony Ryan, Pam Enderby and David Reid (2002), 'Towards a More Inclusive Vision of Dementia Care Practice and Research', *Dementia* 1: 2, pp. 193–211.

Nygård, Louise and Lena Borell (1998), 'A Life-World of Altering Meaning: Expressions of the Illness Experience of Dementia in Everyday Life over 3 Years', *OTJR: Occupation, Participation and Health* 18: 2, pp. 109–36.

Nygård, Louise, and Marianne Johansson (2000), 'The Experience and Management of Temporality in Five Cases of Dementia', *Scandinavian Journal of Occupational Therapy* 8: 2, pp. 85–95.

Ogle, Vanessa (2015), *The Global Transformation of Time 1870–1950*, London: Harvard University Press.

Omar, Maktoba, Nathalia C. Tjandra and John Ensor (2014), 'Retailing to the "Grey Pound": Understanding the Food Shopping Habits and Preferences of Consumers over 50 in Scotland', *Journal of Retailing and Consumer Services* 21, pp. 753–63.

Orona, Celia J. (1990), 'Temporality and Identity Loss Due to Alzheimer's Disease', *Social Science and Medicine* 30: 11, pp. 1247–1256.

Örulv, Linda and Lar-Christer Hydén (2006), 'Confabulation: Sense-Making, Self-Making and World-Making in Dementia', *Discourse Studies* 8: 5, pp. 647–73.

Paradis, Michel (2008), 'Bilingualism and Neuropsychiatric Disorders', *Journal of Neurolinguistics* 21, pp. 199–230.

Paszkiewicz, Katarzyna (2020), 'Cinema and Environment: The Arts of Noticing in the Anthropocene', *Res Rhetorica* 8: 2, pp. 2–21.

Peirce, Charles Sanders (1998), *The Essential Peirce: Selected Philosophical Writings (1893–1913)*, Bloomington: Indiana University Press.

Phelan, Peggy (2003), *Unmarked: The Politics of Performance*, London: Routledge.

Pisters, Patricia (2003), *The Matrix of Visual Culture: Working with Deleuze in Film Theory*, Stanford: Stanford University Press.

Pisters, Patricia (2012), *The Neuro-Image: A Deleuzian Filmphilosophy of Digital Screen Culture*, Stanford: Stanford University Press.

Pisters, Patricia (2015), 'Temporal Explorations in Cosmic Consciousness: Intra-Agential Entanglements and the Neuro-Image', *Cultural Studies Review* 21: 2, pp. 120–44.

Pitches, Jonathan (2020), *Performing Mountains*, London: Palgrave Macmillan.

Powell, Anna (2007), *Deleuze, Altered States and Film*, Edinburgh: Edinburgh University Press.

Prasad, M. Madhava (1998), *Ideology of the Hindi Film: A Historical Construction*, Delhi: Oxford University Press.

Prince, Stephen (2004), 'Introduction: The Dark Genre and Its Paradoxes', in Stephen Prince (ed.), *The Horror Film*, London: Rutgers University Press, pp. 1–11.

Rajadhyaksha, Ashish (2013), 'Why Film Narratives Exist', *Inter-Asia Cultural Studies* 14: 1, pp. 62–75.

Rancière, Jacques (2004), *The Politics of Aesthetics: The Distribution of the Sensible*, trans. Gabriel Rockhill, London: Continuum.

Ratcliffe, Matthew (2012), 'Phenomenology as a Form of Empathy', *Inquiry* 55: 5, pp. 473–95.

Ratcliffe, Matthew (2014), 'The Phenomenology of Depression and the Nature of Empathy', *Medicine, Health Care and Philosophy* 17, pp. 269–80.

Ratcliffe, Matthew (2015), *Experiences of Depression: A Study in Phenomenology*, Oxford: Oxford University Press.

Read, Ala (1993), *Theatre and Everyday Life: An Ethics of Performance*, London: Routledge.

Ricœur, Paul (1984), *Time and Narrative: Volume 1*, trans. Kathleen McLaughlin and David Pellauer, London: University of Chicago Press.
Rodowick, D.N. (1997), *Gilles Deleuze's Time Machine*, Durham, NC: Duke University Press.
Rosen, Philip (2001), *Change Mummified: Cinema, Historicity, Theory*, Minneapolis: University of Minnesota Press.
Rushton, Richard (2011), *The Reality of Film: Theories of Filmic Reality*, Manchester: Manchester University Press.
Sabat, Steven R. (2001), *The Experience of Alzheimer's Disease: Life Through a Tangled Veil*, Oxford: Blackwell Publishers.
Sako, Katsura and Sarah Falcus (2015), 'Dementia, Care and Time in Post-War Japan: *The Twilight Years, Memories of Tomorrow* and *Pecoross' Mother and Her Days*', *Feminist Review* 111, pp. 88–108.
Sandberg, Linn J. and Barbara L. Marshall (2017), 'Queering Aging Futures', *Societies* 7: 21, pp. 1–11.
Sawchuk, Kim (2019), 'Afterword. Relational Entanglements: Ageing, Materialities and Embodiments', *Ageing in Everyday Life: Materialities and Embodiments*, Bristol: Policy Press, pp. 215–24.
Sayad, Cecilia (2016), 'Found-Footage Horror and the Frame's Undoing', *Cinema Journal* 55: 2, pp. 43–66.
Schafer, R. Murray (1994), *The Soundscape: Our Sonic Environment and the Turning of the World*, Rochester, VT: Destiny Books.
Schechner, Richard (1985), *Between Theater and Anthropology*, Philadelphia: University of Pennsylvania Press.
Schechner, Richard (2003), *Performance Theory*, London: Routledge.
Schechner, Richard (2015), *Performed Imaginaries*, London: Routledge.
Schneider, Rebecca (2011), *Performing Remains: Art and War in Times of Theatrical Reenactment*, London: Routledge.
Schnider, Armin (2003), 'Spontaneous Confabulation and the Adaptation of Thought to Ongoing Reality', *Nature Reviews Neuroscience* 4, pp. 662–71.
Schoneveld, Erin (2019), 'Naomi Kawase's "Cinema of Place"', *Arts* 8: 43, pp. 1–18. DOI: 10.3390/arts8020043.
Segal, Lynne (2014), *Out of Time: The Pleasures and Perils of Ageing*, London: Verso.
Segers, Kurt (2007), 'Degenerative Dementias and Their Medical Care in the Movies', *Alzheimer Disease and Associated Disorders: An International Journal* 21: 1, pp. 55–9.
Shakespeare, Tom, Hannah Zeilig and Peter Mittler (2019), 'Rights in Mind: Thinking Differently About Dementia and Disability', *Dementia* 18: 3, pp. 1075–1088.
Sharma, Sarah (2014), *In the Meantime: Temporality and Cultural Politics*, London: Duke University Press.
Shary, Timothy and Nancy McVittie (2016), *Fade to Gray: Aging in American Cinema*, Austin, TX: University of Texas Press.
Shulman, Kenneth I. (2000), 'Clock-Drawing: Is it the Ideal Cognitive Screening Test?', *International Journal of Geriatric Psychiatry* 15, pp. 548–61.
Singh, Bilveer (2015), *Quest for Political Power: Communist Subversion and Militancy in Singapore*, Singapore: Marshall Cavendish.
Slote, Michael (2007), *The Ethics of Care and Empathy*, Abingdon: Routledge.

Sobchack, Vivian (2004), *Carnal Thoughts: Embodiment and Moving Image Culture*, London: University of California Press.
Soderman, Braxton (2007), 'The Index and the Algorithm', *differences: A Journal of Feminist Cultural Studies* 18: 1, pp. 154–86.
Spector, Stanely (1956), 'Students and Politics in Singapore', *Far Eastern Survey* 25: 5, pp. 65–73.
Stacey, Jackie (1994), *Star-Gazing: Hollywood Cinema and Female Spectatorship*, London: Routledge.
Stilwell, Robyn J. (2007), 'The Fantastical Gap between Diegetic and Nondiegetic', in Daniel Goldmark, Lawrence Kramer and Richard Leppert (eds), *Beyond the Soundtrack: Representing Music in Cinema*, London: University of California Press, pp. 184–202.
Stockton, Kathryn Bond (2009), *The Queer Child: Or Growing Sideways in the Twentieth Century*, Durham, NC: Duke University Press.
Stockwell, A. J. (2009), '"The Crucible of the Malayan Nation": The University and the Making of a New Malaya, 1938–62', *Modern Asian Studies* 43: 5, pp. 1149–1187.
Stoler, Ann Laura (2016), *Duress: Imperial Durabilities in Our Times*, Durham, NC: Duke University Press.
Striff, Erin (2003), *Performance Studies*, Basingstoke: Palgrave Macmillan.
Swinnen, Aagje (2013), 'Dementia in Documentary Film: *Mum* by Adelheid Roosen', *The Gerontologist* 53: 1, pp. 113–22.
Tan, Kenneth Paul (2016), 'Choosing What to Remember in Neoliberal Singapore: The Singapore Story, State Censorship and State-Sponsored Nostalgia', *Asian Studies Review* 40: 2, pp. 231–49.
Taylor-Jones, Kate E. (2013), *Rising Sun, Divided Land: Japanese and South Korean Filmmakers*, London: Wallflower Press.
Thompson, E. P. (1967), 'Time, Work Discipline and Industrial Capitalism', *Past and Present* 38, pp. 56–97.
Thompson, James (2020a), 'Towards an Aesthetics of Care', in Amanda Stuart Fisher and James Thompson (eds), *Performing Care: New Perspectives on Socially Engaged Performance*, Manchester: Manchester University Press, pp. 36–48.
Thompson, James (2020b), 'Performing the "Aesthetic of Care"', in Amanda Stuart Fisher and James Thompson (eds), *Performing Care: New Perspectives on Socially Engaged Performance*, Manchester: Manchester University Press, pp. 215–29.
Thum, Ping Tjin (2012), 'The Limitations of Monolingual History', in Nicholas Tarling (ed.), *Studying Singapore's Past: C.M. Turnbull and the History of Modern Singapore*, Singapore: NUS Press, pp. 1–18.
Thum, Ping Tjin (2017), 'Justifying Colonial Rule in Post-Colonial Singapore: The Myths of Vulnerability, Development, and Meritocracy', in Loh Kah Seng, Thum Ping Tjin and Jack Meng-Tat Chia (eds), *Living with Myths in Singapore*, Singpaore: Ethos Books, pp. 15–28.
Todorov, Tzvetan (1975), *The Fantastic: A Structural Approach to a Literary Genre*, trans. Richard Howard, Ithaca, NY: Cornell University Press.
Topo, Päivi, Kristiina Saarikalle, Emer Begley, Suzanne Cahill, Torhild Holthe and Jurate Macijauskiene (2007), '"I Don't Know about the Past or the Future, But Today It's Friday": Evaluation of a Time Aid for People with Dementia', *Technology and Disability* 19: 2–3, pp. 121–31.

Tsing, Anna Lowenhaupt (2015), *The Mushroom at the End of the World: On the Possibility of Life in Capitalist Ruins*, Princeton, NJ: Princeton University Press.
Turim, Maureen (1989), *Flashbacks in Film: Memory and History*, London: Routledge.
Turnbull, C. M. (2016), *A History of Modern Singapore 1819–2005*, Singapore: NUS Press.
Tweedie, James (2013), *The Age of New Waves: Art Cinema and the Staging of Globalization*, Oxford: Oxford University Press.
Twigg, Julia and Wendy Martin (2015a), 'The Challenges of Cultural Gerontology', *The Gerontologist* 55: 3, pp. 353–9.
Twigg, Julia and Wendy Martin (2015b), 'The Field of Cultural Gerontology: An Introduction', in Julia Twigg and Wendy Martin (eds), *The Routledge Handbook to Cultural Gerontology*, Abingdon: Routledge, pp. 1–15.
Uhde, Jan and Yvonne Ng Uhde (2010), *Latent Images: Film in Singapore* (2nd Edition), Singapore: Ridge Books.
United Nations, Department of Economic and Social Affairs, Population Division (2015), *World Population Ageing 2015*, http://www.un.org/en/development/desa/population/publications/pdf/ageing/WPA2015_Report.pdf (accessed 23 October 2017).
Uprichard, Emma (2008), 'Children as "Being and Becomings": Children, Childhood and Temporality', *Children and Society* 22, pp. 303–13.
Valera, Luca (2018), 'From Spontaneous Experience to the Cosmos: Arne Næss's Phenomenology', *Problemos* 93, pp. 142–53.
Van Gorp, Baldwin and Tom Vercruysse (2012), 'Frames and Counter-Frames Giving Meaning to Dementia: A Framing Analysis of Media Content', *Social Sciences and Medicine* 74: 8, pp. 1274–1281.
Van Someren, Eus J. W. et al. (1996), 'Circadian Rest – Activity Rhythm Disturbances in Alzheimer's Disease', *Biological Psychiatry* 40: 4, pp. 259–70.
Wearing, Sadie (2013), 'Dementia and the Biopolitics of the Biopic: From *Iris* to *The Iron Lady*', *Dementia* 12: 3, pp. 315–25.
Wee, CJ W-L (1999), 'The Vanquished: Lim Chin Siong and a Progressivist National Narrative', in Lam Peng Er and Kevin YL Tan (eds), *Lee's Lieutenants: Singapore's Old Guard*, St Leonards, NSW: Allen & Unwin, pp. 169–90.
White, Kate (2018), 'An Attachment Approach to Understanding and Living Well with Dementia', in Kate White, Angela Cotter and Hazel Leventhal (eds), *Dementia: An Attachment Approach*, London: Routledge, pp. 13–42.
Whitehead, Anne (2017), *Medicine and Empathy in Contemporary British Fiction: An Intervention in Medical Humanities*, Edinburgh: Edinburgh University Press.
Wiegman, Robyn (2014), 'The Times We're In: Queer Feminist Criticism and the Reparative "Turn"', *Feminist Theory* 15: 1, pp. 4–25.
Wiegman, Robyn and Elizabeth A. Wilson (2015), 'Introduction: Antinormativity's Queer Conventions', *differences: A Journal of Feminist Cultural Studies* 26: 1, pp. 1–25.
Wiersma, Elaine C. (2008), 'The Experiences of Place: Veterans with Dementia Making Meaning of Their Environments', *Health and Place* 14, pp. 779–94.
Woods, Angela (2011), 'The Limits of Narrative: Provocations for the Medical Humanities', *Medical Humanities* 37, pp. 73–8.
Woodspring, Naomi (2016), *Baby Boomers: Time and Ageing Bodies*, Bristol: Policy Press.
Woodward, Kathleen (1991), *Aging and its Discontents: Freud and Other Fictions*, Bloomington: Indiana University Press.

Woodward, Kathleen (1999), 'Statistical Panic', *differences: A Journal of Feminist Cultural Studies*, 11: 2, pp. 177–203.

Woodward, Kathleen (2016), 'Rereading Simone de Beauvoir's *The Coming of Age*', *Age, Culture, Humanities: An Interdisciplinary Journal* 3, https://ageculturehumanities.org/WP/rereading-simone-de-beauvoirs-the-coming-of-age/ (accessed 19 August 2021).

Woodward, Sophie and Kath Woodward (2019), *Birth and Death: Experience, Ethics, Politics*, London: Routledge.

World Health Organization (2019), 'Dementia', 14 May, https://www.who.int/news-room/fact-sheets/detail/dementia (accessed 17 September 2019).

Yacowar, Maurice (2018), 'Happy End', *maurice yacowar*, 25 January, http://yacowar.blogspot.com/2018/01/happy-end.html (accessed 4 January 2022).

Yew, Leong (2010), 'Managing Plurality: The Politics of the Periphery in Early Cold War Singapore', *International Journal of Asian Studies* 7: 2, pp. 159–77.

Yoshimoto, Mitsuhiro (2006), 'National/International/Transnational: The Concept of Trans-Asian Cinema and the Cultural Politics of Film Criticism', in Valentina Vitali and Paul Willemen (eds), *Theorising National Cinema*, London: BFI Publishing, pp. 254–61.

Zeilig, Hannah (2013), 'Dementia as a Cultural Metaphor', *The Gerontologist* 54: 2, pp. 258–67.

Zendehbad, Azadeh (2015), 'Circadian Rhythm Alteration in Dementia: Implications for Non-Pharmacological Therapies', *Alzheimer's and Dementia* 11: 7, p. 607.

Zimmermann, Martina (2020), *The Diseased Brain and the Failing Mind: Dementia in Science, Medicine and Literature of the Long Twentieth Century*, London: Bloomsbury Academic.

Filmography

2001: A Space Odyssey (Stanley Kubrick, 1968, USA)
3688 (Royston Tan, 2015, Singapore)
After Life (Hirokazu Koreeda, 1998, Japan)
Alzheimer's Case, The (Erik Van Looy, 2003, Belgium)
Amour (Michael Haneke, 2012, Austria/France/Germany)
Ashes (Mat Whitecross, 2012, UK)
Beautiful Memories (Zabou Breitman, 2001, France)
Best Exotic Marigold Hotel, The (John Madden, 2011, UK/USA/UAE)
Blade Runner 2049 (Denis Villeneuve, 2017, USA/UK/Hungary/Canada/Spain)
Bodyguard, The (Sammo Hung, 2010, Hong Kong/China)
Breathless (Jean-Luc Godard, 1960, France)
Coco (Lee Unkrich, 2017, USA)
Ethel and Ernest (Roger Mainwood, 2016, UK)
Evim Sensin (Özcan Deniz, 2012, Turkey)
Expendables, The (Sylvester Stallone, 2010, USA/Bulgaria)
Expendables 2, The (Simon West, 2012, USA/Germany)
Expendables 3, The (Patrick Hughes, 2014, USA/France/Bulgaria/Germany)
Gray Sunset (Shunya Itô, 1985, Japan)
Happiness (Andy Lo, 2016, Hong Kong)
Happy End (Michael Haneke, 2017, France/Austria/Germany)
Howl's Moving Castle (Hayao Miyazaki, 2004, Japan)
Illusionist, The (Sylvain Chomet, 2010, France/UK)
Iris (Richard Eyre, 2001, UK/USA)
King's Speech, The (Tom Hooper, 2010, UK/USA/Australia)
Lady in the Van, The (Nicholas Hynter, 2015, UK)
Logan (James Mangold, 2017, USA)
Magallenes (Salvador del Solar, 2015, Peru/Argentina/Spain)
Marjorie Prime (Michael Almereyda, 2017, USA)

Memoir of a Murderer (Won Shin-yeon, 2017, South Korea)
Memories of Tomorrow (Yukihiko Tsutsumi, 2006, Japan)
Millennium Actress (Satoshi Kon, 2001, Japan)
Mimic, The (Huh Jung, 2017, South Korea)
Moment to Remember, A (John H. Lee, 2004, South Korea)
Mourning Forest, The (Naomi Kawase, 2007, Japan)
My Dog Tulip (Paul Fierlinger, 2009, USA)
Nebraska (Alexander Payne, 2013, USA)
Olive Tree, The (Icíar Bollaín, 2016, Spain/Germany)
On Golden Pond (Mark Rydell, 1981, UK/USA)
Out of the Past (Jacques Tourneur, 1947, USA)
Pandora's Box (Yeşim Ustaoğlu, 2008, Turkey)
Paranormal Activity (Oren Peli, 2007, USA)
Parting (Boo Junfeng, 2015, Singapore)
Passage of Life (Diego Corsini, 2015, Argentina/Spain)
Pecoross' Mother and Her Days (Azuma Morisaki, 2013, Japan)
Philomena (Stephen Frears, 2013, UK/USA/France)
Poetry (Lee Chang-dong, 2010, South Korea)
Quartet (Dustin Hoffman, 2012, UK)
Red (Robert Schwentke, 2010, USA)
Red 2 (Dean Parisot, 2013, USA/France/Canada)
Relic (Natalie Erika James, 2020, Australia/USA)
Ringu (Hideo Nakata, 1998, Japan)
Robot and Frank (Jake Schreier, 2012, USA)
Sandcastle (Boo Junfeng, 2010, Singapore)
Savages, The (Tamara Jenkins, 2007, USA)
Separation, A (Asghar Farhadi, 2011, Iran/France)
Shed Skin Papa (Roy Szeto, 2016, Hong Kong)
Solaris (Andrei Tarkovsky, 1972, Soviet Union)
Star Wars Episode VII: The Force Awakens (J. J. Abrams, 2015, USA)
Still Alice (Richard Glatzer and Wash Westmoreland, 2014, USA/UK/France)
Still Mine (Michael McGowan, 2012, Canada)
Summer Snow (Ann Hui, 1995, Hong Kong)
Taking of Deborah Logan, The (Adam Robitel, 2014, USA)
Thanmathra (Blessy, 2005, India)
Travelling Companion (Peter Del Monte, 1996, Italy)
Triplets of Belleville, The (Sylvain Chomet, 2003, France/Belgium/Canada/UK/Latvia/USA)
Twilight Gangsters (Kang Hyo-Jin, 2010, South Korea)

U Me Aur Hum (Ajay Devgan, 2008, India)
Up (Pete Docter, 2009, USA)
Visit, The (M. Night Shyamalan, 2015, USA)
Week-end (Jean-Luc Godard, 1967, France)
Wrinkles (Ignacio Ferreras, 2011, Spain)

Index

Note: *f* indicates a figure

actual, the, 77, 78, 81, 91, 107
aesthetics, 151
After Life (Koreeda, Hirokazu), 6
ageing, 7, 65, 86, 90, 93–4, 104, 150–1
   bad, 94
   as cultural process, 35
   fear of, 106
   films about, 6–8
   Shyamalan, M. Night, 106
   time, 8–9
   trauma of, 9
   U Me Aur Hum, 34–5
agency, 20, 21–7, 29, 63–4
Al-Saji, Alia, 12, 132
   hesitation, 140, 143–4
   past/present, 142–3
Altamirano, Marco, 87–8, 89, 91
Alzheimer Case, The (Van Looy, Erik), 6
Alzheimer's disease, 10
   agency, 22
   causes, 83–4
Amour (Haneke, Michael), 6, 98–100
amyloid cascade hypothesis, 83–4
Angels in America (Kushner, Tony), 146, 147
anti-normativity/normativity, 35–40
aphasia, 132
apparatus theory, 123
Aquilina, Carmelo, 23
Ashes (Whitecross, Mat), 6
aswang narratives, 114
audiences, 75–6

Baars, Jan, 8
Baby Boomers, 6, 7, 8
Baez, Sandra, 72, 73
Bazin, André, 121
Beautiful Memories (Breitman, Zabou), 10
becoming and change *see* change and becoming
Benjamin, Walter, 134–5
Bergson, Henri, 27–9, 52, 53, 79
Berlant, Lauren, 151
Best Exotic Marigold Hotel, The (Madden, John), 7
Bhabha, Homi, 130
Biggs, Simon, 50–1, 52
biological clock, the, 8
Birth, Kevin K., 2
Bitenc, Rebecca A., 67–9
Blade Runner 2049 (Villeneuve, Denis), 6
body, the, 8
Bodyguard, The (Hung, Sammo), 6
Boyle, Geraldine, 22–3
Breathless (Godard, Jean-Luc), 133
Brockmeier, Jens, 49–50
Bruno, Guliana, 134
Burke, Lucy, 94
Butler, Judith, 24

capitalism, 93–5, 100, 127
care, 66, 67, 84, 99–100
   aesthetics of, 83
   Pandora's Box, 101
CDT (Clock Drawing Test), 1, 2

censorship, 128, 132, 140
change and becoming, 50, 73, 77, 78, 131, 147
    Deleuze, Gilles, 59, 77
    temporal identification, 36, 44
    U Me Aur Hum, 25–7, 33, 36–7
China, 136
Chivers, Sally, 7–8, 99
    Silvering Screen, The, 10
chrononormativity, 31
cinema, 3, 112–13
    analysis, 12–13
    apparatus theory, 123
    Bazin, André, 121
    as change mummified, 121
    clock/non-clock time, 4
    Deleuze, Gilles, 11
    digital technology, 121–6
    found footage horror, 118–20
    frame rates, 4
    horror, 105–6, 107–9, 116–17, 118–20
    material degradation, 124–6
    reality, 113
    representational 10–11
    Rosen, Philip, 121
    Singapore, 128
    sound, 4, 119–20
    temporality, 5
    time, 121
    see also films about dementia
cinema of attractions, 3
Cinematic Representations of Alzheimer's Disease (Medina, Raquel), 10
Clare, Stephanie, 24–5
Clock Drawing Test (CDT), 1, 2
clock time, 2–3, 8, 88, 89
    cinema, 4
clocks, 2–3, 87–8
    as metaphor, 8
close-ups, 68
Coco (Unkrich, Lee), 7
coenaesthesia, 76
coexistence, 91
Cohen-Shalev, Amir, 87, 89, 101–3
colonialism, 130
confabulation 44–52, 59–61, 70

consumption, 93
Coyle, Rebecca, 119–20
crip time, 34
cultural aphasia, 132
curative time, 32

death, 65–6, 94
    Amour, 99
    Happy End, 95, 97–8
    Pandora's, Box, 102
DeFalco, Amelia, 8–9, 51–2
Deleuze, Gilles, 11, 12, 44, 91
    demented time, 58, 140
    difference, 77, 79
    Idea, 77
    identity, 77–8
    movement-images, 131
    past-present paradoxes, 53
    philosophy of difference, 12, 58–9
    real, the, 77–8
    recollection-image, 139
    rhizomatic worldviews, 117–18
    time, syntheses of, 52–3, 58
    time-images, 131
    virtual object, the, 107
demented time, 58–64, 140
dementia, 5, 83–4, 150
    agency, 20, 22–3, 63–4
    capitalism, 93–4
    care, 67
    Clock Drawing Test (CDT), 1, 2
    clocks, 2
    death, 94, 95, 99, 102
    as disability, 40n
    early onset, 9–10
    empathy, 67, 72
    fear of, 106, 150–1
    horror, 105–6, 107–9
    language, 111, 145
    linear, homogeneous time, 2, 5
    memory, 50–1, 146–7
    othering, 13, 51, 66, 67, 72
    real, the, 78
    relationality, 11–12
    sundown syndrome, 106, 109
    temporal identification, 78–9

dementia (*cont.*)
   temporality, 5, 9, 14
   time, performing, 18–20, 147, 151
   wandering, 129, 135–6, 144
   see also Alzheimer's disease; films about dementia
Descartes, René, 88–9, 91
deterritorialisation, 131, 132, 136, 138
difference, 12, 58–9, 61, 63, 77, *Happiness*, 82–3
   in itself, 73, 77, 78, 79, 81, 82, 84
   rhizomatic worldviews, 118
digital surround sound, 119–20
digital technology, 121–6
Doane, Mary Ann, 69, 107, 122–3, 124, 126
double-time, 130–1, 136
duration, 27–8, 79

ecology, 90–1, 92, 93, 97
editing, 133
Eleftheriotis, Dimitris, 69
empathy, 66, 72
   close-ups, 68
   difference in itself, 73, 77, 78, 79, 81, 82, 84
   entangled worlds, 72, 73, 75, 76–7, 81
   as erasing differences, 67–71
   perspective-taking model, 72, 80
   see also radical empathy
enchantment, 103–4
entangled worlds, 72, 73, 75, 76–7, 81
Ethel and Ernest (Mainwood, Roger), 7
euthanasia, 96, 99, 100
Evim Sensin (Deniz, Özcan), 10
Expendables, The franchise (Stallone, Sylvester/West, Simon/Hughes, Patrick), 6

Fade to Gray (Shary, Timothy and McVittie, Nancy), 10
Falcus, Sarah, 67
family, 145–50, 151
fantastic, the, 113–14, 115
film studies, 68–9, 126–7
film watching, 76

films about dementia, 5–10, 145, 150
   agency, 20, 25
   ecology, 93
   enchantment, 103–4
   hesitation, 127
   linear/non-linear time, 20
   radical empathy, 69, 83, 84
   temporal change, 25
   temporal identification, 20, 39–40
flânerie, 134–6
flashbacks, 56–8, 141; *see also* prolepsis
Fletcher, James R., 83–4
Fong, Sylvia S., 22
forgetting, 130
found footage, 118–20
Freeman, Elizabeth, 31
Freeman, Martin, 72–3
Freud, Sigmund, 112
Furstenau, Marc, 123

gender performance, 30–1, 32
Gilleard, Christopher and Higgs, Paul, 7
glitches, 126
GMT (Greenwich Mean Time), 3
grandparents, 145–50, 151
Gray Sunset (Itô, Shunya), 6
Greenwich Mean Time (GMT), 3
Guattari, Félix, 117–18
Gullette, Margaret Morganroth, 35, 94, 99
Gunning, Tom, 3

habit, 52
hallucination, 44–52, 59–61, 62, 70
Haneke, Michael, 98–9
   Amour, 6, 98–9
Happiness (Lo, Andy), 65, 67, 74–5*f*, 76, 79, 81–3
Happy End (Haneke, Michael), 6, 85–6, 91–3, 95–7, 100, 101*f*
Haraway, Donna J., 91
Herrup, Karl
   How Not to Study a Disease, 83
hesitation, 12, 113, 115, 116–17, 120, 126–7
   Al-Saji, Alia, 140, 143–4
   Parting 139–40
   wandering, 144

history, 128, 129
  Singapore, 128, 129–44
horror, 105–6, 107–9, 116–17
  aswang narratives, 114
  found footage, 118–20
  sound, 119–20
  see also uncanny, the
How Not to Study a Disease (Herrup, Karl), 83
Howl's Moving Castle (Miyazaki, Hayao), 7
Hughes, Julian C., 23
Hydén, Lar-Christer, 47

Idea, 77
identification
  agency, 63–4
  see also temporal identification
identity, 51, 77–8
  national, 130–1
Illusionist, The (Chomet, Sylvain), 7
index, the, 106–7, 111, 112–13, 117, 118
  digital technology, 121–6
Industrial Revolution, the, 3
intersectionality, 32
Iris (Eyre, Richard), 6

Jentsch, Wilhelm, 112

Kafer, Alison, 32, 34
Kaplan, E. Ann, 9
Karatsu, Rie, 80
Kaufman, Sharon R., 94
Kawase, Naomi
  empathy, 66
  Mourning Forest, The, 65–6
Keady, John David, 12
Keen, Suzanne, 67, 72
King's Speech, The (Hooper, Tom), 7
Kitwood, Tom, 11–12
Kotwasińska, Agnieszka, 110
Kwok Kian-Woon, 136

Lady in the Van, The, (Hytner, Nicholas), 7
language, 111, 132, 145–6, 148
  Singapore, 136, 141

Latimer, Joanna, 93–4
Lee Kuan Yew, 136–7
Lefebvre, Martin, 123
Lim, Bliss Cua, 114–16
Lim Chin Siong, 136, 137
Logan (Mangold, James), 6

McKechnie, Claire Charlotte, 48–9
Mackenzie, Catriona, 63
Magallanes (del Solar, Salvador), 6
Malaysia, 137, 139
Marcus, Esther-Lee, 87, 89, 101–3
Marjorie Prime (Almereyda, Michael), 6
Marks, Laura U., 122
Martin-Jones, David, 126–7, 131
marvellous, the, 113–14
material degradation, 124–6
MDA (Media Development Authority), 129
Media Development Authority (MDA), 129
Medina, Raquel, 87, 89, 101–3
  Cinematic Representations of Alzheimer's Disease, 10
Memoir of a Murderer (Won Shin-yeon), 42–4, 50, 52
  confabulation/hallucination, 47–8, 49f, 59–61
  demented time, 59–62
  time, syntheses of, 53–8
Memories of Tomorrow (Tsutsumi, Yukihiko), 10, 42, 43–4, 52
  confabulation/hallucination, 45–7, 62
  demented time, 61–3
memory, 50–1, 53, 146–7
men, 31
Menkman, Rosa, 126
Mikesell, Lisa, 19
Millennium Actress (Kon, Satoshi), 7
Mimic, The (Huh Jung), 6, 45
Moment to Remember, A (Lee, John H.), 10, 18–19, 20
  normativity/anti-normativity, 39
  curative time, 32
  gender performance, 30–1
  temporality, 21–2, 23

Moment to Remember, A (Lee, John H.) (*cont.*)
   time, performance of, 318–19, 20, 29–32, 37–40f
   agency, 23, 29
Morton, Timothy, 90–1
Mourning Forest, The (Kawase, Naomi), 65–6, 67, 69–71, 79–81
movement-image narratives, 52–3, 131
Mulvey, Laura, 112–13
My Dog Tulip (Fierlinger, Paul), 7

narratives, 42–4, 48–9, 64
   aswang, 114
   confabulation/hallucination 44–52
   deterritorialisation, 131, 132
   empathy, 67–8
   movement-image, 52–3, 131
   reterritorialisation, 131, 132
   time-image, 53, 131
   time, syntheses of, 52–8
nation, the 129–31
nature, 87–91, 97
Nebraska (Payne, Alexander), 6
neoliberalism, 100
normativity/anti-normativity, 35–40

Olive Tree, The (Bollaín, Icíar), 6
On Golden Pond (Rydell, Mark), 6
Operation Cold Store, 137
Örulv, Linda, 47
othering, 5, 13, 51, 66, 67, 72

Pandora's Box (Ustaoğlu, Yeşim), 6, 85–7, 89–90, 100–3
Paranormal Activity (Peli, Oren), 105
Parting (Boo Junfeng), 128–9, 133–4f
   final sequence, 142–3
   flashbacks, 141
   hesitation, 139–40
   language, 141
   past/present, 142–3
   wandering 133–4, 136, 138, 139–40, 142, 143
Passage of Life (Corsini, Diego), 6
past, the, 126–7
past/present, 108–12, 142–3
past-present paradoxes, 53
Pecoross' Mother and Her Days (Morisaki, Azuma), 6
Peirce, Charles Sanders, 106, 123
performance, 4
   gender, 30–1, 32
   on-screen and off-screen, 76, 79
   see also temporal performance
Philippines, the, 114
Philomena (Frears, Stephen), 7
Pisters, Patricia, 76
Poetry (Chang-dong, Lee), 6
polyphonic assemblage, 94–5
population, ageing, 6
   films about, 6–7
postcolonialism, 114
Prasad, M. Madhava, 43
prolepsis, 43–4; *see also* flashbacks
prosopopoeia, 111

Quartet (Hoffman, Dustin), 7

radical empathy, 66–7, 69–71, 73, 81–4
Rajadhyaksha, Ashish, 43
Ratcliffe, Matthew, 66, 72, 73
real, the, 77–8
reality, 113
recollection-image, 139, 140
Red series (Schwentke, Robert/Parisot, Dean), 6
reflexivity, 22–3
relationality, 11–12
Relic (James, Natalie Erika), 45
reterritorialisation, 131, 132, 136, 138
revisionism, 129
rhizomatic worldviews, 117–20
Ringu (Nakata, Hideo), 105
Robot and Frank (Schreier, Jake), 6
Rosen, Philip, 121
Rushton, Richard, 11, 113

Sako, Katsura, 67
sameness, 59
Sandcastle (Boo Junfeng), 148–9
Savages, The (Jenkins, Tamara), 6

Sayad, Cecilia, 118–19, 120
Schechner, Richard, 4
SEA (situated embodied-agent) view, 23
Segal, Lynne, 9
sensate democracy, 83
sensory cinema, 75–6
Separation, A (Farhadi, Asghar), 6
7 Letters (Boo Junfeng; Khoo, Eric; Neo, Jack; Rajagopal, K.; Tan Pin Pin; Tan, Royston; Tong, Kelvin), 129
SFC (Singapore Film Commission), 129
Shary, Timothy and McVittie, Nancy
   Fade to Gray, 10
Shed Skin Papa (Szeto, Roy), 6
Shyamalan, M. Night, 105–6
   Visit, The, 105–6
signification, 24
Silvering Screen, The (Chivers, Sally), 10
Singapore, 128
   censorship, 128, 132, 140
   Chinese students, 136, 137–8
   Chung Cheng High, 134f, 136, 137–8
   history, 128, 129–30, 131–3, 136–9, 140, 143, 149
   independence, 137
   Keretapi Tanah Melayu (KTM) railway, 133, 138–9, 141
   language, 136, 141
   Malaysia, 137, 139
   national security, 137
   Operation Cold Store, 137
   Parting, 133–4, 136, 138, 139, 141–2
   politics, 136–8
   Sandcastle, 148–9
   Tanjong Pagar Railway Station, 138–9, 141, 142
Singapore Film Commission (SFC), 129
Singapore Story, The 129–30, 131, 132, 143
situated embodied-agent (SEA) view, 23
Sobchack, Vivian, 75–6
society, expectations, 31
Soderman, Braxton, 123–4
Solaris (Tarkovsky, Andrei), 74
sound, 4, 119–20
space, 27–8

Star Wars: Episode VII – The Force Awakens (Abrams, J. J.), 6
Still Alice (Glatzer, Richard and Westmoreland, Wash), 10, 68–9, 75, 145–6, 147
Still Mine (McGowan, Michael), 6
Stoler, Ann Laura, 132
Summer Snow (Hui, Ann), 6, 45
sundown syndrome, 106, 109
surround sound, 119–20
synaesthesia, 75–6

Taking of Deborah Logan, The (Robitel, Adam), 105, 106, 107–8
   digital surround sound, 120
   digital technology, 121, 125f–6
   as found footage horror film, 118, 120
   glitches, 126
   hesitation, 115–16
   past/present, 109–12
Tan, Kenneth Paul, 129–30
Taylor-Jones, Kate E., 80
technology, 121–3
temporal identification, 5, 20, 31, 49–51, 73–4, 78
   Bergson, Henri, 27–9
   change and becoming, 36, 44
   Moment to Remember, A, 32, 37, 38, 39
   U Me Aur Hum, 36–7
temporal performance, 18–20, 27–35, 36–7, 78–9, 147, 151
   ecologies of, 85–6, 95, 97, 103
   Happy End, 92–3, 95, 96, 98, 100, 101f
   nation, the, 130–1
   polyphonic assemblage, 94–5
   rhizomatic worldviews, 118
   Singapore, 140
temporalisation, 49–50
temporality/time, 5
   ageing, 8
   Bergson, Henri, 27–35, 79
   chrononormativity, 31
   cinema, 121
   crip, 34
   curative, 32
   Deleuze, Gilles, 79

temporality/time (*cont.*)
    demented, 58–64, 140
    double-time, 130–1, 136
    experiencing, 5
    experiencing differently, 10–16
    films about ageing, 7–8
    horror, 107–9
    Lim, Bliss Cua, 114–16
    linear, homogeneous, 2, 3, 114
    men, 31
    Moment to Remember, A, 21–2, 23
    narrativisation, 49–50
    nation, the, 130–1
    past, the, 126–7
    past/present, 108–12, 142–3
    past-present-future, 114
    past-present paradoxes, 53
    postcolonialism, 114
    spatialised, 27–8
    syntheses of, 52–8
    women, 31
    see also clock time; temporal identification; temporal performance
Thanmathra (Blessy), 6
Thompson, James, 83
3688 (Hui, Ann), 45
Thum Pin Tjin, 130
time *see* temporality/time
time-image narratives, 53, 131
Todorov, Tzvetan, 113–15
Travelling Companion (Del Monte, Peter), 6
Triplets of Belleville, The (Chomet, Sylvain), 7
Tsing, Anna Lowenhaupt, 94–5
Turnbull, C. M., 136, 137
Tweedie, James, 134
Twilight Gangsters (Kang Hyo-jin), 6
2001: A Space Odyssey (Kubrick, Stanley), 74

U Me Aur Hum (Devgan, Ajay), 10, 18, 20
    ageing, 34–5
    agency, 26–7
    change and becoming, 25–7, 33, 36
    music, 25–7
    normativity/anti-normativity, 37
    sound 33, 34
    time, performance of, 32–5, 36–7f
uncanny, the, 113–14; *see also* horror
Up (Docter, Pete), 7

virtual, the, 77, 78, 79, 82, 91, 93
    past/present, 143
    see also virtual objects
virtual objects, 107
Visit, The (Shyamalan, M. Night), 105–6, 107–8
    digital surround sound, 120
    digital technology, 121, 124–5
    as found footage horror film, 118, 119, 120
    hesitation, 115–17
    past/present, 108–9

wandering, 133–4, 136, 138, 139–40, 142, 143, 144
Week-end (Godard, Jean-Luc), 91–2
Western worldview, 127
Whitehead, Anne, 71, 72
Wiegman, Robyn, 36
Wilson, Elizabeth, 36
women, 31, 32
Woods, Angela, 48
Woodspring, Naomi, 8
Woodward, Kathleen, 150
worldviews, 71, 115
    histories, 126–7
    rhizomatic, 117–20
    Western, 127
    see also entangled worlds
Wrinkles (Ferreras, Ignacio), 7

EU representative:
Easy Access System Europe
Mustamäe tee 50, 10621 Tallinn, Estonia
Gpsr.requests@easproject.com

www.ingramcontent.com/pod-product-compliance
Lightning Source LLC
Chambersburg PA
CBHW071846230426
43671CB00012B/2083